D1091345

TEMPLE GAIRDNER OF CAIRO

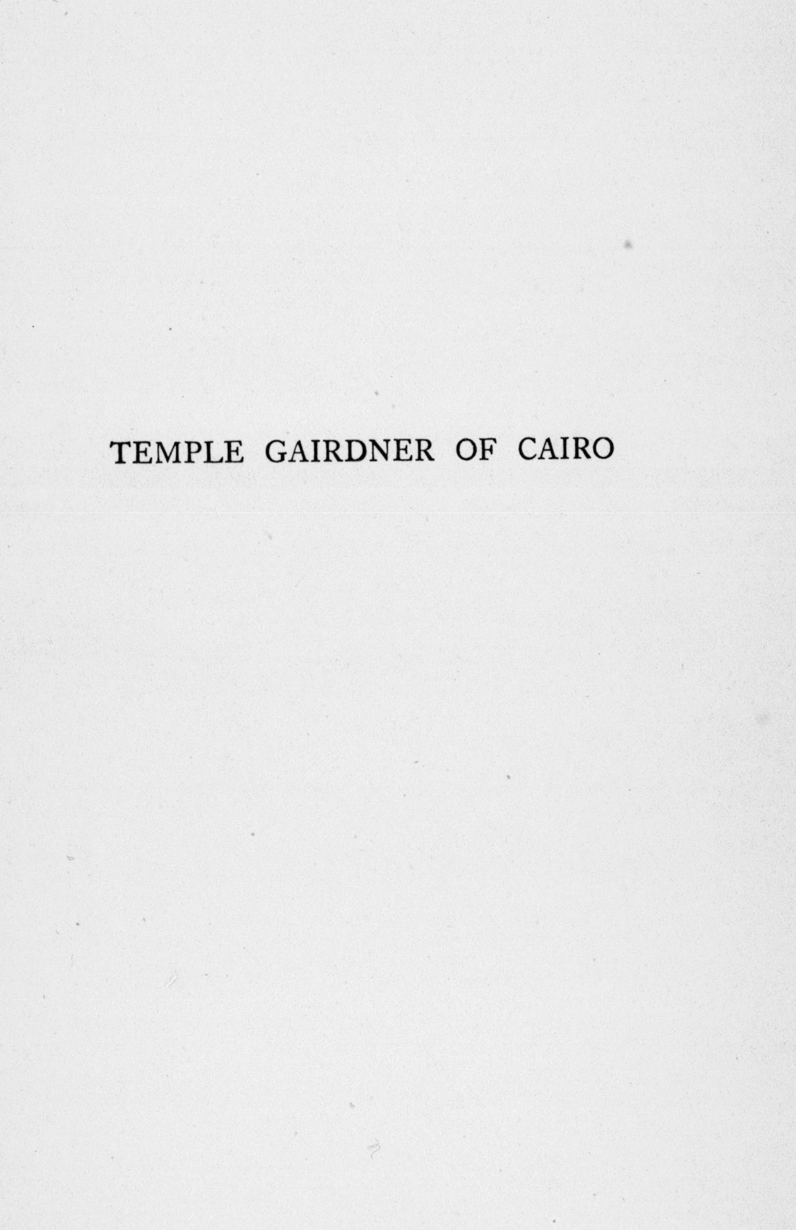

Temple Gairdner
Aged 53

TEMPLE GAIRDNER OF CAIRO

BY
CONSTANCE E. PADWICK

"... and for joy thereof goeth and selleth all that he hath."

"He was made for joy, being contented with the simplest of all things, love."
(*Letter of Temple Gairdner.*)

LONDON
SOCIETY FOR PROMOTING
CHRISTIAN KNOWLEDGE

First published 1929

Printed in Great Britain

TO

THE CHURCH IN BRITAIN
FROM THE CHURCH IN EGYPT

THIS BOOK

IS A

GREETING

AD MAIOREM DEI GLORIAM

PREFACE

For all her faults and struggles, the *Ecclesia Anglicana* is still the mother of saints. Sometimes she makes one of them (poor saint !) carry the burden of a modern bishopric. More often, to their own content, she leaves them in some slum or backwoods settlement, in some Bemerton or Hursley of our day, or in a foreign mission-station. And in her busy life there will sometimes steal upon her a fragrance from such places, as on a summer night the breath of hayfields will reach a city market-place.

Temple Gairdner's was one of these lives, with its vigours, humours, gifts, potentialities and graces half-buried. " Whatever may be said for good or ill about my work in Egypt," he wrote to a son, " it has not been the sort that makes at all an effective biography, or one that is called for, or that the public would be interested in . . . very small beer."

He forgot, so writing, that the man is greater than his work, that if his tasks were sometimes dull, his spirit had the vividness of one who lived " ever beholding that Face that doth minister life to beholders." And without his knowledge, " the house " of the Church in Egypt " was filled " with the fragrance of his life, which some called wasted, in such measure that wafts of its beauty were felt in many lands, as the scent of lime trees in July will steal into incalculable places. So that at Canon Gairdner's death an African leader wrote blessing God for " that soldier and saint of Christ " ; and an Indian comrade wrote, " I saw the news of his passing away and for two days I could not eat " ; and an American friend in Turkey said, " It has been the kind of acquaintance that one associates with a glimpse of some wonderful symbol of strength and beauty—like, say, Niagara Falls or the Matterhorn" ; and Bishop Gore could write of "Temple Gairdner, our common friend, the friend and helper of the whole Church."

To the whole Church, then, his life belongs, and this book is written not as the chronicle of a mission but as a restoration to the wider Church of what is too great to belong to Egypt alone.

In spite of his words just quoted, Temple Gairdner has all but written his own life. In early years, as a discipline in method, he kept diaries. Later, when he left this practice, he wrote, to his separated family, letters into which he seemed to spill his very self. And here, perhaps, a word is necessary. Those letters that trickled so easily and vividly from his pen were full of many-coloured interest in all life and especially in the lives of those to whom he wrote, and the selection for this book of their rarer passages of deliberate self-revelation may have given a false picture of the man. By their utter spontaneity all his letters revealed him, but conscious self-descriptions or interior revelations were neither common nor easy to Temple Gairdner, and those quoted in this book were oftenest made with pastoral intent, when it seemed to him that a child or a friend was passing through some like experience of growth or struggle.

If his own pen has in part written this book, the rest of it is the work of more than three hundred friends of East and West, on whose hearts he had written himself, and who have recorded their memories. These records and the detailed thought and care of Mr. Kenneth Maclennan, with the stimulus and help of friends within and without the Church Missionary Society, have brought the book into being. To these friends and to the help of every member of Canon Gairdner's family it owes its existence, and above all to his wife, who gave with both hands of her best.

One other word must be said. If, for reasons of space, in telling the story of such crowded joys and interests, but slight reference has been made to Canon Gairdner's colleagues in the Egypt mission (among whom the present writer is proud to be numbered), let it not be thought that he was the man to dominate the scene or give scant credit or attention to his colleagues' work. Never was comrade more generous of self-effacing help, of thanks, of appreciation, of all the ministries of friendship.

This book, we have said, is written that Egypt may offer to the whole family of Christ on earth something of a life so richly lived. But the Church in Egypt knows full well that not by reason of this book nor chiefly in this book that dear past of hers will live. "The past was given," Temple Gairdner said, "to live in the present, not in the sad death-life of mere memory." This past, because it *was* 'in Christ' *is* 'in Christ,' and 'Because I live,' says the eternal Voice, 'this past shall live also.'

CONSTANCE E. PADWICK.

OXFORD,
Christmas Eve, 1928.

CONTENTS

Preface . . . . pp. vii–ix

CHAPTER I

"PRELUDE TO ADVENTURE"

1. How Temple Gairdner coming to Oxford in 1892 found there varieties of behaviour in the matter of religion, with some extravagances. 2. How he had a Scottish home and father and a love of that land. 3. How he had an English mother, an English school and church, and a love of that land also. 4. How he came with an exhibition to Trinity College, Oxford, and found there friendships and many delights of the mind . . . . pp. 3–16

CHAPTER II

LOVERS' MEETING

1. How the O.I.C.C.U. had a great part to play in Oxford and in the world. 2. How Temple Gairdner saw his brother die and heard a heavenly call. 3. How he became the lover of Jesus Christ. 4. How he spent a summer term in great joy and spoke in the streets of Oxford. 5. How beside Derwentwater he committed himself to foreign service . . . . pp. 17–31

CHAPTER III

OXFORD

1. How, in his second year, Temple Gairdner had to deny himself some pleasures, and how he was faithful to his college boats. 2. How he lived the life of the O.I.C.C.U. and earned the disapproval of the "bloods" of Trinity. 3. How while he loved the men of the O.I.C.C.U. he sometimes thought other thoughts than theirs on Church and Hell. 4. How the younger men of the O.I.C.C.U. found him a leader and a friend, and how he fought temptation. 5. How he read philosophy and obtained only a second-class in "Greats," and how he bore disappointment . . . . pp. 32–46

CHAPTER IV

THE UNCOMMERCIAL TRAVELLER

CHAPTER V

APPRENTICESHIP

CHAPTER VI

MARRIAGE

CHAPTER VII

THE MUSICIAN

CHAPTER VIII

TWO EVANGELISTS

CHAPTER IX

APOLOGETICS

CHAPTER X

SEVERANCE

CHAPTER XV

ARTIST

CHAPTER XVI

IN CO-OPERATION

CHAPTER XVII

THE CHURCHMAN

CHAPTER XVIII

THE BOULAC HOME AND PASTORATE

CHAPTER XIX

IN EXITU ISRAEL DE EGYPTO

APPENDIX

TEMPLE GAIRDNER OF CAIRO

CHAPTER I

"PRELUDE TO ADVENTURE"

I

THE clash of temperaments within the little world of Oxford was as interesting in 1892 as in any year of her long history. Those were the days when Walter Pater sat behind an oriel window looking on to Radcliffe Square, in a little room where everything was clean and clear; where flowers stood in blue and white vases and the walls were painted a yellow more delicate than daffodils. There he wrote and rewrote, a still figure, modest and unassuming as his room, yet in a kind of priestly concentration, cherishing, as one who carries a frail and precious vase between his two hands carefully, his gift of the felicitous word, the spare and perfect phrase.

He had finished his essay *On the Study of Dante*, and *Plato and Platonism* was in part sent to press in that autumn of 1892. His place among artists and interpreters was now secure, but there was no security in his delicate, quivering mind. He feared, not with a vulgar fear, but as one who is the guardian of a tremulous flame. "I should be afraid to read Kipling," he told a friend, "lest he should come between me and my page when I begin to write." Perhaps only at St. Barnabas' amid the incense, listening to the impersonal-personal voice of Mother Church, did the fear quite leave his "grey-green lighted" eyes. It was observed in those days that from sitting on the backmost bench, a soothed spectator of the Mysteries, he would steal forward to a place among the worshippers.

. . . . .

Bawling down the High Street, not fifty yards from Walter Pater's window, swung a line of twenty undergraduates arm-in-arm. Some with faces tense in an act of daring and others strangely lighted with an inward joy, they chanted to a totally undistinguished tune:

> It is better to shout than to doubt,
> It is better to rise than to fall,
> It is better to let the glory out
> Than to have no glory at all.

The crude words straggled up to heaven past the twisted columns of St. Mary's, past the carved front of All Souls, past Queen Anne, in whose days approved religion was more decent and composed, with less resemblance to intoxication.

Oxford, where devotion had clothed itself in so many an ancient form of dignity and beauty, felt a cold disgust. These were the O.I.C.C.U.[1] men, crude and tasteless Evangelicals, it was said, without two ideas to rub together in their minds. But though some may have fallen short of two, *one* idea at least they all possessed; it pushed them to extravagance, to heroism if need be; it gave a pungent flavour to lives that might have passed through Oxford unremarked and unremarkable, so that instead of drifting down the High Street, unnoted, commonplace, they shouted down it "Hallelujah" or some Keswick ditty "to let the glory out." They passed through Oxford in the 'nineties of the last century as a company of the first Franciscans passed through an Italian market-place, less an order than an ebullition. And the dominant idea, that pushed some of them to easy publicity and others to a publicity that was torture, was witness to a Person and an experienced Life.

Into this Oxford of the 'nineties, where young æsthetes savoured Oscar Wilde; where the spiritual ascendancy of Charles Gore still lingered, though the man himself was

[1] Oxford Inter-Collegiate Christian Union, commonly called "Oiccu."

passing on to Radley ; where a new book called *Barrack-room Ballads* was one of the excitements of a winter in which Mrs. Patrick Campbell first drew crowds—

> To see that interesting play
> *The Second Mrs. Tanqueray ;*

where the ending of Jowett's long reign at Balliol seemed almost as much the closing of an epoch as was the ending, that winter, of Gladstone's last administration ; where Walter Pater haunted St. Barnabas' and the more boisterous spirits of the O.I.C.C.U. infringed the rules of taste and breeding,—into such an Oxford came Temple Gairdner in October 1892.

He was then an enthusiastic, absent-minded lad in a Norfolk jacket and a bow tie. " He was tall and yet well knit," says one of his friends, " and his stride was quick with a determined swing as if he had something very definite to do." His musician's hands were strong and beautiful, and the hazel eyes behind glasses sometimes lighted his whole face with whimsical but entirely good-natured humour, and sometimes looked as if they saw the invisible. He used those eyes to smile with oftener than his mouth. But his friends knew him best by a rather royal backward toss of his head, a legacy of the time when uncontrollable curls had to be thrown back from his eyes in babyhood. They remember him too for his way, when in thought, of drifting round like one in another world and oblivious of this, and for his curiously sudden power of return to be more intensely present and humorously observant of the immediate situation than many who never wandered in worlds not realized. He came with a mass of hungers and aptitudes for Oxford to satisfy, and since she was to do much for Temple Gairdner, it is well to ask what was the endowment that he brought to her.

II

His parentage was Scottish and English ; and the marriage gave to the children a rich and sometimes strange combination of gifts, and also placed their minds under the tension of two sets of sympathies and traditions, both calling to them and both theirs by right. The pull of this double loyalty and kinship may help to account for a certain bigness of outlook which is the family mark.

The Scottish strain was on their father's side. Dr. (afterwards Sir William) Gairdner, then Professor of Medicine at Glasgow University, was in that year of 1892 elected a Fellow of the Royal Society, and in the following year was unanimously requested to become President of the Royal College of Physicians of Edinburgh. He was a great physician and a great teacher, of whom Principal Caird said that he had "long passed beyond the point at which a man's reputation is confined to the circle of professional experts. It is the proud boast of this University [Glasgow] that it numbers among its teachers men, of whom he is one, who are of more than European fame." But the man himself was greater than any professional work or standing. This teacher of science was a rich humanist; music he understood and deeply loved; painting or sculpture had power to bring tears to his eyes; in youth he wrote verses about the "long lines of softened light" on some "beauteous evening," and beauty could always find and move him. He read his Dante; he wrote long letters to his brother, James Gairdner, the historian of Tudor times, about the versification of Shakespeare or the characters of the sixteenth century; he harmonized German student songs; and he went round Rome, always on foot, Shelley in hand, though he knew also how to relish Gibbon, and could refer a friend to Frazer's *Golden Bough* for "Albano and the very old legend connected with the exquisite lakelet." And all this with an endearing Scottish speech that he never tried to change, with a quite phenomenal absence of mind concerning those matters that were not interesting him at the moment (all Scotland was full of stories of his oblivion), and with the simplicity of a little child. "Worldly wisdom he had none," a friend says, "he never graduated in that school. He was a Nathanael."

In religion Dr. Gairdner had been brought up as a Unitarian, only in maturity entering further into Christianity and associating himself with the Church of Scotland. Religion was in every fibre of his being, but he always stood outside and marvelled at Church controversies as strange vagaries of the human intellect. "Cocksureness and narrowness" he found "very irritating," for he had a mind and heart that dearly loved a heretic. His consulting-room contained a noble and venerable portrait of Charles Darwin, still in those days the arch-heretic, and he sharply rebuked a small daughter for referring to him parrot-fashion as "the great agnostic." He would not have such a man summarized, even by a small child, in a merely negative term.

For Dr. Gairdner a facile faith was incomprehensible, but a hard-won faith was all. To such a faith he had himself attained, and this faith he would confess with his own simplicity to his students or to his young sons. "I do not envy the man," he said to a large company of the University on an occasion when they had gathered to do him honour (and the words came with a deeply personal note because his hearers knew him to be fresh from the death-bed of a son)—"I do not envy the man to whom the spiritual world is so shut that he must needs have a materialized ghost to make it palpable. . . . In my most settled and calm thinking I regard spiritual things as the greatest of all realities."

This man, with something of majesty, with dazzling gifts of mind and with a noble innocence, was all but idolized by generation after generation of Scottish medical students. After his death they summed up in a *Times* article the qualities that held them most:

> He was conspicuous for a sort of innocent directness of outlook, a perennial simplicity surviving all the perplexity of life. He possessed in full measure the rich Scotch ethical imagination. His medical ethics were ethereally fine.

So high an achievement in the realm of character was

partly, Dr. Gairdner liked to think, the fruit of a family tradition of high ethical living. Of this he wrote with pride to his son Temple :

> My father was, I think, about the most inflexibly just man, and also one of the least self-seeking men I have ever known in all my life. . . . Of all the Gairdner brotherhood in that generation, it might be said that, whether of greater or less ability and distinction, they were emphatically righteous and pure in their conduct, public and private. . . . That was the inheritance that I really had and valued.

To his young sons Dr. Gairdner was their affectionate, absent-minded father, devoted to babies, whom he was never tired of watching, devoted to family music-making, a little remote from their young world and a little bewildered by their rapid developments (for he married late and his family was large), but dear and conversable and one to whom a mental puzzle could be brought. His children felt the magnanimity of the man and knew well that they had no ordinary father. What his son Temple received from him in character this book must show. In mental endowment the son possessed two outstanding marks of his father's mind. And first of these undoubtedly was that passion of his for all beauty, but especially of music. In later years, after hearing some Beethoven in Berlin, Temple wrote to his mother of the "rush and vividness" with which it had brought his father to his mind :

> He seemed to be simply speaking in the music—from the morning when (at the very beginning of my concert-going days, I suppose about 1886) he took me up to the old Erard in the drawing-room and demonstrated for me the Andante of the *C Minor* which we were to hear that evening, down to the last days, when he would call out from the sofa, "Oh splendid, *splendid* !" He came back with a rush in that music.

From his father, too, Temple Gairdner drew a certain philosophic, balancing turn of mind that very rarely goes with such passionate emotions as were his, and gave birth to certain recurrent phrases of homely wisdom which caused his friends to smile. "You can't have it both ways," was one of these favourites, or, "Let us get back to first principles."

And from this father came to Temple his heritage as a son of the Scottish countryside. William Henry Temple Gairdner was born in Ayrshire, at the little port of Ardrossan, hardly more than a village in his birth-year of 1873. Here for some years was the Gairdners' summer home, in a house set on the rocks where the tongue of a little bay runs out to the western sea. "That corner," says an old friend of the family, "bleak and bare even in summer, the two old houses standing in the free bracing air between sea and sky, looks as if it were meant to be a starting-point for great ventures."

All his life Temple Gairdner would thrill with joy at the unforgettable outline of Arran seen from Ardrossan against the sunset sky. Passing through the Mediterranean in 1902 he saw, it seemed to him, the contours loved since childhood:

> Westward and northward the dark ridges of the Corsican hills showed their profiles darkest blue against the cloudy gold. One ridge I cannot forget—in shape like Arran, the Goatfell range seen from Ardrossan—with an opaque belt of white mist sleeping at its base, but above silhouetted sharp against the glory. . . . There it dreamed, almost a living thing—a soul at peace upon the breast of God.

"What an enormous dynamic power," he once remarked, "that Arran scene must have had, did have, on my subconscious life in those early years, with its mysterious and eternal beauty!" All his life, too, the "sea-road" at Ardrossan, its salt-bitten marshes yielding tiny burnet roses, stood in his mind as the picture of clean, wind-swept sweetness. A baby's cheeks at their freshest were always to him "like the wild roses on the sea-road at Ardrossan."

This, then, was the family's summer haunt for Temple's childish years, the scene of many scrambling joys, of swimming, of sailing, of mackerel fishing with James Craig or Angus McPhail, but the permanent home of his boyhood was in Glasgow. He loved to recall the Glasgow nursery with John Gilpin wallpaper and with a row of porridge-bowls on the window-sill to cool, and a row of hungry children impatient within, for Temple was the third child of a family of nine. His father's house—No. 9, The College—was one of a row of Professors' houses which looked on the one side over a green court to the University buildings, and on the other down the steep fall of Gilmore Hill to the Western Infirmary, where Dr. Gairdner gave his clinical lectures, and beside and beyond that again to the smoke-filled valley and the forest of chimneys that hid the Clyde and the Kelvin and all that clanging heart of Glasgow's life. Temple was always ready to defend his Glasgow and to lead a friend round to different points of view, from which he might prove that his city, for all her hard looks and grimness, had also her beauties and romance—"the college tower standing out full and clear," "the Campsies and the Grampians sleeping in the quiet summer landscape." "He loved Glasgow and he made me love her," a friend writes.

One other part of the Scottish country had become peculiarly his own in love from childhood. He was sent in January 1882 to the preparatory school called St. Ninian's at Moffat, and school days in Dumfriesshire gave him a deep affection for the green hills of the border country, their high sheep-walks and their rolling mists. All his life he had unusually keen pleasure (with its corresponding pain) from the smells of the world, and he liked to rhapsodize about "the holy smell of a Scotch glen on a damp day." "If you only knew what it is to me to see a wet bank," he said on returning to Dumfriesshire after many years of Egypt.

I bicycled, in a storm of wind and rain, over some of those moors [he wrote after his last visit to those parts], unspeakably lonely and wild that afternoon, and haunted by old, old associations, by one's own ancestors, and by tragical, historical memories. That day the gloom and storm of the short winter afternoon, with Hartfell towering and glooming at one from across the deep, dark valley, were marvellous consonant with the many moving associations.

I *must* pass on to my children this almost hereditary family tradition of peculiar devotion to Moffat before my generation passes away!

These were some of Temple Gairdner's Scottish roots, and he gloried in them.

III

His English heritage came from his mother. Dr. Gairdner had surprised himself and his family by marrying, at the age of forty-five, a young wife who brought to Glasgow, always a half-foreign, half-repellent world to her, the traditions of English country life and of the English cathedral close. Helen Bridget Wright was a Norfolk woman who married her Scottish lover in Norwich Cathedral and used to delight her northern brood by making speeches for them in the Norfolk dialect. Temple sent her a long letter about this English part of his heritage after visiting Norfolk in 1908.

I must say how pleased I was to hear the accent on its native soil! Once a servant, as she showed us into a room, apologized for its being in rather a confeüsion, which word when I heard I mentally cheered! Another woman, when she spoke, drooped her eyelids and let her voice sink in a sort of diminuendo singsong *exactly* like a certain Norfolk lady when she makes some sly hit, in the 'umblest but in the most effective way possible!

Well, it fell on a day that I went to Norwich. . . . There was a sense of solemnity in walking along the roads and paths and ways trodden by my mother and her sisters and brothers and parents and forbears: the mysterious feeling of a presence, or presences, accompanying me as I walked; the curious sense of familiarity, and that the place was "mine," that one never feels except in places that are really so—places like Ardrossan, for instance. So there was an Ardrossan feel about the Close. There the lime trees were in bloom, and in the warm, close July day their smell too was strangely familiar. It made it seem as though all these years were a dream, and that from that house now coming into view, the middle one of three at the bottom of the Close, there would emerge two young ladies in the costume of the 'sixties, very pleased with their new summer frocks and charmed with the lime-scented air, and the cathedral shadowing all the scene in that careful, tender, guardianlike way. These two young ladies were, of course, not *chattering*, but it would be quite wrong to say they were *silent*! Out they come, an old gentleman in a white waistcoat and with white whiskers standing in the front garden, looking indulgently at them (evidently *they* know how to get the right side of him, they do). There they come, smiling along as pleased as anything and talking as fast as the Alexandrian ladies in Theocritus. . . . By Jove, they have gone right through me and disappeared . . . shades of the past.

I went to the cathedral and saw the cloister along which that momentous procession wended, before my time, I believe . . . and yet I thought I could see it, somebody with downcast eyes . . . up the steps into the great Norman cathedral. I stood at the altar-rails and made request that I might not be unworthy of that day in April 1870 and of those who met in that cathedral that day. There too the sense of familiarity and mysterious own-ness came down.

The English bride wedded that day in the cathedral gave to Temple Gairdner his rights in the English countryside, and few of England's sons can have loved her so well as this boy from Glasgow. Certain utterly English phrases of Shakespeare could always call out from him a groan of yearning delight.

> *Davy.* Shall we sow the headland with wheat?
> *Shallow.* With red wheat, Davy

was never heard by him unmoved, and his children remember how he bicycled about the Cotswolds looking for "headlands" sown with "red wheat," or pointing out the orchard of pippins where Mr. Justice Shallow ate that dish of "leather jackets."

Not only her country but much of her personality his mother gave to Temple, and also the moulding experiences of an English public school, of Oxford and the life of the English Church.

With a beautiful shapeliness and grace of form and movement, Lady Gairdner had a love of all that was light, elegant, distinguished, and a high-spirited sense of honour. She was irrepressibly and naturally dramatic and vivid in all her thoughts and words, and this was in the very warp of Temple's nature. Her *espièglerie*, her wit, played over everything in what seemed to her the greyness of her northern home. As a reader of Dickens she was inimitable. It is doubtful if she *could* write a dull letter, and she certainly could not suffer bores gladly. Her eldest son remembers a saying of hers that the men and women of her family were all either saints or sinners; and although she had elected for the saints, it was obvious that she sometimes found her fellow-saints dull company. From this quick, vivid mother Temple Gairdner had not only his humour (their letters to one another are those of two people who thoroughly appreciate one another's sparkle), but also his emotional nature. She was a great lover, but a stormy one.

"A perfect character was she," her son said of her, "as individual, inimitable, quaint and notable as one of her own Dickens' characters. It is for love we shall remember her—incessant, passionate, hungry, fond, sometimes jealous ; but always love, and for this her memory will always be passionately dear to us."

Temple's nature, like his mother's, was swept by ecstasies and agonies ; only in him the philosopher with his balancing wisdom supervened and righted the ship just when it seemed she must be over. He became a man of strong emotions so held in control that very few guessed how fierce were the inner storms that tore him.

In girlhood his " loyalist and imperialistic " mother (as he called her) was trained in stiff Tory principles and, like most of Norfolk in those days, in loyalty to a markedly Evangelical section of the English Church. It was in the Church of his mother that Temple ultimately found his home and his life-service. Undoubtedly his deep sense of form, the sacramental tendency of his whole nature, and his natural Catholicism made him more completely at home in the Anglican Church, but it is equally true that his father's son could never feel Scottish religious life to be remote and foreign.

To his mother he owed it that his school days after Moffat were passed at Rossall, where he gained a scholarship. His father, slightly intensifying the Scotchness of his tones for the purpose, girded genially at the one-sidedness of the traditional English education, but in a letter to his schoolboy son he said :

> I must write you a few lines of congratulation—not only on your getting the essay prize, but on your noble resolution to read your Homer, which is far, far in advance of what your father was ever able to do or think of doing. I agree that an English school which has begot that grand ambition in an effective way shows that the classical discipline is not thrown away.

Temple threw himself into that " classical discipline " with an enthusiasm which had been wakened in him when as a little child, sitting in his father's carriage at the door of the Glasgow house, he opened a book to while away the time as he waited for " the grown-ups." It was Kingsley's *Heroes*, and he never forgot the moment :

> O memories of fairyland, and the stirring of my small heart when at the age of seven or eight I read the first chapter of Kingsley's *Heroes* and from it felt the spirit of Hellas come with a flood into mine! . . . I bless Kingsley wherever he sits among the immortals, for in that book is the very soul of Homer and of the Greeks, and to him largely I owe what I feel to-day.

"I think his particular love was Virgil," says Mr. L. R. Furneaux, who in those days helped the Head Master with the Sixth Form, "and I can see him now, as we read the Fourth *Æneid*, thoroughly appreciative of its beauties and quick to pick up or suggest the subtler points of the poem. He was one of six boys, monitors, who used to meet together once a week in my study to read English poetry, and from what he has since told me I think he looked back on those hours as among his happiest at Rossall."

A school friend remembers how he launched out with enormous labour into a poem on Savonarola with "various scenes and cantos and many varieties of English metre"! And he had begun writing to his father about a "difference of opinion" between Milton and St. Paul on the origin of evil. The authentic Gairdner was awake!

In music, the love of his whole life, he never found time, in the crowded round of a public-school day, for laying the foundation of technique as he could afterwards have wished, but his master, Dr. Sweeting, remembers him as—

> Perhaps the most interesting pupil that I ever had at Rossall, with an appreciation and insight that were not only remarkable in a schoolboy but far above that of the average music student of riper years.

His mathematics master would not have echoed these enthusiasms. Temple was captain of his house, and in every sense an active boy, who but for his short sight would have been a Rugby forward. As it was, he won "pots" for running. In the invigoration of those great sea winds he increased the physical hardness in which he always took a pride. Rossall was bleak and bare of trees,[1] but he wrote with great affection of "the beloved low, dull roar of the Irish Sea which I used to hear from the big west dormitory of Hainsworth's," and "the larks with their perpetual madrigal over the playing-fields."

IV

From this austerity of scene he came up in October 1892, with a classical exhibition, to the graciousness of Trinity College, her lime-tree avenue, her lawns and apple trees. Oxford made him her own; he wrote as one of her lovers, "Was oppressed to-day by the beauty of Oxford"; or the service at Magdalen was "*cruelly* beautiful." His first term was all delight and expansion. He put four Greek statues and a piano into his panelled room (on staircase 14 in the Garden Quadrangle at Trinity) and plunged into many welcoming joys. There were Dr. Mee's musical "at homes" every week with a chosen few; there was the Oxford University Musical Society; there were the boats and the knowledge that he was shaping hopefully on the river in a college where athletes had an overwhelming prestige. His school authorities had suggested the Indian Civil Service as his goal; but that was distant yet, and meanwhile there was Greek poetry to read for Honour Moderations. ("My God! I believe half my soul is Greek!" he wrote long afterwards.) And above all there were friendships. There is no doubt that he liked human beings, and the men who write "He was my best friend" are strangely and richly assorted in age, interests, rank, mind and nationality. One who knew him in later days writes of "all the good talk and good music and that enchanting sense of personal companionship which he seemed able to create wherever he went." Certain it is that any

[1] Temple Gairdner once composed a song for a house-concert in honour of the only Rossall forest—a forest of rhubarb, which, being cut for the kitchens in rather firm maturity, caused the young of those days to speak of "hockey-stick tarts."

group which he joined became tenfold more a group. And in this first Oxford term there grew up a close comradeship in the group that sat at the long scholars' table on the fireplace side of the hall at Trinity.

And, of course, there was an innermost circle of intimates who spent evenings in turning heaven and earth upside-down with mighty satisfaction. The Trinity "quintette" which met on Saturday nights included, besides Gairdner, his fellow-exhibitioner G. H. Allen, and F. G. Butler (now Sir Frederick Butler, K.C.M.G., Under-Secretary at the Foreign Office), with J. H. Oldham from the Edinburgh Academy (now Secretary of the International Missionary Council) and T. O. Smith from Gairdner's well-beloved Dumfriesshire country, who was to become a philosophy don at Oriel at the age of twenty-five. Several of the group were good talkers, they were all intimate, and starting from some literary topic (almost any would do—Emerson, Burns, Rossetti, Wordsworth, Carlyle, Homer, Ibsen) they turned their own minds inside-out in the engaging way of youth when the fire burns well at night. The Scottish ethical interest came out on those evenings in Gairdner's young choice of subject. It was only in later, mellower days that he learned to feel at home in the non-moral faery world of *The Merry Wives of Windsor*, of *L'Après-midi d'un Faune*, of *The Beggar's Opera*, or Pavlova's "Swan Dance." "In the early days at Trinity," one of the quintette writes, "he would choose some poem or subject which touched on the deeper problems of life. If he enjoyed conversation or non-formal discussion, he always talked for truth, not for victory. He had no use for mere cleverness or indifference and no time to spare for those who had no keenness or desire for truth."

This boy with his naïve seriousness and care for truth, his magnanimity, his passion for beauty, his quaint humours and dramatic outbursts, somehow came in his circle to an ascendancy that would have surprised himself had he fully known it. There were others in the undergraduate world of his day whose friends knew that they would "achieve greatness." Wadham had two brilliant scholars, successively Presidents of the Union, F. E. Smith and John Simon. (The Union of those days was not wanting in fireworks.) And Balliol had an undergraduate, witty as they, who came from the unusual school of the French *service militaire*, Hilaire Belloc, whose first in the History Schools was followed by the publication of *The Bad Child's Book of Beasts*. All these had every intention of "achieving greatness," and they did it. But some are "born great," and that was the impression that the young Gairdner unconsciously left upon his friends. "I do not doubt," says one of them, "that he was the greatest man among my own contemporaries that I ever came into contact with"; and another is very bold and saith, "He was at Oxford with Sir John Simon, Lord Birkenhead and Hilaire Belloc, and he was the greatest of them all, and the most richly endowed." Whether his friends' impression was a true one, readers of this book must decide for themselves. His countrymen never at any moment in his career showed any inclination to "thrust greatness upon him," and the category which he determined upon for "achieving greatness" was not that of the publicist or politician. "Man," he once said, grasping a friend by the arm and staring out to where a glint of moonlight lay on Morecambe Bay —"man, the only thing in the world worth living for is to find out the will of God and do it."

This mode of greatness he chose, and lived and died unknown while the names of those others are in every newspaper. How the ultimate Tribunal will regard the matter it is not ours to say.

But Gairdner's first term at Oxford was not overtroubled by eternal aspirations. It was a term, he said, of "pure joy." Only as he went down to Glasgow, the Scotch ethicist in him felt with a twinge that it had been almost *too* deep a draught of pleasure, and next term he must be a shade more "altruistic."

CHAPTER II

LOVERS' MEETING

1893

It was for the love that he had to his Prince that he ventured as he did.—*John Bunyan.*

I

DEVOUT churchmanship in Oxford in 1892 roused no hostility. The Oxford Movement after its great ardours had reached that dangerous point in its story when men spoke well of it. It was all but sixty years since Keble had preached the Assize sermon, and life had swung back in some respects to those days when Hurrell Froude had tilted at dull respectability. "We will have a *vocabularium apostolicum*," he had said, "and I will start it with four words: 'pampered aristocrats,' 'resident gentlemen,' 'smug parsons,' and 'pauperes Christi.'"

In spite of the deep reality and strong dominance of Charles Gore, Oxford religion of 1892 showed more "resident gentlemen" than "pauperes Christi." The time was ripe for one of the turbulent winds of God, for one of those movements that reveal afresh the desperate foolhardiness of the Christian life. And this came to Oxford from a source that she hardly appreciated—from that group of ardent Evangelicals that gathered round the O.I.C.C.U. and, not content to make their own devotions, had a lively and aggressive concern for other people's souls. These narrow young desperadoes had some claim to the term "pauperes Christi," for in the evangelistic fury in which they lived every possible penny must be saved from personal expenditure, to buy a Bible or pay for a fraction of a missionary. When W. E. S. Holland bought a luncheon basket at a railway station it was felt that he had all but given away his cause. A sandwich and a glass of milk was lunch enough for one who might save the rest of the luncheon-basket price for evangelistic funds.

In the history of spiritual movements this might be regarded as the last flicker, and a vivid one, springing from what was even yet the great glow of the Evangelical Revival with its passionate soul-seeking, its tracts, its severe standards of separateness from "the world." In Oxford it seemed but a vivid flicker, but in Cambridge (after the visit of Moody and Sankey in 1884) and in the Scottish Universities (through Henry Drummond) and in American colleges (through young leaders like Mott, Speer and Wilder) the flicker kindled into a glowing fire. And there was need of spiritual fire, for this movement had before it a work of the most taxing magnitude, and by its afterwork it must be judged.

If the movement of the Wesleys restored to the orderly and generalizing eighteenth century a sense of the individual value of souls and their incalculable romance; if it killed the slave-trade and raised up or reinspired all the great missionary societies; if the Oxford Movement restored to nineteenth-century England the sense of the visible, divine Community on earth, of the unbroken stream of sacramental life in the historic Church; if it deepened the devotion of Anglican life and quickened vocations; yes, and if by thus heightening the corporate sense it made a Pan-Anglican Congress or a National Missionary Council a natural outgrowth of the Church's strongest life,—if the two former movements did all this, what great thing was now before the men of the 'nineties?

Even this: all that care for the single soul and all that loyalty to the historic community must now, without loss or diminution, be fused with a yet wider care and loyalty.

In the early 'nineties of last century the face of the globe was scattered with the Christian missions that arose out of the Evangelical Revival in England and kindred movements in other lands. But each did its work without relation to the rest, except such neighbourly or unneighbourly relations as resulted from two missions deciding to "occupy" one place. Here was a call to Christian statesmanship that should give unity and the strength of unity to the many-sided, many-minded enterprise.

Again, in religious life there was yet but little sense of Christendom as a whole. There was an Anglican Church, with Rome over against her on the one hand and "the Nonconformists" on the other. Most Churchmen knew and cared next to nothing about the great and ancient or the struggling and oppressed Churches of the East, about the strange, seething religious life of America, about the young Churches growing up in "mission lands," or about the communions other than that of Rome on the Continent of Europe. Here again was work for Christian statesmen who should combine loyalty to their own share in the Catholic heritage with love and care for the whole people of Christ on earth.

These were the tasks before the men of the 'nineties. The crucial work of the decade was to unite in all the colleges of Christendom scattered groups of men desirous of seeking first the Kingdom of God; to build an international love between them; to train an international outlook on the Church's world task; to raise up men who, having tasted the sacrifices and the joys of co-operation, should carry that way of living into the daily life of the Church.

This, then, is the inner meaning of the astonishing and rapid evolution by which in those years little college Christian unions were welded into inter-collegiate unions, and such bodies as the O.I.C.C.U. (Oxford Inter-Collegiate Christian Union) became part of a "British College Christian Union," which in its turn was linked with colleges throughout the world in the "World's Student Christian Federation." This evolution took place with extraordinary rapidity at the close of the nineteenth century; under heavenly inspiration, we must surely say, when we remark that young leaders trained in this school had so changed the face of the missionary enterprise by 1910 that then (and not a moment before) was possible the holding of the Edinburgh World Missionary Conference, binding together the chief non-Roman Catholic missions of the world in a bundle of common life and sympathy ; and when the Great War in 1914 set Christendom by the ears, the World's Student Christian Federation had become strong enough to preserve some reality of fellowship and common work between Christians of all nations and communions. The work done by men at college in the 'nineties held good, weathered the storm, and provided in each country some ready to lead the forces of fellowship and reunion.

The fire that was thus to be scattered through the world had need to be intense, and in the Oxford colleges there was no doubt about the uncalculating devotion of the O.I.C.C.U. men, who were being led by their fellows in Cambridge and in Scotland to take their part in the world evolution just described. " We were prigs and smugs, we really were," says W. E. S. Holland, who was one of the tiny group, " but Archbishop Lang always said that we were much the *livest* group in Oxford when he was a don."[1]

Their shibboleths were terrifying, their narrowness a byword, but upon them something of divine fire had descended, and they stuck at nothing that they could see to be the will of Christ. Years afterwards, when a boy of his own was troubled by the more intrusive type of evangelism, Temple Gairdner wrote to him :

> Yes truly, the language of that sort of layman is often crude and extreme and narrow to a degree. . . . They see a few things clearly, and other things not at all ; those things they will insist on with an insistence that blinds them to all other aspects. Everything will be black or white with them ; no shading of any sort. And their vocabulary will be to match. BUT, I say again, these people have to be reckoned with.

[1] He was Fellow of All Souls 1888–93 and Fellow and Dean of Divinity of Magdalen 1893–6.

Was I not in the midst of them, and one of them at Oxford? And as I look round the world I see everywhere that it is *these men* (perhaps mellowed and developed now) who are doing the big things in the world—the big things for mankind, and God, and the Kingdom of Christ: A. G. Fraser, J. H. Oldham, W. E. S. Holland, to take only those known to yourself.

But up to the end of Gairdner's first term, if this movement touched his life it was with an irritating touch, as when an evangelist on being led into his rooms stared fiercely at the Greek statues and bade him "Smash 'em!—smash 'em!"

II

At Glasgow on his home-comings the whole household took on a new animation. A family friend recalls the boy of those days as bringing home "a magnetic personality, boisterous good-humour and optimism." There was music and singing by the hour; golf or skating; Dickens readings; games with the small children or acting and charades in the long drawing-room. His mother, that lover of all brightness, looked for his coming with her own intensity of emotion. "How often," she wrote to him, "have I looked for you! How often have I pictured your coming in unexpectedly as often you did into the drawing-room, and the joyful surprise and relief and ease from disquietude that your presence brought and the sinking heart when you went away!"

The Christmas vacation of 1892 went with all its accustomed swing, until a blow fell which for ever settled the direction of Temple Gairdner's life. The brother next below him fell ill—his crony and boon companion Hugh, a Loretto boy who had just entered Glasgow University as an engineering student.

Of this son his father wrote, "Even when in his cradle he had that distinctive note of refinement and graciousness of manner which made us call him from the first—and before he knew anything about it—'Gentleman Hugh.' . . . What genuine joy he had in spreading out his little gifts in the family circle, and how little he cared for getting the credit of them!" Their common friend Dr. John McKendrick says that Hugh was "everything to Temple. He was less robust and was championed by Temple wherever he went. A close bond existed between them in music. Hugh played the violin, and for hours they played together."

"My brother Hugh fell ill," Temple Gairdner long afterwards confided to a son of his own. "From the very first I—alone of all the family—had strange fatal presentiments, and for a fortnight I had the solemn and unspeakable experience of watching him die. Sickening anxiety, ebbing hope, and the heart-breaking pathos of that long last night."

To his mother Temple wrote:

> Hugh was out of my reach from Wednesday to the Monday he died. He could not even feel the pressure of the hand or the tender tones; but he knows now. The nothingness of "successful life," "popularity," "influence" and of many things I had before prized was very plain to me when I knelt over him on Monday evening. I felt that unless I could get to a greater extent than ever before the one thing needful—search for it and get it—then I would live in vain: that these were as nothing, the other indeed immortal. . . . Perhaps you never saw much of the spiritual in me; but the spirit is like the wind blowing where it listeth—and even to me it may come. . . . As I knelt over my poor boy I felt precious keenly the need and want of it.

Temple Gairdner never called the great crisis thus brought about his "conversion." There had been in him both a childish and a schoolboy religion, and he had taken with great seriousness the struggle against the temptations of growing boyhood. "I remember each time having a sort of feeling that my whole life depended on that moral decision." He was confirmed at school, "reverently enough," he says, but without any sense of corresponding inward growth. Yet notes of his schoolboy meditations before a Communion in Glasgow could not have been written by an irreligious boy. " Make me pure and good " (he wrote), " so that Thou mayest find in me a response to Thy great love. Make me pure, O my God, now and ever."

In all that now began in him there was no repudiation of the faith of these earlier years.

> I can see my life like a map [he told his mother]. I was being led all along. . . . I can see clear as day a childhood and boyhood marred with all the faults of wilfulness . . . ineradicable selfishness clearly seen but striven against in my own strength. . . . I can see a first term at Oxford wholly given to self . . . then, when I knelt by Hugh's bed I first felt the necessity of putting Christ first and the rest nowhere. It was the absorbing sense that we were not entrusting him to a shadowy future life but indeed into the very arms of Jesus. . . . And then I knew that henceforth there could be but one duty for me, to follow where I heard Him calling.

" I went back to Oxford having tasted eternity first-hand," he told his son. " I sought out men who made no secret of their love and faith. I talked with them and watched them. I joined the College Student Christian Union, at that time a rather looked-down-upon ' Bible-reading,' and began to read the Bible for myself, and with one or two intimates, I can see now with what gorgeous naïveté and want of comprehension ! "

It was an uncomfortable term. The boy was sad; and he became sufficiently intimate with the Christian Union men to make some of his friends feel anxious about these social vagaries. Yet he failed to satisfy the O.I.C.C.U. standards. He wanted to be " a silent witness," they said (a thing impossible to their red-hot evangelism), and he wanted to feel his feet and move step by step. For if Temple Gairdner passed through deep emotional crises and acted on inward experiences, he could not "live the unexamined life," and his new positions had to be thought out as well as lived out. To the brotherhood of the O.I.C.C.U. he seemed to be only very slowly "drawn into the fellowship." And he had none of their shibboleths. They felt it necessary to cover his naked Greek goddess with dusters. Temple Gairdner saw the courage and reality behind their set phrases, and it called to the deeps in him; but "Nothing much happened during the term," he said, "except incommunicable personal grief with a sense of Hugh's living survival."

III

"At the very end of the term, however," he told the sister who knew him best, "came the event that set me in a ferment. There was a Congress at Oxford of the Christian Unions of Oxford, Cambridge, Edinburgh and Glasgow Universities. I went. I heard testimony after testimony of what was being done for Christ by others, and the overwhelming question came home to me, 'What have *you* done? What will *you* do?' And I saw that for me there was no half-way." Years later he told his son of the same event:

> I attended the conference—a *perfectly* new experience for me at that time. I remember that the result of the meetings on me was to focus all the desires and emotions of months into a passionate desire for *service*. Then came the Sunday. . . . I don't believe the addresses were up to much; neither the theme of them, nor much that was said, appealed to me, and the men were speaking a dialect, so to speak, foreign to me, at least foreign to my need then. But the last of the speakers, the President of the O.I.C.C.U., a man named Alvarez, now a missionary in West Africa, rose and spoke. What he *said* wasn't much (he told me afterwards he thought he had made an absolute mess of it), but a *spirit* was in him and in his face, tone and words, which was prepared for me, and I for it. A living Spirit—Christ.

I was deeply moved but not "emoted"—rather taken-possession-of. And immediately on the breaking-up of the meeting I went up to him and asked him if I might speak to him. It was in Hertford hall, and he took me to a room on a staircase to the left of the quad as you enter. He didn't in the least understand what was passing in me, and as *I* didn't understand either, I couldn't possibly tell him. But he solved it by our kneeling together. I can't remember anything of his prayer except the first sentence: "O Lord Jesus, we thank Thee that Thou dost indeed make us to lie down in green pastures, and lead us beside the still waters." . . . There was a silence, and then, to my own amazement, I found myself forced to the utterance of my first audible prayer. It was something like this: "O God, Thou knowest that I do not want anything else but to serve Thee and men, always, all my life. Amen."

When I got to Trinity I seemed unrecognizable to myself and it was as though I was walking on air. I went straight to the room below mine, where my chief pal lived, to tell him about this incredible experience. There were men with him and I merely gaped at him and them—they appeared to me as if one had looked at them from the wrong end of a telescope, phantasms, inhabiting a totally different world from the incredible world I suddenly found myself inhabiting: a new world, breathing new air; all things new. And when I got up the next morning I went straight to Hills & Saunders and put in hand that text which I always had in my rooms and which you may remember in the drawing-room, "BEHOLD, I MAKE ALL THINGS NEW."

It seemed the one text in the Bible for me that day; for I was walking in a world indescribably beautified, indescribably lovely: with my heart exactly as the heart of a bride with her lover, so overmastering was the realization of the Presence—I had almost said the embrace of CHRIST. Yes, I knew it then: and the embrace was returned! It was wonderful. I avoided all company ; I could not bear any. I stayed up a day or two just to enjoy solitude with the unseen Lover. And when I went down to Glasgow, I did not go alone.

Probably no friend of his who ever heard Temple Gairdner say the Name " Jesus " in ordinary talk can forget it. He used the Name very little ; it was too sacred to him and he was never a gushing talker about religion. Yet now and again something in a conversation would induce its use, and always it came out with the shy yet unconcealable note of a lover. Often he revealed himself in the playing of a hymn. " Temple was at the organ," a friend writes, " and we ended up with that hymn ' Jesus, my blessed Redeemer.' I shall never forget the way he played it. If ever music was inspired, that was." Nor is he forgettable in the singing of the old Derbyshire carol of the mystic forest, with its haunting divinely-infantile refrain, " And I love my Lord Jesus above everything." The lover glowed and shone from his whole aspect.

He practically never brought himself to speak in any detail of those experiences of March 1893 from which he once drew the veil in writing to his son. But now and again a phrase in conversation revealed the life-passion then begun, as once when a group at a breakfast table referred pityingly to the man " born blind " of St. John's Gospel, and Temple Gairdner burst out passionately as though he could not help himself, " I know that I would gladly be blind forty years to have Jesus Christ heal me."

IV

" That exquisitely wonderful experience," as he called it, " a first summer term at Oxford," was now before him with all its joys—" the Cherwell that green fairyland . . . green-arching trees making their mystic tunnel for the still, green-reflecting water—the dreamland craft slipping noiselessly along the still waters." On his return to Oxford T. E. Alvarez (whom Gairdner never mentioned without some murmur of affectionate gratiude) "very wisely," he says, put him to tasks which vere in themselves a test of the reality of his experience. The O.I.C.C.U. men of those days were sometimes called on for help by neighbouring clergy. "In those wondrous days of my first summer term," Temple Gairdner ays, "Alvarez got hold of me and enlisted me to help Elwin (who afterwards died as Bishop of Sierra Leone) at the Sunday morning children's service in St. Clement's schoolroom. There I first spoke a Christian address. I knew every plank of that platform!" They went also two and two on Sunday nights to visit the tramps in the common lodging-houses of the town.

And on Sunday afternoons there was a catechizing for which Dr. Whitmarsh, Vicar of Sandford, asked undergraduate help. One or two men walked out three and a half miles from Oxford, taught the children in the little ancient church, consumed a large tea with Dr. Whitmarsh and walked back through the water-meadows. To this work Alvarez introduced Temple Gairdner. "We had week by week," he says, "a seven-mile walk together . . . often an Emmaus walk for us both when the Lord Himself drew near to us, and we returned with hearts burning within us to our College chapels at Jesus and Trinity." T. E. Alvarez was then in his last year; when he left Oxford for West Africa, Gairdner carried on the Sandford work, and the undergraduates whom he persuaded to come with him have vivid memories of his joyousness in the walk through the water-meadows, flinging off his coat ("I don't care *who* sees me"), his head thrown back, his eyes looking into infinities as he rhapsodized about the birds or shyly jerked out his thoughts about eternal verities.

He was all that term in the rapture of his new world, and at the end of it he could still write: "That sense of newness is simply delicious. It makes new the Bible, and friends, and all mankind, and love, and spiritual things, and Sunday, and Church and God Himself. So I've found."

He put himself to the task of confessing to his closest

friends what had come to him. “There can be n concealment,” he told his sister. “It must out. An you can feel, can't you, that had I not said to you what did, I should have been concealing *myself* from you—and so almost sailing under false colours.” The naïv diary entries that record his confessions to his friends ar touching to those who know the natural reserve of th writer. “Butler—clean breast,” or “Had it out wit T. O. S. about last two months. . . . I think we lov each other as much as ever.”

But Alvarez and Elwin and that group of O.I.C.C.U faithfuls had a harder fence for neophytes. Th Rubicon, the test as to whether a man could stan singularity and even mild persecution, the act that brande him socially, and left a man no longer his own but committed member of a brotherhood, was an activ sharing in an open-air evangelistic service at the Martyrs Memorial, held at eight o'clock on Sunday night.

To Temple Gairdner the whole thing was distasteful not because he lacked courage but because his sense o seemliness was hurt. “It was some time before he fel himself able to speak,” says T. E. Alvarez, “his diffidenc being caused only by the very natural feeling that we al shared that there was something bold—if not presumptuous—in such young and callow Christian venturing to obtrude their testimony in a place with such traditions not only of devotion but of learning.”

But if this service was regarded (and it was) as disgracefully branding, as the test of readiness to go all lengths for Christ, then Temple Gairdner was not the man to seek escape.

> I know [he told his mother] that in Oxford one is thought a mild type of imbecile if one displays any *personal* enthusiasm for the cause that is one day to conquer the world. . . . I do feel that at the risk of being thought a prig or a fanatic one must hang out one's colours. . . . I told a great friend of mine this at Trinity, who is a total unbeliever at present, and he

said, " Yes, I see that you cannot but tell of it, since you have had it personally shown to you."

It is hard [he confessed to a sister], I find it awfully so here ; but it will be always hard whatever our sphere of life, and yet it will be always our business. . . . Do I speak at a meeting ? I am asked, " Are you better than those here, that you speak to them ? " Nay, but Christ is better—I do not speak of myself but of Him.

A postscript to this letter informs his schoolgirl sister that he had at last felt " compelled " " to rise up and do something I had never thought possible before—witness for Christ in the principal street here in Oxford." The impossible was happening to him because he was a man in love.

And from the give-and-take of that love was generated a sort of inward brightness so that he would write of " that sun-flooded summer of 1893." " Men often asked to be introduced to him," says T. E. Alvarez, " because of the brightness which was as an atmosphere about him wherever he went." This quite unconscious shining out of an inner illumination was one of his marks through life. " Wherever he is it will be bright," said one of his friends on hearing of his death.

V

A small forerunner of the present summer conferences of the Student Christian Movement had come into being at Keswick, where a students' camp was held immediately before or after the well-known Convention. The students' conference was organized by the new Student Volunteer Missionary Union, founded in this country at Christmas 1891. Groups like the O.I.C.C.U. of that day, not made by common thought so much as by common life and zeal, and sometimes inclined as groups to fear the disintegrating tendency of too many ideas—such groups might have died down into a narrow parochialism, but for the effect of the Student Volunteer

Missionary Union, which kept world-vistas constantl before their eyes, so that men not naturally catholic minded (and who can claim to be so?) grew at leas towards universality in their prayers. By its hard, clea call for life-service anywhere, the S.V.M.U. provided th Christian life in the Universities with that element o ruthlessness and daring that it needed, and gave to Douglas Thornton of Cambridge and others like him the impetus towards a new type of missionary statesmanship. It was to the camp of this union, not yet two years old in Britain, that Temple Gairdner determined to go in his first long vacation.

He arrived at Keswick and found the little camp of those days in a paddock at the end of Blencathra Street, where the inhabitants of the town could lean with elbows on the wall and relish the sight (less common in those days) of young Oxford and Cambridge men acting as camp orderlies. The meetings were held in the Drill Hall, and among the undergraduates in their blazers were the black bonnets of several dear old ladies who could not resist a few extra days in the Keswick which they loved for its Convention, in order to "see the blessed work among the dear students." In spite of these humours, the camp in July 1893 made a deep mark on the lives of several men, and not least on W. H. T. Gairdner. The campers were challenged at their first meeting "to choose out one uncomely characteristic and claim in Jesus' Name to have it forth." Temple Gairdner's choice would have surprised his friends: "I chose cowardice, physical and moral. That night my heart was full: my prayers were inarticulate. Bravery . . . my deepest petition."

Next day: "Resolved at eleven that there was nothing now between me and S.V.M.U.[1] . . . Oh for bravery!"

On the morning of the third day a silent transaction took place. He went out by the lake with his friend J. H. Oldham, his prayer for bravery still burdening his

[1] Membership in the Student Volunteer Missionary Union, involving a declaration of readiness to serve as a foreign missionary.

spirit. Suddenly he burst out, "Look here! If we are not right, let's get right!" They knelt there in the fields. "We did not rise," says Gairdner, "till we had claimed light through Christ and received it. 'Twas God's instruction. I had prayed for BRAVERY and suddenly I felt that I would not mind being beaten for Christ. Then I knew that I was right with God, my prayer was answered."

But the dominant note of that summer, a note that rang in his ears all his life, was heard on a memorable Saturday afternoon, July 22nd, 1893. The campers were out on the lake in a flotilla of little boats moored under an island. Derwentwater was still and sunny; birds were singing on the island and in the boats young figures were lolling at ease. They were in summer mood; the morning meeting had been an unexacting one about the care of the missionary's health in the tropics, which no one felt so immediate a question as to be absorbing. And now the afternoon meeting was held in these enchanting circumstances. Bishop Hill of East Africa was baling out the nearest boat to Temple Gairdner, who was in full, placid enjoyment of the whole scene.

Suddenly a tall, rather majestic figure, standing bareheaded at the prow of one of the boats, uttered an unforgettable call. His hands outstretched, his face with a shining in it that Gairdner never forgot, he cried to that company of happy youth: "AGÔNIA is the measure of success." (It was Robert Stewart, shortly going out to meet martyrdom in China.) "Christ suffered in agony: so must we. Christ died: so perhaps may we. Our life *must* be hard, cruel, wearisome, unknown. So was His."

To Temple Gairdner, fresh from his prayer for "bravery," the speaker sounded a compelling call. "These words and thoughts will, I hope, be with me all my life," he wrote. And his friends know that they were.

Before leaving Keswick he signed the declaration of the Student Volunteer Missionary Union. "It is my purpose, if God permit, to become a foreign missionary."

CHAPTER III

OXFORD

1893—1897

They took great pains with the younger members of the University . . . When they had some interest with any such, they would get then to breakfast and over a dish of tea endeavour to fasten some gooc hint upon them. . . . They seldom took any notice of the accusation brought against them; but if they made any reply, it was commonly such a plain and simple one, as if there was nothing more in the case but that they had just heard some doctrines of the Saviour, and hac believed and done accordingly. . . . He thought prayer to be mor his business than anything else, and I have often seen him come out o his closet with a serenity that was next to shining.—*Description o John Wesley and his friends at Oxford, from letters of the Moravian Bishop Gambold.*

I

Temple Gairdner returned to Oxford for his seconc year, whether he knew it or not, a leader, and one whc must pay the price of leadership. He had in his owr interests a difficult team to drive: his reading, which neither his sense of honour nor his mental hunger woulc allow him to shirk; his intellectual friends, and his musical friends; the boats; and now also the O.I.C.C.U. with its system of prayers and Bible readings its group of comrades and its clear, sharp evangelistic programme.

It was impossible for one life to do justice to all this and it is characteristic of Gairdner that what went first to the wall was his dearest pleasure, music. After a time the piano disappeared from his rooms, and he learnec to be content with an occasional afternoon in the rooms of some friend who owned one. But it was real fasting and at the end of term he would call himself " a musically parched man."

" We struck up a musical partnership," says a friend, " and at intervals during term time he would come round to my rooms and play for a whole afternoon. I remember once at the end we spontaneously fell on our knees, and in burning words he poured out his soul in thanksgiving to God for His great gift of music."

To the boats Gairdner was faithful. It was part of his college patriotism and part of his demand from himself of hardness. He rowed in the torpids of 1894 and 1896, and in the latter year was ninth man for the eight. The Rev. H. Legge, a gigantic rowing blue, known and loved by all the University as " Joe Legge," coached Trinity for the torpids of that year. " I remember Gairdner," he says, " as a plucky, painstaking oarsman, not very brilliant but thoroughly reliable." Being a fairly good second-class oar, Gairdner was sometimes thrust into a crew at the last moment as a substitute, without much opportunity for training, and his friends remember his returning from the boats " absolutely raw and bleeding," and going again the next day " horribly sore." " The pluck of it made an impression."

> There comes to most crews in training [says a friend who rowed with him], a time when they feel heartily sorry for themselves. It was in one of these moments that I remember Gairdner rallying my spirits as we walked together one Sunday afternoon along the Banbury Road. He advanced the theory that all one's appreciation such as it was of the beauty of Oxford, of poetry, of music, of freedom to choose one's own companions, was due to rowing. Rowing " was bringing it all out in me." As for the boredom and slavery of the moment, let us remember our Virgil—*Forsan et haec olim meminisse juvabit.* I can remember his look as he said the words more than thirty years ago—the fast walk, the eager, short-sighted gaze, his half-laughing voice and quick spirit that took every-

thing that had a touch of hardness or difficulty in i
welcomingly ; and yet with a sort of high seriousnes
to do his best with it.

"Bump-suppers" were both a joy and an ordeal tc
Gairdner. He radiated humour on a festive occasion
but neither his artist nature nor his religious devotior
could away with the drunkenness that too often wounc
up these jollities. In a very revealing letter to a sor
he says :

> It may seem prudish, but to the end of the chapte
> I couldn't bear to see anyone—even an undergrad.—
> drunk, with the swinish details which as a matter o
> fact are involved on these occasions.
>
> No one rejoices more than I do in hymning Balliol
> no one would take a more fantastic part in the hymning
> —no one (if you like) would tear up wooden fittings
> more willingly than I to make a bonfire. I stil
> would do all these things and do them with the best
> But the vexation to my spirit is still that undergrad-
> uate human nature appears unable to do these truly
> divine human things without stimuli that make swine
> of the doers.
>
> "Wine that maketh glad the heart of man," I'm
> not forgetting that either, and know the flatness anc
> forcedness which a little of that gladness-maker jus
> expels. As a matter of fact, in the state of excitemen
> and nerves which a bump-supper creates, a thimbleful
> of champagne would be enough to set most mer
> surpassing themselves in drollery and enjoyment.

II

As time went on, the O.I.C.C.U. thought of him more
and more as "one of the inner circle," and he fully livec
their life. In intensity of personal devotion it was very
like the life of the first days of the Oxford Movement.
There was a similar insistence on hard living and on
scrutiny of motive, and the same authentic note of
desperateness, of "all or nothing" that marks every

great return to the spirit of the days when Christ's disciples " left all and followed Him." That this was the temper of the O.I.C.C.U. group is shown by the fact that the leaders of it, almost to a man, offered themselves as foreign missionaries.

The members of this group—at first only one or two in each college, and often ostracized by the leaders of college society—kept in closest touch with one another through a " Daily Prayer Meeting " held in a hired room up many stairs in a house in the High Street. Here at one o'clock daily they prayed for Oxford, for personal devotion, for conversions, and for vocations to the mission field. " I well remember the effect made on me by Gairdner's rapt and subdued behaviour in those meetings," a friend writes. " He would kneel down in the front of the little room, where we met over the tailor's shop in the High Street, muttering New Testament promises. I was aware of a man who believed in prayer and rejoiced in it."

Another mark of the O.I.C.C.U. life was attendance at " Biblers," small circles in various colleges for Bible study.

> I think of him at our College Bible Reading [a friend says], for which he had drawn up the syllabus (and how he could make a printed list of subjects a living thing !) ; how he would stammer out, in his slow, detached way, thoughts and ideas that lived in our memory ; how he would draw the best out of others, even the ignorant or diffident, by his interest in their point of view, his welcome for *ideas*, in whatever guise, his longing after truth, and (be it added) his true Scotsman's love of an argument.

Moreover, the O.I.C.C.U. set before itself that hardest of all tasks—personal evangelism among equals in age and standing. And the street service at the Martyrs' Memorial continued, with its acid test of courage. It was characteristic of Gairdner that, having committed himself to this, he trained a men's quartette to sing at the service, that there might be a touch of real beauty in the business. "I can see him still," says a friend, "standing in his scholar's gown, with a little tuning-fork in his hand." Some who heard him speak there can never forget the head thrown back and the words jerked out from his living experience of Christ, as when he said, "And that Communion is so real that if you are sitting alone in a room with Him and even your dearest friend comes in, you feel it is an interruption."

Growing into deeper touch with the O.I.C.C.U., he found his closest friendships there. With J. H. Oldham of his own college he had a clear, unbroken intimacy, and of W. E. S. Holland of Magdalen he wrote : "He is one of the half-dozen (or less) friends and fellow-workers of Oxford days with whom I always felt and feel in complete sympathy." "I do not think that the O.I.C.C.U. can have included many minds of the rank of Gairdner's," writes one who remained outside it. It did not, but neither did he demand that it should ; to be a real, struggling person was to qualify for his friendship. "In the matter of making friends with uninteresting people," J. H. Oldham says, "and that not as from above, but as really seeing in them something that the rest of us could not see, Temple Gairdner was incomparably the biggest Christian I have known."

But promiscuous friendships, street-preachings and texts on the wall were more than his college could tolerate from a man of parts and breeding. The mute and practical comment on "Behold, I make all things new" was a "rag" in which his furniture and ornaments were smashed. And coming up from the boats one day Gairdner found a group of the "Rugger crowd"[1] standing at the college gate. As he came through the archway, one of the "bloods" stepped forward and hit him in the face. He walked on quickly without a word.

He refused, however, to take up the attitude of a persecuted person or to glory in the isolation of his little

[1] In 1895 five of the University Fifteen were Trinity men, and two were Internationals.

group. He had too many interests to share with men. Was there not Huxley's Romanes lecture to discuss,[1] or the boats, or tennis, or dinners at the Palmerston Club, or the Union, or a Balliol concert, or a Trinity Scholars' Gaudy to sing at, a Schumann quintette to hear at Dr. Mee's "at home," or the Kreutzer Sonata at the Musical Union? He had, through his father, more acquaintances than most undergraduates among senior members of the University—Dr. Caird of Balliol, Dr. Rashdall, Dr. Raper and others knew and liked the boy. "Certainly he never had any want of sympathy with or capacity to enjoy the ordinary interests of life," says his friend Mr. G. H. Allen; and another says, "I think he realized that it was his religion, not himself, that was objected to, and that he might have been popular had he liked."

III

But although in the eyes of the outside undergraduate world Gairdner was branded as an O.I.C.C.U. man, some inside that group were not without their doubts about him.

To some of them his habit of receiving the Communion every Sunday was felt to be dangerously near "leaning on ordinances." He was eager, too, to make more of College chapels, "chiefly regarded at the Trinity of those days," says Sir Frederick Butler, "as a means of getting people out of bed in decent time four mornings in the week. In the evening, when attendance was not compulsory, it was quite the usual thing for the priest and the scholar whose turn it was to read the lessons to have it all to themselves and to give one another wholehearted support in trying to beat all previous speed records."

This state of things Gairdner took to heart. He spoke about the possibilities of the chapel services to his friends of the "Daily Prayer Meeting," and he created a mild sensation by reading, when his own turn came round,

[1] May 18th, 1893, on Evolution and Ethics.

with great reverence, feeling and emphasis. Moreover, he was one of several O.I.C.C.U. men who encouraged the more ardent spirits among Anglo-Catholics to found the Oxford Church Union, with the object of infusing life into the framework of religion provided by the services at college chapels and at the University church.

All this was bewildering to certain members of the O.I.C.C.U., but more of them were puzzled by Gairdner's habits of thought on such subjects as Biblical criticism. His father's son had thought more widely and more tolerantly than the average evangelical of that day and group. "Gairdner we all respected," one of them says, "but he never completely fell in with our shibboleths. We thought his prayers very weird; they came stammering out of his lips, hot with his thought and experience. He was really in all his thinking about twenty years ahead of us. It was all progressive thought with him; he was growing intellectually and spiritually at the same time, and we were troubled as to whether he was 'quite sound.'"

"I think the missionary propaganda we were imbibing and which we regarded as orthodoxy looked on the heathen as destined for the inferior tropics. We had cards on our walls about the number who perished every minute." Gairdner took a strong line and refused to believe in any physical flames of everlasting fire. ("He nearly got butted out of the O.I.C.C.U. on the question," says a friend.) "Not to save them from hell, *but from sin which is hell*" was his dominant thought, adopted before he was twenty. "And when I tried to dissuade him from airing his unorthodoxy," says a friend, "he rounded on me—'My dear man, you don't know anything about truth for truth's sake. Don't you see that your views on hell affect your whole belief as to the character of God?'"

"In youth's mêlée," Gairdner himself says, "every temperament was found, and constant was the clash of views and of methods. The more life the more ferment." "We had queer little theological oddities and some theories of the spiritual life that outdid the mediæval mystics or the sectaries of the seventeenth century," says the Rev. Herbert Whately. "'Keswick' was not hot enough on holiness for some of our number, and for the zeal of some no existing Christian Church provided fervent enough evangelistic methods." Yet with all this the group somehow held together by reason of their common passion for Christ.

In the last year of his life, as he looked back on the O.I.C.C.U. of his day, Temple Gairdner wrote :

> On the whole, men who join these more definite and out-and-out bodies usually get somewhere, whereas so many attachés of broader societies get nowhere in particular. You see, these latter try hard to secure a very wide synthesis which is more naturally the fruit of maturity and experience. . . . Societies like the O.I.C.C.U. make straight for fundamental evangelical experiential Christianity, and make sure of that. Of course, if this crystallizes and nothing further happens, you are apt to get later on in life the hard, stiff, dogmatic shell-backs from whom many things have been suffered during the last ten years. But if only development goes on, then the warm evangelicalism of their origin expands, modifies, mellows, and the result is—power with maturity. The synthesis that such a man attempts later on will very likely have more in it than any precocious one.

"Through all the hurly-burly of this movement of youth," says a friend, "Temple Gairdner, though always utterly humble and apparently unconscious of being a leader, was a dominant figure through sheer force of intellect and personality and the beauty of his Christian life." And another writes :

> Here was a man who could swallow the O.I.C.C.U. and be its president [he was president in 1895], and yet—and yet—have a mind that wanted to see life whole, and that could rise so completely above Low

Church phrases and fads and reach out to bigger things. In spite of a slightly stiff Scotch manner, he had a way of saying a thing—or of praying a thing—that was distinctive, reconciling, sympathetic and arrestingly real. I remember a discussion on the use of one's influence for Christ, when rather extreme things were said. There was a little heat over it. Then I recall "Gairdie" getting up and saying calmly and kindly, "*Some of us have two sets of friends.*" The sentence may seem trivial, but it was characteristic. He *had* two sets of friends, rowing friends, scholarly friends, musical friends, and then on the other side the definitely evangelical set with whom his lot was so courageously identified.

IV

That "slightly stiff Scotch manner" to which the last writer made reference went with Gairdner through life. He had an intense feeling for personal dignity, both his own and that of the other person; and though he could fool divinely among friends, his manner to acquaintances was formal. When in later years he wore also the unconscious dignity of a man who had thought and endured and lived in high ethical regions, acquaintances and pupils sometimes feared him, though no child was ever afraid. Great was his distress and bewilderment if he learnt afterwards that anyone had found him alarming; nor did formality last long. Acquaintances very rapidly passed into the number of his friends and the stiffness was no more. Perhaps it was only for a few of his friends to understand him, but many men loved him, and especially a younger group who reinforced the O.I.C.C.U. when Gairdner was a senior in the college, and when the movement to which he had given his Oxford career was gathering force, and the upper room of the "Daily Prayer Meeting" was sometimes crowded out.

In order to know what manner of man they saw in him, let those friends describe the Gairdner whom they knew:

I don't know what first attracted me to him, but perhaps it was his prayers at the Daily Prayer Meeting [says one], their simplicity and profundity. . . . When he had finished speaking, you felt that at the back of his words lay the unexplored realms of a Great Personality. . . . That rich affectionate chuckle of his, and that upward tilt of his head, with the sideway glint through his spectacles! Ah me! . . . we never shall see his like again.

Gairdner's humour was an affectionate humour [says the Rev. A. G. Fraser, another of the group]. His laugh had more love in it than that of any man I know; if you could make him laugh you were embraced by it.

I shall never forget my first sight of him [says yet another of this younger group]. Asked to a meal, I arrived in his room and sat to wait—when my eye caught the words on the wall, "What is that to thee? follow thou Me!" The clue to the man's character was given to me there. Suddenly he drifted in—you know his "drift"—followed by a friend, and one knew at once, with the instinct one has even in immature years, that one was in contact with a great personality. I hear his first words as if they were spoken yesterday: "Oh! you are W——, and you've come up to Trinity. How jolly! This is X, of Pembroke. We've been round the Parks discussing Free-will and Determinism, and on the whole" (his eyes wandering into infinity) "I am afraid we found that Free-will has got to go!" Any question of affectation or pedantry simply didn't arise. It was just Gairdner, the authentic Gairdner. . . .

I have a vivid remembrance of one day in the summer term when the College garden was what only an Oxford garden in summer sunshine can be, and he took my arm and said, "Let's watch the garden praising God!" and then he began to chant in his strong, virile voice, "O ye delphiniums, bless ye the Lord . . . O ye azaleas, bless ye the Lord" . . . and so on, right round the garden borders. Who but Temple Gairdner could have done it, and made his companion feel that it was the most natural and fitting thing in the world—and feel it with a thrill of inspiration ?

What can we say ? [another writes]. He was my best friend and he did more for me than anyone else ; often, on reflection, I felt that his life and love were the strongest, best evidence of Christianity that ever came my way ; more than books, or Churches, or anything else.

To himself it seemed far otherwise. He had passed from that first surprise of spiritual love to the stage when, educated by the Divine Companionship, a soul knows itself unworthy. His self-scrutiny is merciless :

O God ! Am I playing for my own hand ?

Alone with Thee, through life, the heat of men's praise will not burn me, nor the frost of their blame freeze me ; I shall lose the craving for approbation and influencing men, and the grief at non-success. I am myself the reverse of all this.

Faults still glaring—thoughtlessness, slovenliness, greediness ? Well, *fast* !

But to a man of his rich, vivid life the intensest struggle of those early years was for a blazing purity. A friend still keeps the memory of one of those broken confessions of his that all who love him remember, when on the first day of an Oxford term, he said, " People think me purer than I am : God has given me a certain power over myself, but I still cannot pass the women of the streets " —obviously without feeling the power of temptation. In his diary he wrote : " *Purity* : the occasional (thank God) stumble in thought must and should never occur. . . . For their sakes I sanctify myself, O Lord—for the sake of the men I am going to see ; and women and girls and children ; for their sakes make me reverent and pure and courteous and chivalrous and Christlike. Also make me able to speak with the severity of God upon it—the wound of a friend that is precious."

If ever a prayer was fully answered, this one was. "Gairdner was pure in heart," says a friend, "*not* by shutting his eyes, but by seeing in all beauty and in every variety of gift that which is Divine. He could look at an opera, a dancer, a statue, and for him the divine imperishable beauty of them was separable from the elements of sin that to less pure eyes would tarnish the whole." He was so occupied with the holiness of beauty that he seemed unconscious of what to some was a lurking temptation. Being pure in heart, he saw God. But such purity was not easily come by.

V

Gairdner had a strong sense of honour in regard to the work for which his parents had sent him to Oxford, and he hoped for the first in "Greats" which was predicted for him. He was strict in not allowing himself more time for his religious work than other hard-reading men permitted themselves for their chosen recreations. Perhaps, in his young zeal and vigour, he hardly realized how infinitely more demanding was his form of recreation.

In 1895, the notable year when the Thames froze, when college eights were driven out of the river, and Christ Church meadows were skated over, Gairdner went into lodgings in Pembroke Street, with J. H. Oldham, Paget Wilkes of Lincoln (one of the fiery spirits of the O.I.C.C.U.), and R. J. Wright of Brasenose. The latter gives a picture of the group, then reading for "Greats":

> I stood a little in awe of men so very evangelically disposed. But we pulled along very happily. Gairdner was for his years a capital conversationalist. He was bursting with new interests and topics, and reaching out after things which he couldn't quite express, and always interesting. He had also a broad enough mind to bring together things that seemed

far asunder. Wilkes was a very racy, lively talker, and Oldham a careful, restrained talker. It was good to listen to the three.

We were all four reading for "Greats," and busy with philosophy. I think it was Oldham who said that Wilkes and I were "the extremes" and he and Gairdie "the means." Gairdie's bent was towards philosophy. He was full of it. He revelled in metaphysics.

"As regards his work for the Schools, he naturally brought a challenging mind to what he read. I read Aristotle's *Ethics* with him," says G. H. Allen, "and he had a way of treating his author (Plato or Aristotle, for instance) as if he were discussing the subject with him, and when in Gairdner's judgment Plato or Aristotle or whoever it might be failed at some point, Gairdner loved to pounce down on him and tell him he had gone wrong!"

They were always on the point of discovering the secret of the universe.

"I remember once chatting with him," says the Rev. H. Legge, "and his saying that when he was reading 'Greats' he always felt he was just going to get at the truth, and it always eluded him and seemed a little further on."

Several of his friends remember his excitement over lectures by Professor Edward Caird, Master of Balliol. "He followed keenly the marshalling of the conflicting problems in the early lectures and waited breathlessly for the solution, and I remember his disappointment at the end that nothing had been solved except by a verbal formula, and his sense of the limitations of philosophy."

"He used to come home," says R. J. Wright, "with tales of a remarkable philosophy don they had at Trinity—Cannan by name." Mr. Cannan, Gairdner's "Greats" tutor, was a very able and humorous person who affected the dress and lounge of a bargee. The two were on excellent terms, and Gairdner would report a "long philosophic jaw with Cannan." In lectures Mr. Cannan enjoyed a mock-deferential reference to Gairdner of all questions that touched on religion, and his pupil entered into the spirit of the game. "I remember Gairdner reporting a talk Cannan had with him," R. J. Wright says. "He was imperilling his chance of a 'first' by the pre-occupation of his mind with Christian Union matters. It wasn't that he slacked his work—for he didn't—but his two enthusiasms clashed. There was indeed a third, for he was rowing in the Trinity boat. Eventually Cannan proved to be right. He just missed getting his 'first.'"

The news brought a shock to his circle, as their letters bear witness.

"We all believe you are a first-class man," wrote the Rev. F. J. Chavasse (afterwards Bishop of Liverpool), and Mr. Cannan wrote: "I am very much obliged for your kind way of taking the blame (if any), but we will continue to put it on the examiners—poor wretches. To get both you and Miss R. into the second class was, as I told one of them, a real *tour de force*."

Professor Edward Caird congratulated him on the "free and manly way" in which he took the news, but it was none the less a cutting disappointment, wherein the sharpest sting was his mother's conviction that his missing a "first" was due to absorption in religious affairs. But the news came to him hot-foot upon an interior experience that strangely sweetened those days. He had gone again, immediately after his *viva*, to the Students' Camp at Keswick. There, on his first morning he retired alone for a "long time in church." The transaction that took place in the silence of the empty church by the lake was momentous. As he meditated he heard some words of the Gospel addressed to himself with utterly personal force. "Canst thou drink of the cup that I drink of and be baptized with the baptism wherewith I was baptized?" Gairdner knew that he must answer. He said unto Him, "I can." Jesus said unto him, "Thou shalt."

A week or so later the telegram with the result of the Schools reached Gairdner in a friend's house towards evening. "In spite of oneself, one felt quite sick for a moment," he said. But he talked with one of the ladies and "spent an evening of delightful music" before he went to his room to look his disappointment in the face. There he wrote :

"This night God lays His hand on me. I remember the 'I can' of Keswick. Here is Thy first 'Thou shalt.' Amen, Lord, Amen. . . . I am Thine, O Lord, by a covenant sealed in Thy blood and in this *drop* of mine. . . . Amen."

CHAPTER IV

THE UNCOMMERCIAL TRAVELLER

1897—1899

Yea, I think I may say that his hazardous journey has got many well-wishers to his ways.—*John Bunyan.*

I

To understand the next phase of Gairdner's career it is necessary to return to the Students' Conference at Keswick in the summer of 1894, when the O.I.C.C.U. and similar groups were suddenly called to add to their intense individual evangelistic life a world ambition. Two great young leaders of American student life came to England that year and kindled the will and the imagination of the British leaders.

"Mr. Mott and his fellow-countryman, Mr. R. E. Speer, *par nobile fratrum*, had come over," Gairdner says, and in these two American visitors he found two of the admirations of his life. Of John R. Mott he wrote in 1910, with a quaint little apology to the subject of his portrait—"I wrote it to please myself," he said :

> The whole physique of the man suggested strength, with its frame built on large lines, finely moulded head and rock-strong face. When a point of unusual interest was being hazarded, forward would come the big head, quick as light ; the strong square jowl would be thrust forward, the broad brow knit and scowl (if the word may be used for a sight wholly gracious), the dark shaggy eyebrows almost meet, while from under their shadow shoots a gleam from suddenly-kindling eyes : a very lion preparing to spring at an idea.

And of his speaking he said :

> The sentences of John R. Mott hammer with careful, scientific deliberateness, until at the end the audience finds itself, in a word—smashed. And then the tenderness of the man comes out—as he deals with the fragments.

This man became in 1894 in Gairdner's mind " the Chief." J. R. Mott's comrade that summer, as through many a year, was Robert Speer, who gave a series of Bible readings on " The Man Jesus Christ." " That Man still *lives*," says Gairdner's diary of those days " the Personality which, when we were shown it, burned our hearts is alive, the same, present, our Friend and Lover. I was constrained to nestle into Jesus as never before." There followed a strange expansion of thought and spirit. " Gradually and yet surely it grew in our hearts that this was no ordinary Conference : the more that was claimed, the more was granted. Prayer became daring and inspired. One mind ruled." And on this preparation came " the address in which the watchword (' The Evangelization of the World in this Generation ') was, like a challenge, flung before British university and college men."[1]

Of that great day, Wednesday, August 1st, 1894, the diary says : " Holy Communion . . . deep impression of new era. . . . Evening, Speer simply God-inspired. ' Evangelization of the World in this Generation.' Never heard anything like it. Oldham and I walk up the road and give ourselves to God." It was then unknown to Gairdner that another couple on that same evening, equally moved, " had to get away quietly three miles on the hills to let God speak to us face to face."

[1] " The adopting of this watchword," Gairdner later explained, " was not, of course, a prophecy that the world would be evangelized in the present generation, but simply an affirmation that it might be and should be so evangelized (since every generation of Christians is responsible for evangelizing the world of that generation) ; and a self-dedication to a life consonant with that faith and that aspiration."

They were Douglas Montagu Thornton and a Cambridge friend. What Gairdner wrote later of the effect of this address on the mind of Thornton might describe its enlarging and invigorating effect not on individuals only but on the young movement throughout the British colleges :

> The whole inner man suddenly expanded ; new visions floated before his astonished eyes ; horizon opened out on horizon ; deep called to deep. His flaring zeal settled down into a clear burning flame.

Gairdner gave himself unreservedly to the claims of that demanding watchword, and Dr. Mott keeps vivid memories of him in those Keswick days :

> He impressed me with his natural enthusiasm, his responsiveness to exacting demands in the realm of spiritual discipline, and to the stern challenges sounded out in regard to the extension of the reign of Christ. It is given to but a few men to share in laying the foundations of a movement which within their own lifetime profoundly and extensively influences for good the life of their own nation and the welfare of mankind. Gairdner was one of a small group to whom was given this distinction.

II

After taking his degree, Gairdner was asked to spend one more year in work in Oxford, becoming a lay-brother attached to the clergy who shepherded undergraduates in the Oxford pastorate. "A strange new proposal," his diary called it, but the advice of his friends quieted his anxiety lest he ought perhaps to go abroad at once. "With what fiery intensity," he wrote when the matter was settled, "must I address myself *now* to self-education at home and work at home."

It *was* a year of fiery intensity, that year of 1897, and a prelude to a wider work. For the studious part of his life he was reading theology and attending lectures under the direction of the Rev. F. J. Chavasse (then Principal of Wycliffe Hall, Oxford), whose Greek Testament lectures were his delight. In the active work of the pastorate his "chief" was the Rev. Henry Gibbon (later Chaplain and Fellow of Balliol), a Bayard, formerly of the Indian Army.

Gairdner's rooms became a storm-centre of religious life, a rallying-point, a confessional. "So-and-so opened up" is a recurring phrase in his diary; to the end of his life he used it when confidences had been poured upon him. One week he notes thirteen fresh names of men to be prayed for individually. But all this was carried through in true Gairdnerian fashion with very little sense of time and with a string of appointments forgotten in the intense interest of the conversation of the moment. Mr. Gibbon felt constrained to rebuke his lay-brother. A passage in the diary illustrates the relationship:

> Old Gibbon rebuked me to-night and it was the voice of God. The last week shows well how casual and unsystematic (criminally so) I have been. God brought me very low. My heart was rent. When I got home there was the dear chap back to comfort me. We sat with tears in our eyes.
>
> I sinned against man, and it was against God.
> I was rebuked by man, and it was the voice of God.
> I was forgiven by man, and it was the healing, binding touch of God.
>
> Prayed long to-night.

This year of prelude wound up with two events that meant much to Gairdner—Queen Victoria's Diamond Jubilee and a Student Conference at Curbar.

All his capacity for enthusiasm was lavished on the Diamond Jubilee day. With a brother and a friend he set out to see the show from a tree in the Green Park, only to find the gates closed. "But we spied a man propping up a rotten ladder by which many were scaling the railings at 2*d*. a head. We did too (the ladder soon after broke up into its primordial elements). Now for a tree. . . . Up we go and soon are perched in branches together with half a dozen other human birds, and so command a view of Piccadilly right from Hyde Park Corner." He saw it all, the colonial procession with troops from all the world, the military procession headed by the gigantic Captain Ames, the foreign royalties, "the little Battenberg children, the little girls bowing like machines, two bows a second." Then at last "a venerable aged lady—snow-white hair, shining face—wearing a black bonnet with a white bunch in the middle, and holding a white parasol."

> Men, women and children sprang to their feet and craned forward . . . cheered their very hearts out, cheered out the love that leapt from the heart at that moment to the eyes. All that afternoon I had to choke down the passion that would rise. . . . I left the other two . . . I wanted to be alone . . . I felt something of eternity this morning. . . . Then I read the account of Jesus' procession into Jerusalem. Poor little procession ! . . . To my joy I found that He does not *despise* all this earthly glory, but is going to make it swell the glory of His triumph. Not every monarch's glory will seem glorious in Heaven. But my Queen's will, because the glory of this day was not the procession of the soldiers but a people's love. I should like to serve my Queen. Can I do it better than by taking Christ to her Empire ? She would like that, I think.

A few days after this thrill came the third summer conference of the Student Movement ; for the first time it had moved away from its birthplace at Keswick and was now in a more spacious camping-ground on the banks of the Derwent in the little stone-built village of Curbar among the Derbyshire hills. At this conference Gairdner began his career as a member of the staff ; he was to be travelling secretary for the British College Christian Union[1] in the coming academic year.

[1] This was the name by which the Student Christian Movement of Great Britain and Ireland was known for the first seven years of its existence.

He spoke twice at Curbar, once on "Giving" and once on "Time." Of Gairdner as a speaker his friends give very various accounts. "He never attained to anything like eloquence," says one who has a gift of rapid speech. "There he stood," says another, "his head thrown back, tying himself in knots, jerking the words out with a terrible reality. He always held me riveted." "Perhaps," another says, "he would begin in a very quiet and commonplace way, so that the censorious would say 'There is nothing here'; when suddenly in a flash there would come an utterance, so it seemed, from the Throne of God itself, the inspired word of the authentic man of God, lightning in a dark world."

"I remember that muttering unself-conscious way of his as he came into the tent on the night of his address on 'Giving,' saying under his breath, 'Lord, save me from temptation,'" writes Mr. Malcolm Spencer. And another says: "That address changed the character of the Student Movement. I don't suppose any of the men who heard it ever again gave so little as a tenth. It sent me back to Oxford not only to pay my debts but to live on half of what I had lived on before."

Instantly on this address came a humiliation that Gairdner remembered to the end of his life:

> *July 31st.*—My birthday. I fasted and gave the year to God, confessing my serious sins, especially carelessness. . . . Alas! it was the hour of judgment. At this very hour God punished me for the countless lightly-considered carelessnesses of years. I left my pocket-book with £15 inside it, somewhere by or in the tent. In the evening missed it, and it has not turned up. I repent, receive "the doom assigned": but oh, let it cure.

He was at that time a poor man and the money represented some Oxford fees. "But his financial loss hardly seemed to strike him," says a friend; "he was so disconsolate at having failed of the standard he had set himself and others."

III

That autumn Gairdner became a member of the Student Movement team that had for its centre a fusty little office at 93 Aldersgate Street—an office with one desk and three chairs. The desk was the property of the General Secretary, in Gairdner's time H. C. Duncan. The walls on both sides were stacked with open boxes full of literature.

> It was terrible literature imported wholesale from America, and not in the least suited to British colleges [one of the secretaries says]. Gairdie had not yet written his little *Studies in Prayer* which was our very first British textbook. I remember piles and piles of white pamphlets with the title *Murdered Millions* in blood-red letters. It had something to do with medical missions.
>
> When we had committees, the women sat on the three chairs and all the men on packing-cases. We were in such desperate earnest that we not only did not spare ourselves, we did not spare one another, if we thought we saw signs of obstinacy or exaggeration or snobbishness. We were all living hard and giving every penny we could save to missions. I remember A. G. Fraser being taken to task for having gold waistcoat buttons.

"I remember that Gairdner was always afraid we should gravitate to people of our own social background or education. He was specially anxious to make friends in certain colleges which in those days had a rather different social standing." "I can see Gairdner now," says a fellow-secretary, "when someone at a committee said in a rather superior way, 'Oh, his father was a brewer.' Out came Gairdie's hand with that familiar gesture of his. 'Hush!' he said, leaning across the table in his eagerness—'Hush! we're not speaking of fathers.'" He himself had friends in walks of life in which a young scholar sometimes fails of friendship. There was "my old friend Philips, the fried-fish man," in a Midland town, and Mr. Gilham, the porter of Trinity College, to whom Gairdner sent a Christmas card to the end of his life. "In our young days," Mr. Gilham says, "we were great friends and used to write to one another."

A group so young and so free in friendship could not be without its jests. "All Gairdner's accounts of work, interviews and the rest were given with a great deal of mimicry, verve and humour," says Tissington Tatlow. One of the "stunts" was to get "Gairdie" to imitate a certain Irish member of the O.I.C.C.U. in an impassioned missionary address. "He recounted with the chuckle which all his friends remember," says one of them, "how X, describing the sufferings of a pioneer mission party, made more than a hundred per cent. of them die not once but over and over again."

"We always had a day or a half-day of prayer before our executive meetings," says a committee member of that time, "and we became so much of one mind in those hours of devotion that we often made the biggest and most daring decisions quickly without argument."

"No one before or since has ever led a quiet day for the committee as Gairdner did," Tissington Tatlow says. "As a young man of twenty-two he could bring a company of students into the Presence of God, helping them to a spiritual experience of an unforgettable kind."

IV

After an executive committee they parted to the four winds of heaven, careering over Great Britain and Ireland. Temple Gairdner, whose business it was to plant and sustain Christian Unions in all types of colleges, threaded the whole railway system together with prayers as he had once threaded the lanes of Oxford. This was no sudden development. "Gairdner's life was steeped in prayer," writes an Oxford friend. "He had a way of praying as he walked along the street. It was a revelation to me to meet a robust mystic of that kind, a fellow as gay of spirit and as buoyant and springy as all that and yet with a life hid with Christ in God." "I remember," says Dr. Donald Fraser, "when we went out for walks together at Glasgow he would suddenly break off into prayer in the middle of Sauchiehall Street (in the heart of the city), praying as he walked along, with his eyes open, just as naturally as if he were still talking to me."

So he wandered about the British Isles, extremely detached in both the spiritual and the physical sense from his possessions. One of the favourite stories against him told of his meeting a man in New Street, Birmingham, putting down his bag while he noted an engagement in his pocket-book, and proceeding along New Street minus the bag. "I imagine," Dr. Tatlow says, "that every garment he possessed came back to the office through the post while he was travelling secretary. Shoes, Bible, sponge, pyjamas, toothbrush, waistcoat, and I know not what, followed one another in an unending stream, to the delight of our office-boy."

But this feckless wanderer was proving himself a statesman and a leader. In his first fortnight of work he was sent to Wales as an outsider admitted slightly on sufferance to a Welsh Conference. (He attended the first Graduation Ceremony of the University of Wales, October 22nd, 1897.) His summing-up of the situation was sympathetic :

> The country feels its own personality and wishes to retain it ; this extends itself to the student Christian life. "Wales for Christ" is the cry. Welsh religion has been always national. . . . We should recognize this national energy *and not chafe against it*, . . . but the British College Christian Union should continually bring forward the *world-wide* movement, and not suffer Wales to cut herself off from the larger life.

His summings-up as he travelled were often trenchant :

> The B.C.C.U. here is a failure owing to flabby committee, no head, no policy, no *idiosyncrasy*. There is only one thing—fire the centre. The core, the

five or six men in dead earnest, must become in more dead earnest and draw in the next circle, and then the next, and so on, into the life of seeking after God.

He was all the while putting *himself* to spiritual fences :

> How shall I love *there* [i.e. in the mission-field] if I walk with my heart like a stone through the streets here ?
>
> Let me love every man, woman and child I meet and be Jesus to them and see Jesus in them.
>
> Not I, but Christ loveth in me.
>
> Actually loved the waiter at the hotel.

And again next day :

> Further loved waiter !

To a fellow-passenger in a train, Gairdner suddenly remarked one day that he had " been praying for him." It transpired that he had prayed to be able to love the man who should sit opposite to him, and that God would speak to that man. The acquaintance then made and followed up by letter was the beginning of new life for the older man, an Irish manufacturer who became one of Gairdner's valued friends.

Of his own Oxford he had great joy. " Joseph remembered his dream," was his comment on finding large and thriving Bible study groups. " The shout of a King is in Oxford this term." He acted as lieutenant to Dr. Mott in a mission at Oxford in the summer of 1898. " What do I not owe," Dr. Mott says, " to his loyal, thoughtful and unselfish co-operation manifested so beautifully ! As we daily prayed together he revealed most remarkable insight and complete identification with my spiritual aims and burdens, as few men have ever done. Our union in prayer was very genuine and precious, and his faith excited upon me an uplifting influence like unto that of the tides lifting ships."

> I can't tell you what an intimate joy it was—pure happiness [Gairdner wrote long after to the man he

greatly loved]—to be associated with you that week . . . introducing you to people and trying to serve you in any way. I nurse that memory pretty tenderly to-day.

His return after his travels was to London, and the ondon colleges weighed much upon him. "Found ondon colleges are going to be tough," is his entry fter his first day at the office. A letter to Tissington atlow shows the characteristic action taken :

> Will you turn up an hour before the Quiet Day? . . . We will then like children bring London before our Father and *claim victory*.

The base for his London operations was the house of olonel Oldham, father of his Oxford friend. He was eceived as a son of the house, and no son could have iven more honour to Colonel Oldham, that chivalrous igure, for whom he conceived a great devotion. "Gair-ie's" comings were a longed-for joy to the youngest hild of that house (now the Rev. J. E. Oldham).

> I was rather a shy and solitary small boy. But busy as he was with work as Travelling Secretary, he always seemed to have some time to devote to me. After dinner he would take his seat on the piano-stool and go through a series of old favourites : "Widdecombe Fair," "There was an old wife of Pee-ee-ee-bles who made a potato pie." I had to occupy a particular chair close to the piano in order to be directly addressed at the climax of the narrative ; often I was in convulsions.
>
> Then there were our games together. I was very keen on soldiers, and "Gairdie" would enter into the campaign most realistically, and suggested a helpful device for moving detachments about on bits of cardboard instead of man by man. One day stands out unique—two cousins, a boy and a girl a few years younger than I, were playing with me our pet game of a journey by coach, when Gairdner looked in. I can see him still, with a towel draped on his head, as old

" Aunt Jane," an imaginary personage encountered o
our travels.

And there were our walks in Kensington Garden
and Hyde Park. He would suggest to me that w
should pretend that everyone else was *pretending* t
be the opposite of what he really was : the well
dressed people in their carriages or on horseback wer
the veriest loafers and paupers, while the familia
figures lying about the grass were the titled nobilit
in disguise.

V

From moving platoons of toy soldiers with Jac
Oldham, Temple Gairdner would go off to the office t
enter into the schemes of another strategist, his colleague
fast becoming his friend of friends, Douglas Thornton.
Thornton, " the young man who thinks in continents an
archbishops," had been one of a dauntless few who drew
up a " Memorial to the Churches " in which the infan
Student Movement urged its watchword on the Churc
life of Britain. With G. T. Manley he had visite
Archbishop Temple on the matter and urged the adoptio
of the "watchword " by the Lambeth Conference of 1897
The Archbishop seems to have been very communicativ
to his boyish deputation. " I only hope you'll get th
Bishops to take it up," he said. " I've been trying t
move them for the past ten years, but they're hard t
move."

Thornton had no more fear of dictating to his Churc
than during an earlier movement had the young Hurre
Froude, when, as he stretched out his long length o
Newman's sofa, he broke out : " I don't see why w
should disguise from ourselves that our object is to dictat
to the clergy of this country, and I for one do not wan
anyone else to get on the box." Both men were prophets
with a message to the Church that was like fire in thei
bones.

When Gairdner joined the staff of the movement, th
travelling secretaries had neat little leaflets for distributio

among Anglican clergy, bearing a commendation of the Student Volunteer Movement by the Lambeth Conference, by committees of S.P.G. and C.M.S., and by the Archbishop of Armagh. But that is a far cry from the adoption of the "watchword" as a working policy by the rank and file of Anglican life. It was Thornton who now saw that the way to reach the life whether of his Church or of the Free Church Communions was to impregnate the theological colleges with missionary fervour, and he came to the executive of the last day but one of 1897 with a complete scheme for a conference of all types of theological students to be held the following Easter.

Within four hours the scheme had been agreed to with "wonderful unanimity," and a triumvirate appointed to arrange the whole conference and enlist its membership. "The Trinity," Gairdner called the group appointed, for it consisted of Thornton of Trinity College Cambridge, Tatlow of Trinity College Dublin, and Gairdner of Trinity College Oxford.

The next months were feverish. Gairdner was set to rush at full speed round the Anglican theological colleges, while Tissington Tatlow visited those of the Free Churches, approaching the Principals with suitable explanations and enlisting the membership of the conference. Except for the fact that Thornton had made a speech at a Church Congress, it is doubtful if any of the young promoters were known by name to the responsible heads of theological colleges, but of that they recked little. "Gairdie and Thornton," says one of their colleagues, "were always afraid of the movement becoming dependent on big names. It seemed better to them to go with the weight of their message alone than with the weight of influence."

At intervals during Gairdner's rapid career round the colleges he was recalled by telegram to meet with Tatlow and Thornton in committee, furiously threshing out plans and details.

The Conference was to be held at Birmingham in the days following Easter. In preparation the three protagonists spent their Easter together at Malvern. "Do you remember last Easter?" Gairdner wrote to Thornton a year later:

> We have thanked God for it. Let us linger over the details of that sweet mercy. . . . Good Friday came. We went to service, afterwards up the Hill. *Benedicite*, O all ye green things of the earth, O lovely hill, O plain receding away and away with an ever-deepening bluish haze, O dotted hamlets and Worcester with the cathedral tower. *Benedicite!* We sang hymns on the top, *duetto*! . . . Easter morning—early to the tomb. He was risen indeed. . . . After dinner, in the spirit of Easter, we slaved from 2.30 till 11 p.m. I drove my pen over the paper, finishing the second draft of the report. [It was an apologia for the life and work of the Student Volunteer Movement, to be presented to the coming conference.] At last the report is finished—Douglas settles himself down with a grunt of satisfaction and a blue pencil, and to the chagrin of the author proceeds to slash away at the report like a fourth-form essay. Author cranes over your shoulder on tenterhooks. Peace of Easter nearly spoiled. And so to bed and next day on to struggle and victory at Birmingham.

One more vignette Tissington Tatlow has preserved of those Malvern days. "I shared a bedroom with Gairdner," he says, "and remember waking in the middle of the night to see his figure in pyjamas kneeling under the window, with a curious white light upon him from the moon outside, as he swayed in prayer, praying aloud (he thought me asleep) and pouring out his soul for the conference, the speakers, and the men who were coming to it."

"That conference," Gairdner wrote years afterwards, "was a time agonized with anxiety, want of sleep and overwork. The idea was new, the men who came were strange to each other and to the work—far more curious than enthusiastic. Moreover, they were theological tudents and therefore—critical. . . . But the end was peace. After some difficult crises the delegates went away convinced, and from that time the Theological College Department of the Student Movement has been a working reality."

Gairdner went on that summer to his first International Conference. It was held at Eisenach, the German student hosts having three years previously entered the new World Federation. Eisenach was Gairdner's first foreign travel, and he went to see the Wartburg :

> Outside, the homely-mysterious romantic Germany of our childhood and the fairy-tales. Inside, the narrow winding courtyard . . . the galleries, the picturesque rooms, the glorious banqueting-hall, Luther's room ! Little children were playing in the courtyard ; and the Grand Duke and Grand Duchess of Saxe-Weimar-Eisenach, lord and lady of this mediæval fairy-tale castle, were dining in the light of the setting sun in a verandah looking west.
>
> Who's the coward would not die for such a land as this ? This is the Fatherland indeed.

VI

In October 1898 Douglas Thornton was ordained at St. Paul's Cathedral for service in Egypt. Gairdner wrote to him :

> I want you not to fret at what I am going to tell you. I cannot be at St. Paul's to-morrow. . . . I want you not to regret. For if there is anything in the Communion of Saints, any truth in the glorified universal presence of the Lord or in the power of prayer, or in the membership of the Body of Christ, I declare to you I *shall be present* with your spirit on Sunday. . . . Our whole faith is staked on the reality of these things. . . . I shall help in separating you for your life-mission to Islam. . . . May you be glorified with the glory of Jesus—that is the glory of self-loss, of

the cross. May you spend and be spent. May God honour you by giving you to drink of Christ's Cup baptizing you with Christ's baptism. These are thoughts I shall be thinking to-morrow.

A month later Douglas Thornton sailed for Egypt. Gairdner had yet some services to render to the Student Movement ere he followed.

He was exercised by the difficulty which the "High Church" leaders of those days felt in working with the Student Christian Movement. "We have a difficult position," he said in a letter to Thornton, "on the one hand deepening every day in our devotion to the Church of England . . . on the other accepting in the fullest way things as they are as a basis of things as they should be and will be."

That December he was sent to visit Dr. Mandell Creighton, then Bishop of London, and obtained from him a letter, written expressly for publication by the Student Christian Movement, and which largely set at rest the minds of dubious theological students. The letter was crystal clear :

My dear Mr. Gairdner,

The practical point on which you ask my opinion is this: Do I think that members of theological colleges in connection with the Church of England would in any way compromise their position as thorough and loyal members of that Communion by joining the British College Christian Union, which aims at uniting students of all denominations for the purpose of promoting missionary zeal? I do not think so. . . . Such union for the general purpose of promoting missionary work does not involve any surrender of individual convictions about the best form in which the Christian truth can be expressed. . . . No one religious body can undertake all the work that is to be done. Combination among students might help to remove misunderstandings, which are too often engendered by the ignorance which comes from exclusiveness. Your endeavour has my warm sympathy.

I am,
Yours truly,
M. LONDON.

W. H. T. GAIRDNER, ESQ.

Another and most characteristic fruit of Gairdner's ast year in England was his little series of Bible study extbooks,[1] the first published by the British Movement nd revealing a depth and closeness of exegesis unusual n that type of book. Had Gairdner overestimated the general attainment in these things or was the standard higher in those days? The deeper souls at least found nutriment to their taste. These textbooks were written in all the pauses of the rapid career of a travelling secretary, and he tried to combine such writing with summer holidays at home, but cursed himself when he felt that he had not entered enough into the family life.

> Have been no use in the house. . . . X took me to task about this and it was clear. I was very sad. At home more than anywhere else one must not "appear to fast." I should take holidays while I do and be absolutely at their disposal.

His home relationships had regained their old charm and joy. After his brother's death and his own religious crisis it seemed for a time as if his sense of humour had received a check. But he was himself again now, the bubbling centre of family merriment and the confidant of his sisters, who brought him their difficulties and christened him "Mr. Interpreter."

A great part of the book on St. John was written at Birmingham, where his friend W. E. S. Holland had a curacy. Miss Woosnam, his hostess, describes how he would spring up instantly from his meditations, at the

[1] *Studies in Prayer*, 1897; *Helps to the Study of St. John's Gospel*, 1898; *Helps to the Study of the Epistle to the Romans*, 1899.

of the palace at Khartoum and straining his vision northwards."

He saw the *Punch* cartoon with the title " At last," and a picture of the meeting of Gordon and Wolseley outside the city. Then he heard the sickening news. Khartoum was sighted forty-eight hours too late. " Too late " was the title of the *Punch* cartoon that week, awful and unforgettable to Temple Gairdner.

> To those who were adults [he wrote long afterwards] the next dozen years—they were only a dozen !—must have passed swiftly enough. To those who were young they appeared a lifetime ; which deepened the sense of excitement and wonder when once more British-led troops were discerned quietly making their way upstream, round the historic bends, across the historic short-cuts, past the historic landmarks, Wadi Halfa, Korosko and Abu Hamed, Dongola and Merowe.

Instead of a preparatory schoolboy he was now a fourth-year man at Oxford, but all the old hero-worship woke again in the incurable romantic that Gairdner always was. He sent for Major Seton Churchill's *Life of General Gordon*. It reached him when he was staying with friends in the country, and his diary shows what an event it was.

> Sussex landscape — lawns — clover — solitude—music after dinner and before bed. I opened Seton Churchill's *Gordon*. Quo ducis Domine ? In Africam Domine ?
>
> If *he* was like this, what wast *Thou*, Jesus ? And I—I am cowardly and vain and conceited, and pleasure-loving and paltry and lazy and mean, impure too, sometimes, in thought. But I long to be otherwise. Come in, then, Jesus, his Jesus and mine, and make me otherwise, brave, retiring, humble, hardy, large-hearted, strenuous, pure, loving. And I praise Thee for him—what he was and is to me.

He shared this hero-worship—for when did Gairdner ever have an unshared enthusiasm?—with his friend Douglas Thornton. On all sorts of occasions and in many quaint situations they sang Gounod's "For ever with the Lord" together. It was Gordon's favourite hymn! And since they were both young strategists, their missionary thinking became full of Gordon's Sudan, and their thoughts turned to the whole Mohammedan world of the Near East.

> In the early days of the Student Movement [Temple Gairdner wrote] no one ever heard of the Near East. About 1898, however, a number of coincident causes awoke interest in the Mohammedans of the Levant. Douglas Thornton . . . was led deliberately to single out Cairo as perhaps the most strategic as well as most difficult field in the world. At the same time Kitchener was methodically working his way up the Nile, so that the eyes of all Gordon admirers were being turned once more to the Nile Valley. Finally, one of the chief features of the notable summer conference at Curbar in 1897 was the presence of some members of the "Egypt Mission Band"[1] and of Miss Van Sommer, then, as to-day, an Egypt and Mohammedan mission enthusiast.

Miss Van Sommer well remembers an afternoon at the Curbar Conference:

> Directly I entered the room, Mr. Gairdner came up to me and said, "I was wanting to speak to you. Will you please come outside with me?" We went out on the lawn and sat down on a plank. He said, "I heard you speak for Egypt the other evening. If you remember, I came in just as you began to speak, and it was just as though a voice said to me, 'Why not you?' I have been thinking a great deal lately about the Nile Valley."

Another visitor to the Curbar Conference was the Rev. H. E. Fox, Secretary of the Church Missionary

[1] It developed later into the "Egypt General Mission."

Society, which, through its station in Cairo, was *the most likely British missionary society to reach Khartoum.* Unknown to one another, Thornton and Gairdner both asked for interviews with Mr. Fox and propounded their thoughts on the Near East.

Mr. Fox encouraged both young men to make a formal offer in writing to the Society, and the upshot was that, each without any knowledge of the other's action, they made their offers to the C.M.S. within a few days of one another.

Yet, after all, it was neither desire to serve in Gordon's country, nor any Christian imperialistic strategy, nor any itch for propagating even the most glorious of dogmas, that sent Gairdner abroad, but rather his resolve that the Passion of Christ should not go unrequited in the hearts of men :

> If these things are so [he had written after reading the story of that Passion], then my life must be changed : *of course* it must be an ignoble[1] life. *The true appeal for missions is that if Christ prayed those prayers* (*the prayers of Gethsemane and Calvary*), *then of course the world must know.*

Temple Gairdner was accepted by the Church Missionary Society on November 16th, 1897. His diary says :

> Went to C.M. House. Prayed for a good time and felt quiet and peaceful. Lunched with F[ox] and at 2.15 was accepted. Very kind. A step, but very quiet and logical.

Never had the committee a more loyal servant than the man they accepted that day. He took a pride in discovering glories of sainthood and heroism, great doings and great characters connected with his Society throughout the world ; and when (as would not happen to-day) a personal decision which he and his fellows had reached

[1] In those years he constantly used the word " ignoble " with the meaning of " ignominious."

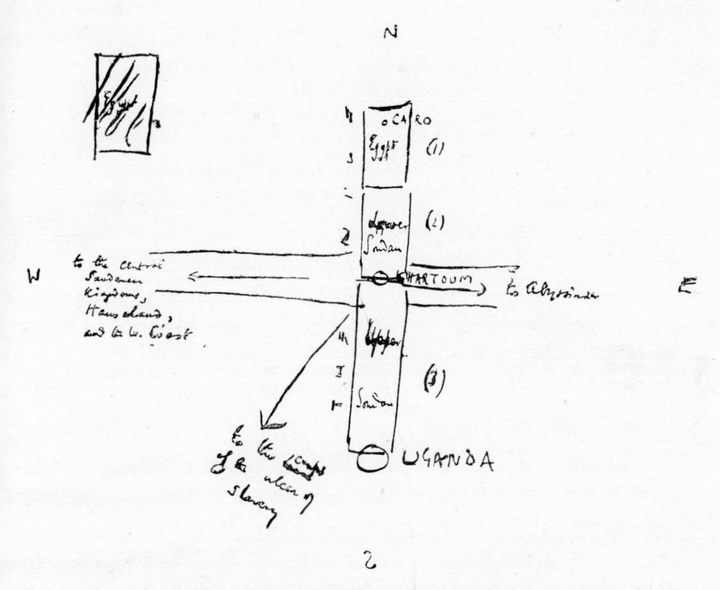

THE KEY-POSITION OF KHARTOUM

When making his offer to the Church Missionary Society, Gairdner enclosed this diagram in a letter to the Secretary.

" It represents," he said, " roughly the key-position of Khartoum, and the three stages of the Nile Valley with their ascending degrees of difficulty : (3) far the most difficult yet important because of its proximity to Uganda and its bearing on the slave question ; (2) hard, but being opened up now and leading to Khartoum, the key to both East and West.

" From this point of view Cairo is worth occupying, not only for its own sake, but because it is the base for (2) and possibly (3), and especially for Khartoum, the focus of the four rays."

with travail in their station was reversed by a home committee, he said in a letter accepting the ignominious situation, " Be sure that we shall do our best to prove you right and ourselves wrong."

II

Douglas Thornton sailed for Egypt in November 1898, and Temple Gairdner's farewell letter to him is illustrative of their friendship and their temper :

> You are having the privilege and joy of going to the very land and the very people of one whom we love. May you go in the quietness and peace with which Gordon went (by the same route as you) nearly fifteen years ago to his death.
>
> Thanks be to God, loneliness, anxiety, danger, were *less of realities* to him than the still atmosphere where dwell Christ and the spirit which loves Him, knowing His love. Gordon is our friend, our brother. My prayer is that you and I may be accounted worthy to give our lives for these lands if it be God's will—to spend our whole lives in them and there lay them down.
>
> The mighty plan of God for these lands which has been unrolling, unrolling, through and in spite of the fever of men of a day, is unrolling to-day ; we enter on the heritage of saints and of martyrs : yes, we ! with all our littleness and unworthiness, *we* are called now to bear the torch and to hand it on unquenched.

So he saw it in moments of aspiration. But there were other moments when he shrank from the life he had set before himself. For some time after his offer to the Society he would wake at night overcome with reluctance and shrinking. " I have found *ambition* dreadfully difficult to cope with," he told his sister-confidante. " It seems so natural, especially with one's upbringing and education, to look forward to making a mark and a name, and so awfully hard to resign oneself to the idea of living and dying tucked away in some corner."

Throughout the diary of those tremendous years before he became a foreign missionary are little jerky ejaculations (generally of prayer) sandwiched in between notes of journeys and committees, and showing clearly enough that this mental fight was not finished in a day :

> [I ask] to do Thy will in some humble, unambitious way, O Lord, and to live a pure, bright, self-abandoned life.
>
> Lord, I am willing to appear to the world and to all to have lost my life if I may only have made it good in Thy sight.

Yet when his own sailing time came, he realized that in this matter of crushed ambition he was not the only or the chief sufferer. He knew that friends at Oxford were disappointed in his choice. " Several of us who had known Gairdner at Trinity and in part at least appreciated his gifts amounting almost to genius," says one of them, " deplored his devoting his life to a mission to educated Mohammedans—spending years of labour, we hear, in making one proselyte." He knew this, expected it, and reckoned with it. But he had not realized that to his parents, for all their genuine piety, his self-burial (as apart from his mere physical absence) was hard. His father, though accepting his vocation, now told him that he had not been able to do so without " considerable struggles and searching of heart." " You seemed to me a man so much made for social life and for the stir and bustle of this great and complex national organism." And for Lady Gairdner, to whom in an acuter degree than to most all partings were hard, this was a parting that brought with it the quenching of treasured hopes. To that passionate lover, her son wrote at his going :

> The worst of partings is with those who remain. When I think of you all, I feel almost as if I had played the traitor. And then comes the meaning of the verse, " He shall *hate* his father and mother." Yes, I see it now. My conduct looks as if I hated you

I couldn't have behaved more unkindly. I couldn't have struck at you deeper, my dearest.

To his father he said :

> Perhaps it was a comparatively light thing for me to take the path I have. But I see now how different it is—must be, with a father whose ambition for a son is so far more legitimate and unselfish than a man's for himself—and therefore all the sorer to forgo. I can't enough thank you for dealing thus with me, and now you see, though late, I do appreciate.
>
> I don't believe I could have stood anything like a public life in this country. God is putting me in a sphere of life where it is *easier* to take the Christ-view of success and honour and fame ; easier resolutely to refuse to seek them in themselves. . . . It needs a very strong man really to stick to these views in the full blaze of modern life, with its competition and seething ambitions. Some are made so ingenuous and unself-conscious that they can preserve their purity under these conditions. But I know only too well, I'm not of that make.

III

His destination was Cairo and his sailing instructions said :

> You are appointed to join Mr. Douglas Thornton in Cairo with a special view to work, when your experience qualifies you for it, among students and others of the educated classes of Moslems.

He more than accepted this decision; he embraced it. His developing thought had passed away from the purely geographical or numerical view of evangelistic work (the early Student Christian magazines are full of calculations as to how many Student Volunteers can evangelize populations of a given size), and he began to see before him the stupendous system of Islam, a system of devotion, of thought, of social life, of law, entrenched, impressive, and deliberately defiant of the Spirit of Jesus. Cairo he saw now as the very heart of that Islamic life. After all, there *was* something great, something to stir the imagination in the vocation of his choice. He wrote to his father outlining his life-work in strangely prophetic words :

> Cairo is my destination for the present and perhaps for good. Though I am ready to go further, I have an idea that I shall not go. I believe that Cairo is the important centre : good work done there would certainly be felt in the Sudan. Cairo is *the* centre of Islam, *par excellence.* It is to Islam that I go—not to any particular phase of it. My ideal is to become a master in Arabic (an awful aim) ; and perhaps to help in creating a Christian literature in that tongue ; and thus to get at the heart of the problem of Islam. Well, that might easily keep me at Cairo till the end of my days.

To Cairo, then, he went, and Cairo became his city, half loved, half hated, but his own. The love came first. He would go off to the Mokattam hills above the citadel and gaze down at Cairo stretched before him, that great city wherein are more than six score thousand persons that cannot discern between their right hand and their left hand.

> Below me is the citadel with its great mosque and two slender minarets, and billowy cupolas and semi-cupolas swelling like breasts. Beyond it, far beneath lies the city with its thousands of flat roofs broken only by the minarets or quadrangles of its mosques. To my left, southwards, stretches the white desert, away and away.

He loved this city of international jostlings because he loved men; and because he loved her he hated part of her life. He hated the shoddiness of the invariable stucco buildings in the new town and the imitation of Brussels in its architecture and gilt-legged furniture. He feared that to live in a world of stucco must bring contentment with insincere work, and the son of Glasgow and of Oxford longed for stone. He grew sick with Cairo's demimonde, its vice, the jealousies and antipathies of national or religious groups. After visiting his people he would come back marvelling that they could live Christianly in a world built on suspicion. "There isn't enough affection to go round," he would say. "In the hard glare of the Orient romance may quite easily wither away." And with all the outward ordinariness of life in a city of telephones and electric trams, committees and tourists, he was yet aware of a sweet, sickening poison in the air, a spiritual atmosphere tainted by hidden foulness—the palpable influence of thousands of lives enslaved in the sensual. "Cairo is a subtly deadening place," he said.

To keep clean and strong, to be able to carry cleanness and strength into the alleys where his people lived, he would go off for days alone in the desert, his water-bottle on his back. Once an adder came out to bask on the rock where he was lying perfectly still, and they rested side by side, he pleased and admiring the beauty of her markings. The desert was his playground and his sanctuary. "Take it out into the desert with Christ and throttle it," is scribbled at the end of a notebook, with reference to some temptation. He gloried in piloting a friend through the narrow wadis near Helouan or the old rock-quarries behind Tura, the dry clashing of their footsteps the only disturber of the empty silences.

When a day of desert solitude was out of the question, it refreshed him most to bicycle out of the city along the Pyramids road, and let the spaciousness of the level fields quiet his spirit. His figure on a bicycle soon became legendary in Cairo. He passed miraculously through the traffic on a battered and long-suffering machine, sometimes with a newspaper open on the handlebars and a tennis-racket under his arm. In later years he had a broken bell with a rather sinister click and resented the attentions of a friend who mended it for him. "Why, man, every camel-driver in Cairo knows the sound of that bell."

IV

Gairdner's beginnings in Cairo were sweetened by a deep triple friendship. Douglas Thornton, to whom he ever felt as a soldier to his comrade and him the doughtiest and most valiant of warriors, was newly married to Miss Elaine Anderson and invited him to live with them in their tiny flat up seventy steps at 19 Sharia Gamia Sherkess.

> If I *may* live with you and your Elaine, I only hope that I shall not spoil your newly-wedded bliss. Remember that two is company, three is none. So the world says: perhaps you, she and I know better, "Where two or *three*——"

The event proved the world wrong and the experiment an unqualified success. "My almost brother and sister here," Gairdner called his host and hostess, and Mrs. Thornton said, "No one less delicate than Temple could have lived with newly married people, but he was a joy to both of us."

The strength of this friendship was what both men needed at that time. Gairdner, for all his readiness to stand *contra mundum* if need arose, was curiously dependent on his friends. "I feel that life to me is so involved, nay, so consists in my relationship to those I love," he wrote, "that in a very special sense *vox amicorum* is to me *vox Dei*."

Even though, especially as years went on, he was in friendship more the giver than the receiver, yet his were real friendships, not patronages or mere spiritual protectorates. He seemed by his very longing for it to call out whatever another soul had to give of response and sympathy. It was characteristic that when he played the piano his enjoyment was not complete unless he had a friend, no matter how incompetent, in the room to share the music. So for one coming from the rich companionship of the student world it was a sweetening of his first Egyptian years that they should be lived in a house of great friendships.

And for Douglas Thornton, the coming of Gairdner with his intuition and sympathy was an unspeakable boon. He was passing through a time of difficult adjustment, so difficult that he could even speak of "the total darkness of the first eight months." With the coming of his bride and then of his friend that "total darkness" was ended, but there were still difficulties for a man of Thornton's build. In the student world he had been a leader of the leaders. Suddenly he found himself in a mission with a secretary who was a saintly invalid, obliged to live outside the city, and haunted whenever new proposals were made, by the invalid's instinctive dread of seeing work grow beyond his strength to handle. The mission was running quietly along narrow though useful grooves; but, beyond a general purpose of Moslem evangelization, it had no policy or thought-out plan for the use of its narrow resources in any concentrated way. There was a small hospital here, a school for girls there, for boys in another place, a meeting for boatmen at one end of the city, an open-air meeting for anyone who would come into a courtyard elsewhere, a book depot with a room for conversation at yet another point—good work all of it, and started for good reasons by good men and women, but disconnected, fragmentary.[1]

All this was a trumpet-call to one like Thornton, "who started," says Gairdner, "from the point of view of missionary strategy, unlike most missionaries, full-grown, mature from the very first." Bitter was it, then, to find himself discouraged as a junior from planning the policy of the mission, and regarded by older folk as too "uppish" for a new-comer. It speaks for the greatness of the student-leaders of those days that a Thornton in these circumstances did not try to build up

[1] The reader will not judge the policy of the mission of to-day (of which the writer is more than proud to be a member) by its early shapelessness.

round himself a group of younger men, like-minded. There is quite an anxious letter from him on hearing of Gairdner's destination to Cairo—anxious to have it quite clear that *he* has not claimed him or influenced his location. "God has brought us independently." And this self-restraint was the result of a resolute world-outlook. "I dare not be so selfish as to ask that many S.V.M.U. leaders should be sent to one centre of the world."

To him, then, the coming of Gairdner was a great and unasked sweetness, and Gairdner brought from those struggles of his against "ambition," a deep personal humility that went far as a solvent of difficulties. Of the secretary of the mission he wrote: "I testify that in these four years never a word passed between us that was not—I will not say, not unfriendly—but was not actually charged with real affection. When he criticized, it was most justly and delicately."

Yet neither for him was it all easy, though with some of his comrades he stepped at once into deep and lifelong friendship. Others, who came from homes of propriety, criticized his manners, nor were they beyond criticism. This group thought him "queer," not realizing either his short sight or his quite unconscious absorption in the master-idea of the moment, nor again understanding the spontaneity of a nature more than half artist. One outraged hostess found it hard to forget that when she set him to amuse her tea-party he swung round the piano to a more convenient angle and revealed the fact that its back had not been dusted! "I think some of us just *missed* his friendship," says a contemporary, "because we were paralysed by his unusualness. You never knew what he would think or do. Certainly no one in our circle can ever have provoked more thought or cut adrift more self-complacency." "Probably he was a little too big for the missionary world to take in," says an observer from another mission.

And real though the new friendships were, he missed the old. In a letter to Dr. Mott he said:

> It is one of the mysteries and the abiding sadness of my life that so much, so very much of what I prized in the brief crowded four years before sailing has been lopped off. Perhaps one lived too fast, made too many friends, accumulated too many interests. Now one has come to a life where letter-writing seems next to impossible, and where, consequently, friendships seem almost to perish through atrophy. But the Christ who was between us as we knelt together at Oxford is still my Christ, and still *the* Christ.

And beyond all this was the inevitable sense of maiming, which came to these two gifted men as to the rest of us, when a man has to acquire again the power of speech from its beginnings.

What Temple Gairdner wrote of Thornton in this connection might have been written of himself :

> He must be a dumb man first, then a stammering blunderer, to the very people whom he longs to reach ; he must, further, become responsible for some work or works which he never started—work that may be a mere piece of trivial detail compared with the plan drawn in his own mind. Even to a dull missionary this apprenticeship is extremely trying ; to a man like Thornton it is simply a death that he undergoes.

V

But they were friends, and they were ardent and they were young ; they hurled themselves gaily upon Arabic.

"Those were great days," says Gairdner. "Thornton would be in one room intoning loudly, the lodger in another intoning equally loudly, and his bride, in a room between the two fires, would be trying to extract grammatical information from a meek-voiced Egyptian effendi." The flat was small and sounds were audible from room to room. Mrs. Thornton remembers a day when Temple Gairdner, in bed with tonsilitis, surrendered his language teacher to her, and as she boggled with the pronunciation of an Arabic letter she heard a hoarse voice from the adjoining bedroom cry, " Caw like a crow, ma'am—caw like a crow."

At the end of a year he wrote to the Society :

> I have had unusual opportunities for language study—and Arabic truly needs unusual opportunities : much leisure, by reason of not too heavy outside work, and being mercifully relieved, through the great kindness of my friends, of household cares ; a good method, cheerfully imparted to me by Mr. Thornton, the fruit of his own hardly-won experience ; and as much teaching as I liked to ask for.
>
> One does specially value in this connection being a minister of a Church which has a liturgy because it sets before one the ideal of being soon able to read in church, and makes one more inclined to aim high in the matter of pronunciation and finish. You practise some prayers perhaps fifty times or more before reading them in church. One minute's delivery at the rate of one hour's preparation, that was nearly the equation of my first sermon.

And for everyone there are ups and downs, days when Arabic flows like water, and days when it ebbs rather than flows. " Dr. Watson, our senior American missionary in Egypt, of over forty years' standing," D. M. Thornton wrote, " has well said, ' It takes a man seven years to feel his tongue loosed, though he can be of some use after four years in the country.' "

But Gairdner moved fast : however imperfectly, he was at the end of six months teaching a class in Arabic and reading in church, and at the end of a year he would give several addresses a week, with Herculean preparations beforehand.

Some of those first Arabic addresses were given to the Nile boatmen, where the wheat-barges moored side to side at Rod el Farag.

> Yesterday [says one of Gairdner's letters] I preached the Gospel of the love of God (yes, I did !) to the

sailors of the Nile boats at their moorings in the river. What a scene it was—the full moon, "looking round her with delight when the heavens are bare"; the soft silver-yellow light; the huge spars and crowded rigging of the boats; the dusky faces in the shadow with the white eyes and teeth gleaming in the light of a smoking lamp. Palms rose like ebony against the Milky Way and the river slipped quietly by the fleet of wherries. I like going down there. One can use such freedom. By God's help I am beginning to emerge from being a fourth-form schoolboy to be a minister of the Gospel.

His final language examination was passed in November 1901, with special commendation from the examiners. He had not been quite two years in the country: "For eighteen years I have been steadily examined, and lo! here is the last. Or can you conceive any occasion which should necessitate an examination after this? No, dear, not even for the archbishopric of Canterbury!"

In reporting to his Society he said, "I have passed my language examination, and so am free to go on working at Arabic harder than ever."

VI

His beginnings of work outside language study were in part congenial and in part against the grain. On February 16th, 1901, he went down all alone (a strange contrast from the crowds of friends at St. Paul's just over a year before) to Alexandria to be ordained to the priesthood by Bishop Blyth in the church dedicated to St. Mark, the first evangelist of Egypt. It was characteristic that, having called in the aid of the ladies of the mission to provide him with a clean surplice which it was of the utmost importance to put on at a given moment, when that moment came, Temple was in another world, absorbed in the awful joy of his commission "to teach and to premonish, to feed and provide for the Lord's family, to seek for Christ's sheep that are dispersed abroad and for His children who are in the midst of this naughty world, that they may be saved through Christ for ever." The surplice returned to Cairo at the bottom of his bag in spotless virginity.

From the first he put a passion of interest into the life of the Church :

> Church music has proved intensely interesting [he said], and I claim to have baptized, received or stood godfather to my full share of the little brown babies of my Egyptian brothers and sisters. Also to have done the difficult feat of marrying an Eastern couple.

He had other tasks less congenial than the services of the Church. The young philosopher, sent out for apologetic to educated Mohammedans, found himself required by the mission to take charge of a boys' elementary school. Moreover, it was a school which brought him no satisfaction, for he thought it to be educationally unsound. It was drawing boys, he saw, from the craftsman class and breeding them up to swell the inflated ranks of a clerkly class that dislikes to soil its hands. Here, as in the O.I.C.C.U., his thinking, accepted by us all to-day, was some twenty years ahead of his time. When he confided these difficulties to a visiting secretary of his Society on the top of the Great Pyramid, he was told to think purely of evangelism and cease to worry over educational efficiency. He obeyed the injunction to think of evangelism, and spent himself in prayer, but it was not in Gairdner to believe that bad education should be done in the name of Christ.

His acceptance of the mandate for uncongenial work is explained in the following lines :

> When I came out I had a greater idea of my own importance than I have now—thinking that so important a person should be in the centre of things. I now see myself in a clearer light. I feel so strongly that a really good man will make his mark in any place : the inferior man will fail to make his mark with

the best chances in the world. I now know that one's importance is to be measured by one's readiness to take up *any* work.

So he became a schoolmaster, and of course with his usual vigour. He spent hours hanging pictures, moving desks, inspecting the dress and cleanliness of small boys, drilling them and taking classes.

"All the superintendents before him," says an Egyptian friend, "had come into the schoolroom very quickly and looked round sharply as much as to say, 'I want to know what goes on in my absence.' When we saw Mr. Gairdner, though he moved fast enough as a rule, always open the schoolroom doors very slowly and stand in the doorway with his head turned away for a moment, so as to give us time to be in perfect order—well, we said, 'He is a saint.'"

His masters were partly mystified and partly delighted at his unpredictable ways of doing things, with a little flicker of humour playing over all his work.

It was not so easy in those days to engage trained teachers, and Gairdner would give his Saturday mornings to carrying his teaching staff a little further in information and ideas. At one time it was English translation, and a more advanced teacher having helped two younger men, Gairdner was not told for fear he should be angry. When the class met, he held up the doctored translations to his nose and sniffed at them gently. "I seem to smell the translation of X. Effendi in these papers," he said genially, and they laughed in happy confusion.

When a series of criticism lessons was arranged, they all remember that he gave the first lesson himself. "And he made some mistakes to encourage us. When he was asked what elephants' feet were useful for, he answered, 'Soup.'"

At the Birmingham Conference in 1898 Gairdner had appealed to the men of his own age to start on the adventure of a simpler way of living. "Do we not need a new age and order of friars, without obtrusiveness o professionalism ? "

As such a friar his Egyptian friends remember him for when he had to leave the Thorntons' home for a time he went to live at his school. He had two rooms and the German wife of a restaurant-keeper next door catered and cared for him.

" Gairdner is not at all a man to manage for himself," was the mission secretary's not surprising comment. But an Egyptian friend has treasured memories of those days :

> When Mr. Gairdner was living at the school in Sharia Mohammed Ali, I used to be very much struck by the simplicity of his personal life. He had two rooms—not up to much. His bed was like the bed of any servant and there was no cloth on his table ; the floor and the window-sills were covered with his books. I often used to go to his room and find him kneeling on the bare stones. One day I thought I would go to see him, and I found him kneeling there on the stones, so I came away without his hearing me. Two hours later I went back and he was still kneeling there.
>
> I often used to ask him to speak to one of the junior teachers (I was the senior), saying that a word from him as head master would set right something that had gone wrong. He would never scold them until he had first called me and said, " Let us pray together for so-and-so. My words will have no power unless God's Spirit is in them ; or at least they might have power to make a teacher keep a rule, but no power to help him *in himself*. Come and pray first."
>
> One night he said to me, " Let us go to the pyramids," so we went and supped there. Suddenly he said, " I want to go up to the top of the Great Pyramid. The moon is shining. I want to go up there and talk with God."
>
> He came back, however, after only going half-way

up. I said "Why?" and he told me, "I have torn my trousers on the rock."

"But do you mind about your trousers?"

"No, I don't mind; but, you see, I'm rather poor and I can't afford to buy another pair, so I mustn't tear them any more." Yet when my baby brother died, Mr. Gairdner, who buried him, said to me at the funeral, "I know you have not enough money to pay for all this; accept this two pounds to help you with the extra expenses."

He was growing into many Egyptian friendships. "He was like a very friendly boy in those days," says one of his Egyptian comrades, "and his ways were so charming that those who went to visit him could not bear to leave. His room was filled with kindness."

One of his staff, Elias Effendi Yusef, remembers him above all as a friend.

> When Mr. Gairdner became head of the school, he became my great friend, coming often to the house and always playing with my baby brother, and when my wife and I had our first baby he said to me, "I should like to come and see your wife and the baby, and to bring the baby some little present. Please tell me what to bring."
>
> I said, of course, "Bring whatever you like, and we shall like it too."
>
> He went to an English shop, and bought a little pair of baby's shoes. Then he bought some socks, six pairs of socks, but each one of a size larger than the last to allow for growing!

Of himself Gairdner said, "I do feel insight into the mind of the people painfully slow." But this teacher of his, looking back to those early days, can say, "What surprised me about him was how he knew my thoughts before I spoke, and how patient he was. He was more Egyptian than the Egyptians. I am an Egyptian, but my Egyptianness is weak beside his. He was *truly* Egyptian."

So the unsought and uncongenial work was carried through, no doubt with many a forgotten business detail, but with an individual flavour that has lived in the hearts of his Egyptian friends.

And his own chosen work, the great apologetic task of the man who said, " It is to Islam I go," was taking its beginning :

> I have had the joy of really starting a meeting of my own, in which there is definite first-hand work of dealing with Moslems. It has taken the form of consecutive readings in St. John's Gospel. Not many strangers come, nor do I want many as yet. I cannot say what a pleasure it is to feel oneself really one with this people as we sit side by side in free, vivacious, amicable yet regulated exchange of thought. I regard this meeting as indicating what I conceive to be my proper line of work—I mean as a step towards that for which I was sent out here—" work among educated Moslems."
>
> I shall be glad when I am set free of the school, in order that I may become equipped for this immense task.

VII

At the end of his first year, writing from his holiday camp at Aboukir with the Mediterranean breeze rustling his paper, he said :

> There has been such a complete upset, such a turning over and over of all one's life, that the things that won't stand the shaking go to pieces. After a while you find what has stood the shaking and abides.
>
> You were active in England ; you were in a responsible post ; many eyes were upon you ; many sympathetic voices were ready to encourage you and make you feel the immediate success of your work and word ; your reputation was wide, at least the circle of

it was not narrow. All that is smashed to pieces when you come out : you are a junior in a single mission-station, you have next to no opportunity ; no eyes watch you and no voices applaud you, nor is there anything particular to applaud, for your work is humdrum. Therefore woe unto you if there is not an eternal something which " remains " when once again the Lord shaketh your heavens and your earth ! Thank God there *is* something, though one feels forlorn sometimes amidst the ruins of what seemed so fine.

All my associates, all my surroundings, are charming. My lot has indeed fallen in a good ground ; I have a goodly heritage. There is no spot in the wide world I would be shipped to, and no work I would exchange for my own.

And at the end of the second year, often a harder time when the zest of newness has worn off, he wrote :

For me the die has been cast : the only way to peace and that self-realization which is indeed Salvation is, for me, the way of spirituality. God has shown me this and has closed every other path. Only sometimes, in the weakness of the spirit, the heart looks wistfully back at some of those closed avenues, which one sees other men treading, and whispers, " you have aimed too high, and may miss all ; aim lower, and you will at least attain something." It cannot be, it cannot be. " Onward to the starry track, glimmering up the heights beyond me, on and ever on."

CHAPTER VI

MARRIAGE

1901—1902

I want to love you as a noble woman longs to be loved and is worthy of being loved: as God's noblemen love their women.—*Temple Gairdner to his Wife.*

I

By his second summer in Egypt, Gairdner needed a holiday in higher air. He went with an Irish friend to the Tyrol, and although part of the holiday was spent in fever, it was a time treasured in many delicious memories after his return to Egypt.

They walked among the Austrian hills and bathed in mountain-streams, and often on a dusty day in Egypt his thoughts would turn to that cool shock.

> Ineffably refreshing to soul and body were those glorious Tyrolean hills! In this land of tepid water my soul and my skin (excuse the apparent incompatibility) cry out after the divine, the Elysian frigidity of those mountain-streams, from which in their cool translucent cells we drank, and drank, and drank, blessing God, and after the superb shock when we plunged therein and every hair-like nerve-extremity tingled and glowed.

Or some little human scene would come back to him:

> . . . That perfect face of the girl—poorest of the poor—that gave us to drink that evening after sunset.

But the holiday was memorable for more than gathered fragments of beauty. He could not but be conscious hat his friends believed him, with his affectionate nature and his feckless ways, to need the love and security of a home as a basis for his work, as the best liberation of his spirit for his life-task.

It was true that Temple Gairdner was made for love. In his last year at Oxford when he went to play the organ at the wedding of a friend, he had been deeply stirred at the sight of lovers meeting :

> Prayed definitely that I may be a *man* and have a heart one day pure and noble enough to be owned by and to own one woman's heart. May that day come, O Lord. Amen.

And having prayed that prayer, by a real and repeated effort he put the whole subject aside during his work for the Student Movement. He came out to Egypt with no hint of love spoken between him and any woman, but with awful, tender thoughts of marriage.

> Sullivan was right in making, by his music, a wedding day to seem a compound of grave and gay. It seemed so strange, so wonderful, so mystic. A man and woman standing at the altar seem to assume heroic proportions. Around you and L., as you stood there, there was to my gaze something of an unearthly light. . . . Yes, it was a dream : but unlike ordinary dreams in this, that it was more real than reality, whereas dreams are less than reality.

But this dream, he believed, could not be for him. Must he not be ready to be sent at any moment into the depths of the Sudan ? "It seemed to me," he said, "that God was calling me to a single life."

He came to Egypt, and he found that missions in the Moslem Sudan were barred by Government prohibition, and Mr. (afterwards Bishop) Gwynne was allowed in Khartoum only on sufferance as chaplain to the British rather than as a missionary to the Sudanese. Gairdner saw a vista before him of Cairo life, and he saw his friend Douglas Thornton strengthened, enriched, equipped for such life by his wife. Clearly the subject might b thought out anew, and through those summer weeks i was never far from his mind. On the last day in th Tyrol, Temple Gairdner went out alone amid lowerin mists on a hillside at Pieve, and there finally "fough and prayed" through the question. "God would no mislead me, I knew, I knew."

In a home letter he later on revealed what was then passing through his mind.

> The main reason I stuck up for celibacy was that it enabled me to live a simpler life and to make (as I thought) the people to whom I had been sent the first and chief thing instead of the second. And therefore not until I realized that this idea was not radically sound or necessarily true was I able to entertain the least idea of marriage. Will you therefore join me in the earnest prayer—yes, for it is life and death to me and the rescue of my life from failure—that this union so far from alienating me from the Egyptians, will draw me immeasurably closer than I could have been drawn otherwise. This is a great prayer, but I see how it can be fulfilled. A wife, if she is the right sort, will enable a man to reach them *at more points of their hearts* ; their wives more, their boys and girls more, their home-life more.

"A wife, if she is the right sort." Yes—and his thoughts were turning to one who would, he believed, be ready as himself to put the work of Christ always before her natural inclinations. He came down from his hill-side to start on the return to Egypt, with sweet hopes admitted at last to play in his mind.

He took boat from Trieste, and no sooner left port than fever caught him, and perhaps there was also a certain fever of mind in those first hours at sea. He realized that if his new decision were to be put into action it must be without delay ; for the partner to whom his whole heart was turning had herself obeyed a missionary call and was soon to sail from Scotland for a college in India. If he were to change the sphere of her missionary service, it must be at once. When the boat reached Brindisi, sick man as he was, sprawling uncomfortably on the floor of his cabin he wrote the letter of letters to Miss Margaret Dundas Mitchell and asked for the answer of her heart.

> Written in fever in that hot cabin at the Brindisi quay [he afterwards said to her of the proposal] and flung on shore literally as the boat moved away—then or never !—on so fine a thread hung our two fates. . . . I adore the great Fate who is also the great Father.

He flung himself back on his berth, feverish but in a strange quiet and content of spirit which stayed with him through the days till her letter reached him on September 23rd, 1901.

> Your letter arrived this afternoon : I got it at five o'clock, and put it unopened in my pocket, got on to my bicycle and rode out into the country. I felt I must read it alone and with God. I will show you the place one day. Then I raised my heart in prayer to God as I have been doing many times each day since the day at Brindisi. I had utterly committed the whole matter to Him. . . . Then, in the quiet light of the setting sun, I broke the seal and saw the Yes. I bowed my head and took you from the hands of God : then gave yourself and myself back to Him to fulfil His utter will. . . . Please God these things will make something heavenly, something spiritual and ethereal in our relations one to another. Something that God may have pleasure in and use to His own glory.

Miss Margaret Mitchell was the daughter of an old friend and neighbour, Dr. J. O. Mitchell, a well-known citizen, lover and historian of his Glasgow, from a family which had, like the Gairdners, a heritage of piety and character. The two lovers had already very close and dear associations. As little children they had scrambled over the Ardrossan rocks together or shared Glasgow nursery teas ; as boy and girl Temple's piano and the violin of his future bride had joined in family music-makings ; as man and woman each had accepted the loneliness of a missionary vocation. But during Temple's work-filled years they had seen but little of one another, and since he came to Egypt not even that little.

The way of letters now seemed terribly slow : " I know that heavy-footed letter has not yet crawled to your door : not till to-morrow. It seems almost human, that letter !—like some irritating old pompous gentleman who *can't* understand what there is to hurry about, and is the more leisurely in his movements the more everybody fumes all round."

II

Love in absence it had to be till the very wedding-day, save for a brief spell in December 1901 when Miss Mitchell paid a halcyon visit to Egypt on her way to Palestine ; for the Church Missionary Society changed her destination from a South Indian college to the Girls' Orphanage in Nazareth in order that she might begin the study of Arabic. " I wish to thank you for the handsome, the more than handsome way in which you have greeted my engagement," Gairdner wrote to them.

By the regulations of the Society permission for the marriage could not be given till the autumn of 1902. During the intervening months of separation, Temple Gairdner, in the absence of a listening ear, set down in writing the high, selfless ideals that these " two people very thoroughly in love," as he said, accepted for their joint life as servants of Egypt and of Christ :

> To-morrow is a solemn day. Not only is it the anniversary of my ordination as deacon (reckoning by the Church, not the civil year) : but it is the first Communion since our engagement. . . . To-morrow therefore I am going to lay you upon the altar

of God as my present to Him. I received you at His hands, and now I give Him you—my best—a sacrifice, holy, well-pleasing, acceptable. . . . Oh that love might be satisfied : to love even unto death. Thrice happy, and thrice honoured, those to whom it has been given to love even unto death—the love than which " greater hath no man."

But because these words are high words, and more easily conceived and uttered than carried out, God calls me simply to small, daily feats of love. . . . Until one has learned *them*, how can one aspire to the higher things !

Help me ; and you can : for if you suffer me to give *you*, my own and my only possession, to them, you will have enabled me to lose myself. . . . I think I could have the satisfaction . . . of loving with something of the love of God if I were conscious of sacrificing even my darling wife and our married life to this people. . . . What a joy if you can creep into corners of hearts, perhaps very vacant corners some of them, which I am for one reason or another prevented from reaching, and comfort, brighten, gladden them, make life sweeter and more livable for them.

As you say, Love, when divided, is really only multiplied. And I have laid our love on the altar that it may be divided, aye, divided and subdivided and ever grow in the process. It is my earnest prayer that the very passion of mutual attachment may involve a breaking forth of compassion and friendliness and simple affectionateness and faithful friendship and deep charity towards this people to whom we are sent, and towards the fellow-workers with whom we are sent. . . .

Of her before whom was laid so stern and selfless an ideal, let it suffice to say that in these matters she met her lover half-way. There was no sacrificing on his part (as with some idealists) of another life caught unwillingly into the swift current of his aspirations. Together and as one they "sought first the Kingdom o God." And if their love thus dwelt in the mountain tops, the love that is "of the valley" was not withheld from them. They sought first the Kingdom, and there was "added unto" their love a bloom of tenderness that only drew fuller beauty and sweetness from the stern ideal set.

> Others would say [Gairdner wrote] that a love which attempts to be spiritual before all else will be colourless, warmthless, passionless. *I* say, seek ye first the love that is spiritual (the Kingdom of God) and all these things—colour, warmth and passion shall be added to you. And I am experiencing the truth of my belief.

The year of waiting before their marriage was called by Temple Gairdner his year of vigil, spent in a yet deeper self-discipline to fit him to become "worthy of this holy, holy, holy thing." The prayer of that vigil is recorded in his diary, a revelation of the deep springs of his life:

> That I may come near to her, draw me nearer to Thee than to her; that I may know her, make me to know Thee more than her: that I may love her with the perfect love of a perfectly whole heart, cause me to love Thee more than her and most of all. Amen. Amen.
>
> That nothing may be between me and her, be Thou between us, every moment. That we may be constantly together, draw us into separate loneliness with Thyself. And when we meet breast to breast, my God, let it be on Thine own. Amen. Amen.

The new love brought a sense of expansion and joy, a grace of colour and warmth into his life. His beloved, motherly Mrs. Bywater sent him "an angel note," and he was so grateful to her that he "kissed her hand." The depth of love in his home letters, too, was an unforgettable revelation. "Oh, you women!" he wrote to sister, " don't you know that your love to all the sons of men save the Son of Man is more than its object is really worth ? " When Sir William Gairdner told him that he had often wished for this very match and " believed that the union might indeed be made in heaven," Temple went to bed " tired with the weight of glory."

III

The " weight of glory " and the security of love were given just in time to fortify him for what was to him a descent into hell, when during the winter after his engagement Temple Gairdner for the first time met with treachery. He was to know it again and again and to learn to read its sinuous, cringing secrecies, and always it brought horror and pain to that " unshielded heart " of his. But this first experience came with the shock of unpreparedness to a spirit clear and delicately true.

It was a story only too familiar to those who know the Near East, but his first reading of it was determinative for his whole life. The little band of Christian ex-Moslems was tampered with in the all too common way, by newspaper editors and others, with various forms of bribery and threat. Two members of the Church gave way to these temptations ; one (A.) had taken the position of an evangelist in the mission (" He is not exactly like St. Paul," said Gairdner wistfully after their early contacts), the other (B.) had been baptized only at the previous Easter Eve. Both made public recantations of Christianity for Islam, as usual accompanied with slanders concerning the leaders of the Church they left. It darkened all the sky for Gairdner. He could not rest for thinking of the failure of these souls, of the failure of the Church to hold them, and it was well for him that from tormenting thoughts he could turn with confidence and joy to his betrothed.

> D. M. T. met me with terrible news about A. ; mad letter to *Al Haqq* [an Arabic journal] attacking Protestant missions and missionaries. . . .

A terrible meeting with A. quite unstrung me. *now* begin for the first time to see that the characte of Judas Iscariot is possible and human.

[*To his betrothed :*] We are in the middle of th most terribly unpleasant and grievous business have yet had to do with since coming out. In th midst of it all and from it all I turn to your love—sc trustful, confiding, loving : such a contrast ! That is what we want out here : of such is the Kingdom of God.

When you come I am going to show you round with pride, and *especially* to my native friends. Dear, do you know that *that* may do more to heal wounds than anything else ? I believe that they will *know* they are loved when they find me proud to show my future bride to them. . . . I am praying and believing that you may without an effort love these people from the first.

Had a good time of confidences with them [his Egyptian fellow workers]. I was enabled to see behind the scenes a bit, and how they watch us and what they find a stumbling-block in us.

One must steadily press for more truthfulness without petulantly or bitterly or (perhaps) even indignantly castigating the deep untruthfulness of the East.

The first shock, then, only drove him into closer love and understanding of Egyptian friends. The second was harder to face. It was the case of a young sheikh undoubtedly convinced in intellect of the truth of Christianity, but morally yet to make, and flabby as a jellyfish.

The worst that I feared. B. has been publicly received back to Islam, together with wholesale abuse of those who have been his only friends and lovers for the past year.

Some of the surface causes I know, but the psychological history of the whole matter I cannot even imagine. [Alas, Gairdner, less pure spirits find these imaginings all too easy!] It is Satanic. I never felt as I have this week the fact of the hideous existence of a kingdom of darkness and of evil. It has come down on us like the night.

To his betrothed he wrote in deep depression :

I seem to have left the uncloudedness, the boyhood of life behind me for ever, and have entered into what I feel to be a sadder life. . . . For I look ahead, darling, and I see the same thing in front—this apparently hopeless effort to cope with Islam, the weariness of the climate and the sense of duties left untouched, and above all, these terrible disappointments. That's the life I've chosen ; that's the life—God help me—I've asked you to come and share.

Sordid miseries, and unheroic and uninteresting. . . . You have thrown in your lot with a life that must, in the natural course of things, expect many sadnesses like these. . . . Indeed, I grieve that I am not *more* sad, for this is a call to enter into a very inner chamber of the sufferings of Christ. The danger is that one should remain in the ante-room of mere disappointment and grow hard and cold in it, and settle down to a faithless, hopeless sort of existence.

All the thoughts of Holy Week and Easter were that year coloured for Gairdner by this first taste of the hardness of Moslem work :

I think if one let oneself go, one's heart would really be broken and we should then be free to love all men. . . . It is very easy to overdo the advice about "not sentimentalizing over the physical sufferings of Christ." On the whole, I think the danger lies towards callousness. Why are we given such extraordinary minuteness in the Gospel narrative unless we are meant to draw nigh and follow it all—all ? . . . I am finding the indifference of the Moslems to this tale of pity most shocking. But how shall I rouse them if I am not pierced by it ?

[*At the Easter Communion* :] I looked squarely at the sad experience of these months and deliberately yielded myself to the altar for this and more than this if He will.

I feel that there is a terrible cleavage between us and them (the Egyptians). I yield my life to Him to be so fashioned as to understand and be understood by them.

I won't waste more time hating myself. The self that I hate and that He hates I leave on the Cross or in the tomb. And that which rises with Him is a new self.

B. returned ere long, penitent, but with the facile unrealizing penitence of an immature conscience, blind to spiritual depths. He was admitted to probation with the condition that he cut off all intercourse with his tempters, and at the end of probation a public confession must be made before the Church which he had publicly repudiated.

"This my son was dead, and is alive again ; he was lost, and is found" : B. has come back to us, and my heart has peace. There is joy, I trust, in heaven and there is a quiet restful thankfulness on earth. One is too much used up to be exultant : but quietly thankful like the tone of Handel's "But thou didst not leave my soul in Hell" after the agonizing Passion music.

The crisis then was over, the temptation to harden and sour was refused. But the extravagance of it all, the cost of it ! Can Gairdner have been the man for Moslem work when one shallow, calculating little soul could bring such a "night of anguish" to his spirit ? "A ridiculous expenditure of her finest material," says the world of the Church. And the Church of the ages knows that such costing love, more often than physical martyrdom, is the price of "blood and tears" that she must pay for the Moslem world. It is no new story n every age her tenderest hearts must be put to her ıardest work.

IV

It was true, as Gairdner said, that this business of B. had left him " used up." With the early summer his weariness gained on him, and the malaria which he had contracted in the previous year came on with several very sharp attacks. He made good recoveries, but Dr. Harpur decided that the malaria must be taken seriously and defeated once for all, and ordered sick-leave in England before Gairdner's marriage in the autumn.

He went home, then, in July 1902, and although the voyage was not free from fever, with every knot his buoyancy returned. The very smell of the sea was life-giving. " O associations of Ardrossan first, then Rossall, I greet it with full heart as one greets a known friend." The man who thought he " had left the boyhood of life behind for ever " was radiant again. When he reached England, " even the sulphur of the Underground was delightful."

> I have claimed the heart that enjoys [he said]. Only the coward, slavish, " dolish " spirit cannot. Lord, I know that Thou desirest a holy freedom in Thy children : if the Son makes me free, I shall be free indeed. Deliver me from slavishness. Give me a heart so at leisure as to enjoy Thy gifts, and be utterly open to mankind.

And because he always had to philosophize his keen sensations, he was thinking out the relationship between his life in God and his radiant enjoyment that summer of " a bush of privet smelling divinely " ; or " the dear dirty little cheering Scotch children who lined to fill the gutters " when colonial troops marched through the Lawnmarket at Edinburgh ; or " the pure air from the mountains, scented with wet bracken, heather and myrtle, and all things clean and health-giving." " It was glory ! On we went, laughing, talking, quoting."

Some of his most " Gairdnerish " thoughts, the

thoughts by which his friends best knew his mind, wer
sent that summer to his betrothed in Nazareth.

> I believe that the man in the ocean depth of whos heart reigns the Lord is perfectly free : for every talent enjoyment, interest is brought to His feet and receive His glad sanction. They are " sanctified by praye and the giving of thanks."
>
> I know perfectly well that if my face is sullen it i because of failure in . . . communion with God. Loving nature in God. . . . There you have the synthesis of the eternal antithesis between culture and abnegation. The creation (the creature) groans, we are told : she does so because through the fall of man she is either loved not at all, or loved for her own sake, and so made in her own despite " the world." If we can love her for her Maker's sake, she feels the beginning of her " redemption," " the glorious liberty of the sons of God."

" His religious experience," says a friend, " so far from cramping him, led him out into a broad room and made him heir to the wondrous and varied riches of heaven and earth."

He went to the Matlock Student Conference that July :

> In the latter part of the Conference I quite began to do travelling secretary work and felt as young as ever before ! I saw men individually, and went to discussions in the tents after cocoa at night, and addressed meetings—all like the old days. Judge therefore how I felt when I was made to realize that I was considered an old hand whose words were words of wisdom. . . . You may imagine I let in an element of chaff to prevent the thing becoming absurd. Dear, I felt as young as I did when in England, and this is surprising, for last Easter I thought I should never feel really young again.

And after the comparative repression of the first years in Egypt, how exhilarating to be greeted on all sides as a man greatly beloved !

> I want to tell you that at this time I have been made to feel conscious that a good many people love me a great deal. Isn't it utterly strange? Apart from all questions of desert, love is in itself a good thing, a Godlike thing. God loves to see it existing from whatever cause or absence of cause. . . . God is very good: my narrow heart feels like bursting from this excess of the richnesses of His goodness. The more they become, the richer they become, the more I yearn after that life of sacrifice—of the cross—of the life laid down in Egypt.

The rest of the holiday was spent in visiting his own family and his bride's. "Music flowed like water" in his home (now moved to Edinburgh), and his luggage, when he went to a sister's house, included "Dr. Yellowlees' travelling case, all full of music."

And there were wedding preparations, too—his happiness that summer casting a glow over details that did not always interest him! He and his tailor plainly took some little pride in an "ineffable silky white duck" suit, and a "creamy white serge." He hoped that his bride would like him to be married in white!

> Saw a Punch and Judy show and laffed immoderately. I told the man that I considered his profession a most honourable one. By the way, I told Borland [the tailor of the "ineffable white duck"] that I considered tailoring a fine art, whereat he was quite delighted. He said, "We educate people up to appreciate a good coat."

V

Temple Gairdner left Edinburgh at the end of September for what he called "The Bridegroom's Progress" that was to bring him to Nazareth on his wedding-day, October 16th, 1902.

He started from London with a few of his bride's

relatives : none of his own could come to his wedding. The last night in England was spent, to his great joy, with his much-honoured Colonel Oldham, " and it was the best of send-offs, for it was with prayer to God."

The whole journey from first to last had a gaiety about it. " The vigil " was all but ended. He was to be dubbed knight not many days hence at Nazareth, the city of his Master, and his joy broke out in bubbling boyish spirits and a contented amusement with all common things and people. He was never more care-free.

> I leaned over the taffrail and with delight indescribable drank in the softness and beauty of the night. There was not a breath on the water : no motion to the ship more than the motion of one " breathing very softly in the fields of sleep." I utterly yielded to the complete carelessness of the hour. Nothing to catch, nothing to go back for, nothing to recall, nothing to arrange.

The party joined a French boat at Marseilles that called at the Piræus and there broke down. A Greek coaster from Smyrna was chartered to carry on the passengers of her derelict sister to Syria. Meanwhile, the delay of " four divine days " brought pure gold to Temple Gairdner. To be stranded, unasked, at the doorway of Athens, on a coast where every headland and island had its story, to see with his own eyes places " more familiar to imagination than my native land itself " ! And to be cut off from all duties but to enjoy it, to drink it in and worship its beauty! It was one of the great holiday moments of his life.

From the deck he noted every stage of the approach to Greece :

> There lies Sparta, dreaming in its solitude, owing to its very mystery and proud loneliness the strange fact that the most unintellectual city in Greece was the ideal state of Greece's rarest mind—Plato. . . .
>
> I heard it with the hearing of mine ears, but now

mine eyes see it. For that is "the pleasant vale of Argos," and this is the sea over which drifted the chest with poor Danæ and her baby the infant Perseus. . . .

That patch of mainland suddenly flooded with light from the west and backed by a ring of grey sentinel mountains, what is it? Lycabettus, the Acropolis, Athens, Piræus! We are nearing the heart now.

The sun has just set behind Salamis, and everything, water, ships, city, hills, harbour, swarming boats of yelling Greeks, all are floating in ruby light.

He went to Athens in "a passion of Hellenism":

The cream of the whole day to me, the thing that above all things appealed to my soul, was the Theatre of Dionysus. As I looked at that stage and that central exit I was more moved than by anything else for many a day: that vacant doorway, through it went Agamemnon as a sheep to the slaughter, through it rushed Jocasta with shrieks that chilled the hearer as she realized the hideous truth. . . . Can it indeed have been two millenniums ago? It seems as if it must have been last year.

Or there was Salamis:

After wasting the morning in chess, I had a palpitating afternoon. I went a long walk by myself to the very top of "the rocky brow that looks on Salamis"—Mount Aigaleon. The boatman said something to me about robbers on the hills, so I spoke to a smart officer on the quay. Speaking being useless, I wrote in ancient Greek: "I want to go upon those hills and I wish to know if there are robbers." After touching up this composition a little, he replied that he did not know and led me to a police office hard by. There he wrote: "Come here at 4.30 and the sergeant will give you a policeman to go with you"! A policeman for the "rocky brow"! I sloped off minus my policeman. . . . There, stretched like a stage at the foot of an amphitheatre, lay the scene of the battle.

> Ye gods, what a sight for a king on that October morning. . . . Not a single duel between galley and trireme but he saw it ; not a single shout but he heard it—for I could hear distinctly the shouting of a drover on the coast road far beneath. What a war must have beat about his ears ! . . . It was on this crest that Xerxes certainly sat. Well, he lost ! But he saw a sight fit for a king !

And there was a last idyll on the day before he left, when Gairdner walked at Salamis along "a real Ardrossan-like coast-road, with a single telegraph wire, and complications of the salt smell from the sea and whiffs of wild plants from the land."

> This afternoon I went over to the Bay of Salamis by myself and bathed . . . off clean, warm rock, like Ardrossan ! smelling of clean, fresh, wet seaweeds like Ardrossan ! into pellucid water with coloured stones, seaweeds, rock-gardens ! into warm, warm water ! And then I sate me down on a hot rock and let the sun dry my body. There I sat and basked in a state of utter bliss, with feet on the warm stone and little blue waves lapping and gurgling into the crevices.

VI

They reached Syria in cheerful discomfort on their "corky" little Greek coaster, and "passing down that long, shining Syrian shore, over the bells in the sea-depths at Tyre," they came to Haifa. Here Gairdner was to meet his bride for the civil marriage before the British Consul, passing on to Nazareth of Galilee for what was to both of them the real marriage on the following day in the little Anglican Church.

At Haifa he wrote :

> The sun rose on me this morning over Nazareth. I take the omen. Never have I beheld a scene more mysteriously beautiful than Carmel rose-red in the fore-glow of the dawn . . . "the awful rose of dawn."

So they came to Nazareth for the wedding, which had for its keynote the words they had chosen for that day and for their life together—" Father, glorify Thy Name."

He told his mother about his wedding on " that wondrous dream-day ":

> The beautiful service I had " insetted " into the Communion Service . . . the nice hymns which we both sang with good heart . . . the Communion so right and satisfying . . . the blessing by the old Syrian clergyman with hands uplifted, high-priestlike [some of the service was in Arabic], . . . and as we turned the corner out of Nazareth a pretty sight—little Syrian children from the orphanage with flowers and pomegranates to greet us.

A week of honeymoon was spent on Mount Carmel, and there in " the glory of Carmel " they laid down their plans for the new home they were to make in what he called " the prosaic, humdrum, semi-European, difficult, unsatisfactory life of Cairo." Down on the plain they were to build a home " after the pattern that was shown unto them in the Mount," " our dear shining ideal," he would call it in after-years. This home, a place of solace, love and strength to many, was their joint achievement, his and hers, not more the work of one than of the other. In the training of their children, in the caring for their guests, Eastern or Western, they were as one. And henceforth, not the building of the home only, but the whole achievement of his life was also her achievement, who gave him the strength and comfort of her love and loyalty, the powers of her heart and mind.

VII

At the beginning of the courtship they had agreed that their married life should not alter his old ideal of simplicity, which was hers also.

> From the very outset every penny shall be consecrated to God. I think there is an *art* of simplicity. It

will need no end of thinking out, and it is worth learning.

In Scotland, too, while various purchases were being made, he wrote to his bride:

> Pray specially at this time of buying that nothing may be done to commit us to life alien to our best ideal. [*And again at a Communion :*] Refreshed by the Sacrament, dear, I especially laid on the altar all our wedding gifts and all the many things we are buying at this time, that each several thing may glorify God and give pleasure to others.

He was half-appalled by those wedding presents, though he glowed over the love behind them.

"Feeling how none of these things had been really coveted, I could clearly say, 'If Thou takest them away again, they were never mine.'" Very few "things" became "his" in an intimate way. Small possessions he invariably lost, except a little brown Prayer Book given at his ordination. And he never let any peaceful domestic corner and well-worn armchair enter deeply into his life. In part he was too electric for that and too taut-strung at his work, and in part life made it hard for them. It was nearly a year before they had a house of their own in which the wedding gifts could be unpacked. And when the home and the babies came together, its standard of physical comfort was not high. His writing-chair, a rude native-made desk (it was years before he possessed an orthodox roll-top), a battered bicycle, his piano and baby organ and a few pictures of dear association but no intrinsic worth (hanging pictures was a ceremony of delight to him, kept in the early years for Christmas Eve)—those were his chief domestic gods. Books he had: one cannot think of him without them. He bought what he needed for his work, but was strict with himself about unnecessary book-buying. The bulk of the scholarly Arabic or Islamic books that he amassed he passed on to a central library for missionaries, so that a visitor,

TEMPLE GAIRDNER.

Aged 29.

knowing him to be an Arabist, when shown his study, said, "But where are Gairdner's books?" He kept a cupboard full of commentaries much borrowed by his comrades, and three or four bookcases of general literature which he resolutely cleared from time to time of superfluities. Little enough in quantity he allowed himself, but that little was very wide in range of interest, and the interests grew with the years. It was a hard year with Gairdner that saw no fresh enthusiasm.

VIII

The luxuries of their home were music, children, and the peace of utter loyalty.

What fatherhood meant to him words cannot express. He seemed to find in his children with a sort of rapture his vocation. When he wrote to a tiny nephew, "I am William's and Hugh's and Eleanor's and Douglas's and Patria's Daddy, that's who I mostly am," he was not far from expressing what he really thought about himself. In the earliest days he did not teach his babes to call him "Father"; it seemed too sacred.

> I have been thinking over my disinclination hitherto to be called "Father" by the children [he wrote to his wife during an absence in 1906]. It is simply too tremendous a name. It seems almost like blasphemy. One might almost as well be called God. I feel so awfully unworthy of it. Yet one of my prayers during these weeks is that I just *may* be able to tell them to call me so when we begin the new life together again.

So he entered with awe and rapture on a vocation on the night in November 1903 when he first heard that "strange, new, thrilling, indescribable sound that was not the voice of any human being or other animal that was or ever had been: the unforgettable, wholly indescribable first cry of a first child." "That dear little tiny, red, villainously ugly, muckle-mouthed, shivering, whining, snivelling, beloved, healthy, weakly-kicking blob of pinkish jelly which I took into my arms. Wondrous scenes !—dirt common, the commonest of the common, daily, hourly, momently occurring, yet each one a miracle as unique as the Fiat Lux of the First Day."

He was an abandoned baby-worshipper. "We think we kiss them because we love them," he would say, "but it's really the most delicious self-indulgence. The very smell of a baby is delicious. And there's that perfect little spot at the back of their necks that is just made for kissing." His letters are full of vignettes of his babes :

> This evening, lying on his back, his legs simply flickered with intuitive Sandow's exercises, so rapid, so symmetrical, so agile as nearly took one's breath away. And he as grave as possible, working those little flickering pins as if it was his profession.

He baptized his own first baby, William Tennant, on Holy Innocents' Day of 1903.

> He was fast asleep as I signed him with the cross, his face very calm and innocent beneath me. The utter unconsciousness was touching. Yet who doubts the reality ? Grant that he may be indeed a Holy Innocent.

Temple Gairdner could instantly set up a good understanding between himself and a baby, and at a baptism his reassuring hold, his comforting support of a small back, would nearly always still a wailing mite. Moreover, he who often seemed to see nothing on his wild bicycling career through the city, somehow always had eyes for a baby. One of his Arabic classes remembers an occasion when, coming in late for his lesson, he excused himself on the ground that having met a young lady in the street who was a friend of his, it was necessary to stop and kiss her. The "young lady," they found, had been riding in a perambulator. Professor Wendell Cleland, of the American University, tells how after such a meeting between his baby daughter Ann and Temple Gairdner, the latter leapt on to his bicycle and was off, only to swoop back again when they thought he was gone, leaping once more from his bicycle to adjust Ann's hat and veil. "The sun was shining in her eyes," he said.

Through the busiest years of his life his nursery party was his solace. He loved to come in while nursery tea was in progress—fair heads, blue cups and plates, and solid slabs of bread and butter. He would walk round the table, unconsciously or half-consciously caressing each little head of fair hair, and then settle down perhaps to tell everybody about the mangy camel who looked like a broken-down dowager duchess in a slum, destitute but always supported by the thought of her grand relations: he *became* that camel while he told about her, and there were gurgles over the bread and butter. And at games he was inimitable. The height of joy at Christmas or on a birthday was to have "dumb crambo with Father."

He and his wife were generous in appreciation of those who helped their children, nurses, teachers, godparents, kindest aunts. "My heart does go out to nurses in general," he said, "mothers in all but physical fact and name, and yet condemned to the most cruel periodic terminations, deaths, you might almost call them, of their motherhood."

As the children grew older and the separation came upon them which all Anglo-Oriental families must know, there was no slackening of the intimacy. Many of the best letters of his life were written to his boys and girls, letters in which he seemed to live their life and to feel in himself what it was to be a child or a schoolboy or girl; letters that ended "Your own Father," "Your ancient, loving Father," or, when the boy or girl was in the throes of new experience, "Your still very own Father," "Your same, usual old Father." For years at the back of his desk where men will put a motto or a memorandum he had a grubby postcard written by a small schoolboy in large printed letters with the legend: "You are loved by your boy."

On his English visits he gave himself wholly to the family life, eagerly helping each child on to the next small conquest while he gloried in the last. Their friendship was life to him, and they gave him that and their admiration without stint. "The praises of children are like Christ's 'Well done,'" he would say, "to an extreme degree humbling and exalting at the same time."

Perhaps no letter ever gave him more joy (though the intense joy that he had of his children's letters was as great and as steady as what he called "my imperious craving" for news of them) than when a son of his, on going to Oxford, said that one touch was needed for perfection—if only his father could be an undergraduate with him! "Having hardly any memories of my own father, I used to think how I should have liked him to be mine," one of his comrades said, "not at all from pride in his achievements, but because of the ideal personal relation between him and his children." And this art of being a father passed over into his relations with the Egyptians whom he had come to serve with his love. If when he first came out they saw him, as one said, "like a very friendly boy," later they said of him, "He was a very tender father to us all." "He was the only one who kissed our little babies when they were lying dead."

CHAPTER VII

THE MUSICIAN

And the Interpreter did usually entertain those that lodged with him with music.—*John Bunyan.*

I

"COLLECT all the music that ever was heard of—don't stint! We have the whole range of classical music before us," Temple Gairdner had written to his betrothed. This music and a good piano were the only extravagances of their furnishing, and his bride brought her violin, a perpetual joy to him. Scores of friends remember their home best for the gift of music that it brought to Cairo.

Not many of his comrades realized the steady, perpetual discipline under which in Egypt he kept his finely critical musical nature. For in music he was always pursuing the unattainable, ideal Beauty :

> In music I know I am critical—at least of amateur effort, my own included. I will confess to you how seldom one gets any nutriment from amateur performances either instrumental or vocal. You know the frightful slovenliness of technique, unredeemed by any particular power of taste or knowledge or expression.

Or of a Church service in a great city :

> Paid choir, good, machine-like singing, fine organ, good organist as far as playing went, expensive (and empty) church—AND the music bad, bad, bad—vicious through and through. Vulgarity and blatancy added to the banality of average machine-made "church music." I draw a veil.

How did this critic tolerate the sloppy amateur performances that were Cairo's average, or the ragged-edged drag of the hymns at some little missionary gathering, or the piercing tunelessness of Egyptian voices forced into European airs ? And that year in, year out, with so little of relief ? The fact remains that he so threw himself into these little amateur performances that the amateurs excelled themselves or felt sure that they had done so. " I never saw so much in that song before," they would say. He so dealt with a baby organ at a meeting that the assembly had to sing a little better than its wont : so eagerly beat time (with Prayer Book or whatever came to hand) that his lagging " Bulls of Bashan " at the back of the Arabic congregation lagged a little less. And people smiled indulgently and said, " How he was enjoying himself in that hymn ! " He *was*, but it was an enjoyment built on strong self-discipline. " A musically starved man " he would call himself to an intimate, but most of his friends saw no sign of fasting in the genial enthusiast at the piano or the baby organ.

Since with Gairdner any enthusiasm brought a real need of sharing the new joy, he must always play with exposition the latest work that had captured him. " Demonstrating " was his word for that marvellous process by which he brought his friends into the communion of the beauty that enchanted him, and " I demonstrated *The Meistersingers* or *The Apostles*," the commonest of phrases in his letters. Many houses where he stayed have memories of those " demonstrations ":

> After dinner at a visit to the Clergy House in Khartoum on a Sunday evening, Gairdner sat down at the villainous piano—all pianos were villainous in the Sudan—and played to three of us the piano transcription of Elgar's Second *Symphony*. Suddenly he stopped, repeated a phrase and said, " Voilà la femme ! Here she enters just like a serpent in the grass—the

notes, even, have the sinuous appearance of a serpent. Elgar drives her out backwards at the end of the movement."

Or in a house in Wimbledon :

He was full of some opera that he had just heard. He wished to reproduce it for our little household and could hardly wait till the maids—for whose presence he specially stipulated—had washed up the dinner-things. Then he began. Rapidly he sketched the story, then with almost incredible skill he reproduced solo, chorus or orchestra on a rather indifferent piano with a delicacy and a volume of sound which made one marvel, stopping now and again to call attention to some recurring phrase, or to interpret.

With a home of his own he could " demonstrate " to his heart's content, and the hospitality of that home became mainly musical. It was a natural growth—three or four friends would wander in on the evening kept for music, and give themselves up to the peacefulness of a dark room lighted only at the piano. In that house one listened to music in silence. Long works were not shirked and repeats were faithfully observed. When the last chord died away, Gairdner would swing round on the music-stool murmuring " Heavenly ! " or " Too beautiful for words ! " Then a light would be turned up, to find the music for the next player, and some new guest would be discovered and greeted with a cheer before the room plunged once more into darkness and harmony.

It was good music in a city of poor music, and the audience grew to the capacity of the room. " He seemed," one guest said, " in a real ecstasy of music and fun, that helped him and us through some dark times." Or again : " It had been a Wagner evening and at 11 p.m., when it was over, he said, ' Oh, do let's do it all over again ! ' " Many men may have been greater musicians than Gairdner, but few can have had greater power of sharing music, of infecting a whole roomful and making them enter into his enthusiasm. "We'll play Schubert's *Rosamund* and send them all dancing down the stairs," he said once; and dance down the stairs those men and women did, in sheer abandonment to the spirit of the music.

> I remember how when we went away Mrs. Gairdner sent her husband out to help us on with our cloaks, but he was so carried away by the music that he strode up and down the hall humming to himself, while we with great amusement and sympathy put on our wraps.

With the growing audience (and the qualification for those musical evenings was not social standing or even musical education, but simply the capacity for enjoyment) the programme became of necessity slightly more formal. And the meetings could no longer be once a week when about eighty people were involved. The planning of these bigger evenings was an intense delight; Gairdner would bicycle through the city for days with the music singing in his head:

> I am making quite a thing of that Forest Music from *Siegfried*; it is in bits, you remember, but by a little piecing together we can make a longish thing and *absolutely restful* to listen to throughout.

A Danish-American friend whose violin played a great part in the musical evenings of later years says of her own impressions:

> Anyone with a soul for music could immediately find in Canon Gairdner a kindred spirit, and it was his own great delight to discover such spirits. What used to impress me so much about him was his seemingly complete forgetfulness of self in all that he did, his complete absorption in the expression of beauty. One always felt that he was thoroughly Christian and that this fact was the secret of the purity of his enjoyment of art in its various forms. To Christ be the glory.

II

It is hard to tell what was the true place as a musician of a man who had to let this gift go largely undeveloped. "Your husband has a genius for music and given training could have gone *any* lengths," a Jewish musician once told Mrs. Gairdner, but this was not her husband's own opinion. Conscious though Gairdner was that he might with opportunity have gone very much further, he did not think that he would ever have gained the technique of a really great performer. On his lack of technique he wrote wistfully to his former Rossall music-master, Dr. E. T. Sweeting:

> I think I noticed in your last letter a characteristic hit at myself, made with that delicate obliquity which made "Sweeting" such a successful disciplinarian at Rossall—your remark, I mean, about two boys, "musicians—but wanting in the necessary grit which will stick to and overcome technical difficulties and so make greater things possible hereafter." Point by point I must confess to the accuracy of the description.
>
> I had never been in the least *inspired* to tackle the technical drudgery. When I came to you I fancy you felt it was already too late. Being a slacker at best, I sought my inspiration in bungling over the works of the great masters—which line I keep to this day, now finding that I have no other one possible for me. None the less, I keep a sore place when I think of the might-have-been, and your little riposte flicked the skin off it nicely.

What he undoubtedly might have been was a supremely great conductor, for he thought orchestrally and his personality and teaching power would bring concerted music out of the most unpromising groups. He composed little in the way of independent creation, but he was for ever adapting, setting, orchestrating on a small scale, working creatively on the music before him—

8

thinking out a delicate little obbligato for his wife's violin to play to a friend's song, fitting in a part for his son's clarinet, adding a descant to a hymn-tune or harmonies to an air heard in the street. His was not pure creation but rather creative interpretation, and the same was in the main true of his work in literature. "Mr. Interpreter" he still remained.

When Gairdner sat down to a piano, "it was not the instrument he played that mattered to him," a good observer writes, "but the sounds that the composer intended. I think he must have considered himself conductor of a full orchestra whenever he sat at piano or organ to produce rather than to play his favourite music. Inside himself he could hear all the instruments of the orchestra, and somehow, anyhow, he wanted to make what he heard perceptible to his audience. He hummed or sang or shouted when necessary: with sufficient hands I think he would have played a comb and tissue paper if he thought it supplied what the piano lacked."

Short of the comb, he managed in an astonishing way to give broad impressions of orchestral music with his wife's violin (representing all the strings), his American organ (tuned to the piano and representing all the wood-wind), and the piano and his voice filling in the rest! For a few happy years he had a fellow-missionary who was an excellent pianist, but as a rule he had to play both piano and organ himself. Most people were amused at the first sight of Gairdner seated in an angle between the two instruments, swinging round from one to the other as the music demanded, or giving a hand and foot to each. "A new instrument called the pionium or harmano has been evolved," he said. At the first glance it looked uncommonly like some monkey-trick; but those who came to scoff remained to be thankful for a serious and often entirely beautiful reproduction in little of an orchestral composer's meaning, a reproduction that could only have been given by one who read the score with a comprehension of the whole balance of parts.

A story which, rather to Gairdner's disgust, went the round of Cairo, showed a feat of musical concentration.

> He came to my house for a musical evening [says a friend], and he and his wife were to play us the *Siegfried Idyll*, she playing violin and he piano and organ. When he arrived, I met him, saying, "I'm afraid we shall have to give up the *Siegfried Idyll*, because I find the piano and organ are not tuned to one another; the organ is a semitone lower." "I think we can manage," he said, and sat down to play with one hand the music as it was written, while with the other hand on the second instrument he played it transposed to a key a semitone higher.

He asked that the audience might not be told of the difficulty for fear they should be occupied with his brain-feat and miss the full beauty of the music. He would not have his methods thought of, whether as tricks or feats. All that mattered was to express the soul of the music by any and every method he could contrive. (A brass tray was once introduced behind the piano for the great final crash of Hamish MacCunn's *Ship of the Fiend!*) There in Cairo, with all his limitations, he would ponder a score, crooning over it with his little organ and *hear* the music and become so ravished at that almost silent hearing that sometimes the reality in cathedral or opera-house came short of his imagined beauty.

"*For the Fallen* had not the infinite climactic effect that I was waiting for in the last page but two—I expect it needs the Albert Hall and a big organ for that," he said at the end of a concert. And after a feast of music in London he wrote:

> When all is said and done, I came to the conclusion that I with my score and baby organ in Cairo had not such a bad time of it after all. You get your imagination to work and emotional effects clothe the skeleton strains, more moving (I found) than the actual effect produced even by the Terninas and Van Rooys. It

was the unutterable surpassing the uttered. Every now and then—particularly in the Quintette of *The Meistersingers* and the *Liebestod* of *Tristan*—I felt quite disappointed. I could have cried out " No, no, no ! ! Not *so*—you haven't felt that in the least ! " One had dreamed of an infinite beauty, and lo ! the best finite did not seem to touch it.

Gairdner at a concert was *devout*. It was a great, rare joy to be well savoured, rolled on the palate like the finer vintages. At a musical festival he told his children, " I would go down to the hall an hour before time so as to enjoy to the full the pleasures of anticipation and study the programme with its annotations—it seemed more luxurious and ample and prolonging the business of the pleasure, so to speak."

He was not of those who rushed away either. In this respect London audiences seemed to him lacking both in reverence to fine music and in gratitude to artists. At the poorest little show he would give full meed of that unselfish clapping at the very last, the clapping that has no hope of an encore.

III

And what was the music that meant so much to this man and that he made to live and glow for his friends ? For one who spent seven-eighths of his working life completely out of touch with the musical world, both the catholicity and the steady development of his musical taste were notable : hints of it are scattered up and down his letters.

At last I am penetrating into the sanctuary. I mean the musical significance of the great D Major Mass. To fail here is rather serious, for Beethoven's own superscription is " From the heart it came ; to the heart it must go." And it is true. It is a truly religious piece of music. It derives from Palestrina, and I seem to detect, too, that those who came after have not been able to get away from it—fore-echoes of strains in Brahms's *Requiem*, in Dvořák's *Requiem* and in Elgar I am sure I have discovered. When I find this great godlike, reserved soul confiding its secrets—and sometimes such intimate, tender ones—to me, how should I not feel indescribably honoured and moved?

A group of songs from the inexhaustible Schubert ocean, all of them new and very arresting—I *must* know more about Schubert.

Once again one saw what a master of *orchestral* effect was Bach in addition to everything else—especially from his superb use of the *oboe d'amore*.

How gloriously eerie and mysterious is the middle portion of *Euryanthe*—sheer witchery. . . . The almost antique but never-to-be-antiquated beauty of Weber.

There was some music, too, that became dear in his home because of the honest, sweet, homeliness of its beauty, or its nursery, fairy-tale note. Peter Cornelius's *Brautlieder* (of these he wrote an English translation) or the rollick of *The Barber of Seville*, or the Hans Andersen romance of Humperdinck's *Hansel and Gretel*. And he gave notable lectures on Scottish folk-songs and the history of Western hymnology.

English folk-music, too, had a real hold on him, whether the music of old English dances (he bought every book published by Cecil Sharp) or the music of old carols, or the work of Vaughan Williams and Holst with its folk-song basis. "Folk-music appealed to the English essence of him," says his son, "the same which made him love Shakespeare and Dickens and all homely and simple things."

It was not easy for a man who went to Egypt in 1899 to follow the new musical developments of the next quarter of a century, but Gairdner was loth to renounce kinship with any development of beauty.

The moderns, Vaughan Williams and others, such difficult atonality, such difficult idiom, but arresting and with a new sort of beauty, and a new method and aim which have to be perceived and accepted before the music can be judged upon [he said].

The splendid way in which the moderns use the instruments of percussion. Just as in the case of the brass, what strikes the tyro as prodigality in use is seen in time to be *economy*. For unsuccessful and blurring use of brass in *tuttis* you have to go to the early composers, who used it much more sparingly. The moderns who use it lavishly never get it ill-balanced or coarse. So with the percussion which Strauss and others have tremendously developed. Effects with kettle-drums, big drum and perhaps side-drum too, and cymbals, run across the sound-tissue of a big *tutti* like a slat of rattling hail with a rumbling thunder at its heels.

And of Holst's *Ode to Death* he said :

I did like it. Towards the end, the crotchets of the slow six-four measure are picked out by the celeste. That clear, far-away tintinnabulation mixing with Holst's dark harmonies—exceedingly beautiful.

He was, then, under all difficulties a " catholic man," but he had his particularities, his musical intimacies, and they were closest of all with the music of Wagner and Elgar.

IV

His love for Wagner began before the days when it was fashionable among Englishmen and continued into the days when among purists it was *démodé*. The enthusiasm sprang up in his Oxford years and went with him all through life. He " demonstrated " Wagner wherever he went with his astonishing power of making others hear or see through his own intense perceptions. Two of his little children, admitted in dressing-gown and pyjamas to hear him " demonstrate " the *Rheingold*

Overture on the piano, have never forgotten how their father conveyed to them the splutter and swirl of the water, the flashing of a Rhinemaiden's white shoulder or her high lilting call, in a beauty which, young as they were, was an experience both seen and heard for their whole lifetime.

His letters are full of his joy in Wagner :

> I always thought that the sailor's song in the first scene of *Tristan* was of the sea, sea–y, of the salt, salty, and I have now proved it : as the wind sings over the bows I have been singing it, shouting it : it is as airy as the air itself.
>
> *The Meistersingers*—that embodiment of youth and sunlight and joy, I enjoyed it with all my soul. Surely it is the most entirely poetical thing he ever wrote. It has quite a Shakespearean feel about it.
>
> Some of the great thrilling chords, orchestrated with terrible glory, seemed to tear at my very bowels, so that it was difficult to repress a cry of mixed pain and joy. . . . One feels more and more that even if the *Ring* gets left by the taste or the thought of future ages, it will be impossible for any future age to dispense with *Die Meistersinger*.

The culminating experience was in 1906, when he and his wife spent nine days of wonder at Bayreuth :

> The last act of *Götterdämmerung* is a fit climax. It somehow reminds me of the closing movement of Schubert's big symphony which you feel to be a wordless tragedy. The agitated triplets and racing dotted-quavers which are the peculiar features of the symphony are found identically at the close of the *Götterdämmerung*. I was completely done up when it ended and took quite a long time to recover.
>
> I should say that a friend has given us an introduction to Wagner's daughters. We saw the drawing-room where the musical parties with Liszt went on, and Wagner's library. They seemed glad to speak about

their father's work. When they began the usual style of thing about missions I slung in a telling shot—that the ideas of Islam were the very ideas that every music-drama of Wagner combated, and that the Moslem Allah was Wotan to the *n*th power. Immediate effect on Fräulein Wagner, "Ah yes, it is so! But you would not evangelize the Buddhists." I was politic enough to say that Islam was quite enough for me to tackle.

The reasons for affinities between soul and soul in the domain of beauty are as secret as the springs of love itself. But there were certain intellectual conditions of Wagner's work that made it irresistibly fascinating to Gairdner. It represented in the first place an ideal concerning the theatre, and Gairdner was an artist not in music alone but of a strong dramatic gift. It was true that he would not have music enslaved to mere description of fact and incident. But neither would he claim for it aloofness from man's story. "I believe thoroughly in music as an interpreter of facts and incidents and persons so far as they can be simply, broadly and emotionally treated."

To a Gairdner, then, with two powers within him, that of the actor and of the musician, Wagner's marriage of the two arts was in itself a fascination. And the Hellenistic thought behind it appealed to the Hellenistic in him.

Wagner's music-dramas a preparation for the art-work of the future, the recovery of the Hellenic succession. . . . It must be an art that springs out of the life of the people. The tragedy of Æschylus and Sophocles was the work of *Athens*. Only a whole people can throw up a true drama.

Temple Gairdner longed often for some great art-expression that would bring home the unity of all beauty. "The drama is the most salutary of the arts because it leads back to the unity of the arts," he said. "Art must permeate and pervade the totality of life and draw its inspiration from everything in life."

To Gairdner as an artist, then, the appeal of Wagner's work was very strong, but there was another side in him that had to be satisfied too: he was part philosopher. And the mere fact that Wagner's art was the conscious expression of his philosophy was in itself alluring. And when that philosophy had for its main theme man's redemption, how could Temple Gairdner fail to respond with deepest interest?

The instinctive leap of the soul to the beauty most akin to it remains incalculable, but Gairdner would not have been Gairdner had not these root ideas of Wagner's work met with instant response in his mind.

V

Elgar was the other composer whose work became most intimately his, and again there was an appeal to more than one side of Gairdner; the dramatist in him and the saint in him were attracted as well as the musician.

The Apostles was produced at the Birmingham Festival in 1903. By June of 1904 Gairdner was "looking through it" and feeling that he had found something new and great.

> What strikes one is his grasp on the *whole* and the wonderful spirituality of that whole. Elgar seems to me to be tapping a new spring in art—dramatizing the oratorio. What can be more dramatic than the Magdalen-storm section? The *absence* of the stage enables him to disregard necessities introduced by time and space, and, grouping together events ideally connected, though in time and space sundered, to suggest a novel and most powerful dramatic situation.

He longed for the conclusion of the *Apostles* cycle, and when in 1919 Sir Edward Elgar told him something of the outline of this conclusion he was eagerness itself:

> . . . The work is to close with the unspeakably touching close of the Revelation, "Even so, come,

Lord Jesus!" Merely to see Elgar's setting of *that* it will be worth while to pray for the completion of the work.

He wrote in Cairo an interpretation of the second *Symphony*, a guess at the composer's inner thought and intention, and happy was he when Sir Edward Elgar told him that he had interpreted aright. *The Dream of Gerontius* he first heard (not by his Cairo method of baby-organ-cum-imagination, but in London) in 1919.

I can't say much: it overpowered me. I should have liked to sit in perfect silence for half an hour after it, . . . but the Albert Hall audience behaved extraordinarily badly. The Kyrie and Intercession music in Part I shook me like an aspen. I had just come from seeing X. [X. was in deep mental trouble.] It seemed suddenly to me as if not only we, I, but the choir, all spiritual powers in earth and heaven were praying for him, and the thought broke one up, yet inspired and calmed as well.

One of the happiest afternoons of his life was that on which he heard for the first time Elgar's *Quintet*, brand-new from the composer's hand and played in his own home.[1]

The scene in the fine music-room was very picturesque. The grand piano on the oak floor. The dim light, and the fire burning silently and fitfully in the deeply recessed fireplace with its ingle-nooks, in one of which sat Elgar's rather elf-like daughter. That fire-vignette had almost an air of illusion about it—it reminded me of the fireside scene in *Valkyrie*, Act I—you know how curiously unconcerned, and therefore illusory, homely fire seems on a stage when the impossible-fantastic is being played. A fit setting then to the weird quintet. I heard it twice clean

[1] Sir Edward Elgar, who had, he says, "a very great esteem for Canon Gairdner," kindly allows the reproduction of the description written at the time.

through and part of a third time that afternoon, and got to know it really well. It is glorious. The second subject of the first Allegro is one of the most haunting Elgar ever wrote—I found myself quite unconsciously using it as a prayer at my orisons that night.

The first movement begins with some pianissimo mutterings, like souls turning from side to side in mortal discomfort and numb pain ; then the first subject proper, weird chords, very eerie, with terrible appealing broken utterances from the first violin. " Spirits in prison." An inferno scene—not so much in hell as in an earthly Tartarus of some evil spell. The beautiful slow movement is clearly the redemption scene. And the finale is the resurrection of those damned ones, not to a heavenly Paradise, but rather to a second chance of a blessed, healthy, sane life in a restored world. It is most moving. . . . I don't think that chamber-music ever *could* have been heard under more exquisite conditions.

" I never knew that music could be so spiritual and sacramental," says Gairdner's friend Brother Douglas Downs, " until I heard his interpretation of some passages of Elgar. He showed me for the first time in my life that music may be the very language of heaven."

VI

One little-known service this musician-missionary did to the lands of the Near East, a service which has not yet borne full fruit but has within it many fructifying possibilities.

From the year 1906 he began a collection of Near Eastern airs taken down at the lips of many singers from Syria to Assouan, and used or suitable for use in Christian worship. Some of these were ancient Christian Church tunes handed down by ear from one blind '*arîf* (Coptic choir leader) to another. Some were airs sung by Moslem dervishes or Nile boatmen or Syrian peasants. This collection of some three hundred tunes he prepared for the press during his last illness.[1]

His collecting work confronted him with the question of the scale system on which the Near Eastern music was built—a question which puzzled him for years. He had heard before leaving England of the "quarter-tones" of the Oriental scale. He soon discovered them to be mythical. There was no such regular division of the Western semi-tone. And the conditions of Egyptian singing (Egypt being the least musically gifted of the lands of the Near East) made it very difficult to discover any rule for the more delicate intervals.

In the year 1911 an enlightenment came to him through some gifted musicians of the Greek Catholic Church in Aleppo. "They asserted and proved to me that the modes practised under Oriental names by Arab musicians in the Levant are one and the same with the modes known and used in the services of the Greek Church to-day," modes, that is to say, in which the octave is invariably divided into sixty-eight parts, but the ratios between intervals instead of being regular are various, as (in the case of the first mode) 9, 7, 12, 12, 9, 7, 12 = 68.

Gairdner wrote[2] a very clear and succinct explanation of the modes which he found to be now actually used, and when noting down Eastern tunes, this knowledge of their fundamental structure helped him to express them as accurately as might be in the Western notation, although with the utmost care this notation must, as he sadly owned, cause the evaporation of part of the peculiar aroma of the airs composed in Oriental modes.

He always looked for a modification of the bad musical taste encouraged in the Church in the Near East by some Western missionaries, who teach a not very happy selection of the hymn-tunes of a strange land. He was

[1] They had previously been privately printed, but are now to be published by the S.P.C.K., London.

[2] In an article called *The Sources of Oriental Music* for *The Moslem World*, October 1916.

for improving that selection and offering the best, not the feeblest music of the West, but he also hoped for the day when the Church would discover and use the beauty of her own Eastern airs. For this renaissance he was content to wait. The reward that he saw in his lifetime for his patient scholarly work was to have some member of his congregation (once a Moslem) ring him up begging that a best beloved Eastern tune of his collection might be sung in Church next Sunday, or to hear the utterly pure beauty of a few girls' voices as they sang on Good Friday one of his haunting Eastern airs.

CHAPTER VIII

TWO EVANGELISTS

1902—1907

But what do we talk of them ? They were a couple of lion-like men ; they had set their faces like flints.—*John Bunyan.*

I

At the first Christmas season after Gairdner's marriage, on St. John the Evangelist's Day of 1902, the delicate, ailing secretary of the mission, the Rev. F. F. Adeney, died at the desert town of Helouan.

> I loved Adeney and love him still. He knows it [Temple Gairdner said]. . . . I asked that our house might be to some what his has been to me—that I might do the work among Moslems that he wanted to do and could not.

The group that was left to lead the Egypt mission of C.M.S. was a group of *young* men, all much of an age and able to speak with freedom and deal hard knocks to one another. They had to learn to work together as a free group, a lesson with as much in it of self-discipline as the ordered life of a community under holy obedience. Gairdner saw from the beginning the all-importance of this discipline. In his first months in Egypt, writing of that " agreement " without which miracle-working prayer is not attained, and of the " stern yet most tender conditions of it," he said :

> So unique and so God-like a thing is real unity on earth, absolute disinterested agreement in heart and

motive, that its occurrence is not, and cannot be, anything short of the presence of God Himself. We know the agreement of the Triune God : earthly agreement is its manifestation.

This, then, cuts at the root of all envy, jealousy, petty irritation, personal dislike, contempt, conceit, self-assertiveness.

It is often more a sign of grace and love and humility to say "Amen" to another's prayers than to lead in prayer oneself.

The mission did attain in these years the spirit of a family in which love and freedom of speech were both conserved. And one of the welding forces was the shock of repeated sorrow, for in Gairdner's first years of married life there were several tragic deaths in the little group. "Singular in their lives as those who made for union and love and happiness," Gairdner wrote of the departed, "their very deaths continued and helped this work which is stamped as the outstanding work of the children of God." And at these times of tragedy the mission learned to expect from Temple Gairdner all his strength and all his delicate sympathy.

One such day of sorrow and breaking of heart came to the community on December 8th, 1903, when the young wife of the well-beloved Dr. Maynard Pain died in childbirth. To Gairdner it was the loss of a friend—"Perhaps the most absolutely charitable soul I ever met, with her cheerful, quaint, benevolent ways and words and tones," he said ; and it was a tragedy into which he could the more deeply enter with the stricken husband, that he was himself still vibrant with the emotions of the birth of his own firstborn exactly one month earlier.

Our loved and truly lovely Mrs. Pain died in childbirth [he wrote]. O my God ! lying still and lifeless with her little lifeless child on her arm ! They looked strangely beautiful ; a sight terribly sweet. A sight to shame from me or anyone else who saw it everything ignoble or vile or sinful. The poor stricken body sank : God, I cannot think of that ! Help her husband to forget it. Show us her sweet triumphant soul . . . it is one more triumph, and it must be a triumph-song to-morrow. A triumph of Christian character ; one more triumph for Christ. I know that if I only finished a course like hers my friends might well simply shout in triumph.

And there are some who will never forget the sight of Temple Gairdner with Maynard Pain, the two of them, arm-in-arm, hour after hour pacing up and down the hospital garden, looking the horror in the face and mastering it. Next day, when they buried her, the triumphal note was clear.

"I remember," says a fellow-missionary, "at that funeral service how Gairdner's steadfast voice rang out in songs of praise, making the guttural Arabic beautiful. And then, his duty completed, I saw him hidden behind a small building and giving way to his tears. I have never known anyone so able to weep with those who weep and to rejoice with the rejoicing."

II

It was through such sharing of human experiences that the mission grew close-knit, and within that family sprang up the marvellous dual unity in work between Thornton and Gairdner which has left their names inseparable.

"Their close working friendship," Maurice Richmond says, "recalls historic combinations of men whose twin genius united extensive and intensive, prophecy and scholarship, the world of action and the world of ideas. We think of Luther and Melanchthon, of John and Charles Wesley, and in another sphere of Garibaldi and Mazzini. Thornton was the dauntless Cambridge evangelist, the man who 'thought in continents and archbishops' with prescient vision of openings years before they became visible to others."

"In rides through the streets," Gairdner says,

'Thornton's conversation would be incessantly on the houses and localities, and he would throw out ideas all along the way (because he could not help doing so, not because there was any chance of carrying them out) about the possibilities of work in those localities."

And now Thornton envisaged a great Christian apologetic, saw the types of men to be met, saw lines of action, secured premises, advertised fiercely, collected an audience, dreamed of a literature, bore down objections, toiled at estimates, wrote appeals, and Gairdner behind him all the time ("saying Amen to another man's prayers") was thinking out the detailed content of that apologetic, pursuing an individual soul with prayer, mastering the niceties of Arabic style and courteous phrase, and above all interpreting his friend and his friend's plans to those who were annoyed or scared at the rush and sweep of their unceasing evolution. Gairdner was still "Mr. Interpreter."

"Mr. Gairdner said, 'You know that Mr. Thornton has many things on his mind. Have patience with him, only have patience,'" says an Egyptian friend—"that's what he always taught." And especially in thought was Gairdner the interpreter. Thornton the prophet reached his ideas by great intuitions, knew they were right, and was not over-careful in the logical support he gave to them. It was Gairdner's task to fill in the logic and show the sweet reasonableness of what looked like some wild leap.

Gairdner played the part of interpreter then, but not more from necessity than from delight. He gloried in this friend of his, in his sweep and power. With joy he gave himself to a wonderful self-identification in Thornton's plans. "I thought I could be content," he said, "to spend my whole life in helping him 'make' his far more valuable life."

They came only gradually and with a struggle into freedom for their marvellous co-operation. With more mastery of the language and of the general situation both longed to be off to that work 'among educated Moslems'

for which they had been set apart. But Gairdner wa
still uncomfortably married to his school until his fur
lough in 1904.

> They say that the virtue of the school of *Liter.*
> *Humaniores* is that it fits a man for any duty. Hov
> thankful should I be then that I have its philosophic
> aid behind me as I cope with the gigantic task of the
> *Push Forward Reader*, Part I. B I T, H I T, K I T
> To this sort of thing I give hours of my time. It
> sometimes needs a very broad view of life to see where
> it all works in. No, not so broad neither. One sees
> clearly enough when one thinks a moment.

He was able to tell his Society that he had "introduced many reforms." "At last my limping old school is beginning to keep step." But none the less, when a secretary of the mission on a pastoral visit from London counselled a continued policy of accepting any or every task, Gairdner held another view:

> As for my own future, I hardly agreed with his apparent point of view, which was that a missionary should do what turns up to do and *not* have a definite aim to which he will try to subordinate all smaller works. I hold that unless you to some extent resist the pressure of events, you tend to become their sport. I have already suffered too much in this way.

After schoolmastering by day he was at nights pressing forward to the work he felt to be his call:

> I have been taking a class of catechumens, very interesting, a sheikh from Khartoum who tells me he was by no means the only one seeking after the truth there, a tailor, the two bootmakers, two Aleppo men.

It was this direct dealing with men as individuals or in small groups that most deeply appealed to Gairdner, and in this shone out his insight and his sympathy.

Douglas Thornton, too, was pressing on towards their characteristic work. The Society had a small book depôt, very dearly beloved of the late secretary, Mr. Adeney, who toiled at its accounts with meticulous care and never failed to report to headquarters with modest pride the number of New Testaments there sold. On his death, when Rennie MacInnes (later Bishop in Jerusalem) became secretary of the mission, the little book depôt, its accounts and its future were handed over to Douglas Thornton. He was not the man to leave a work as he found it. In that little shop (front and back rooms) in the very heart of the city he saw, says Gairdner, " a means of securing personal contact and work among individuals and a means of circulating the message through literature."

> With characteristic energy he set to work and soon had shifted all the furniture and shelves about and transformed the appearance of the place, making of it a sitting-room as well as a shop. Then he threw it open *at nights*, organizing a succession of voluntary workers to welcome men in from the street, seat them with all due courtesy, give them books to read, or discuss with them if discussion were preferred.

" It is not a beautiful place," even Douglas Thornton had to own ; but here, night after night, taking duty alternately, Thornton and Gairdner learnt in close talk all the twists of argument that their Moslem friends would bring forward, and many of the difficulties deeper than argument that beset their lives. It was a perfect training-ground for direct personal exchange of thought with Moslems of many types.

> Went to depôt [Gairdner says]. One Sudanese talked faster and more volubly than I have ever seen anybody talk. Heavens, how his thick negro lips vibrated with the speed of their movement ! . . . Very useful conversation with Turkish sheikh. . . . A Persian Babi tackled me on all the points that are the most difficult not to say insusceptible of explanation, e.g. the nature of Christ's Resurrection Body,

the Second Coming, and so forth. Oh, how this wearies me! Yet a man has perfect right to seek enlightenment on points like these. If they are essentially beyond intelligence, why do they enter so deeply into the warp and woof of the Faith? . . . It may be enough for me to cling to what I can see clearly and leave the rest, but it is a hard position for a *teacher* to take up.

This evening at depôt had one of those experiences which, though rare, compensate for many of the little miseries that attach themselves to missionary life—to see a simple, uneducated man like Muhammad Hasan grasping for the first time some of the deeper things of faith—the Incarnation, the Trinity—and far more than that *perceiving that there was ethical significance in these high mysteries*, to see a light positively coming into face and eyes; to hear him say, in language halting like a child's, that his mind was full of a new comprehension; to listen to his prayer of thanks for the light and that every night might be like "this evening." All this was wonderful and delightful. God bless him.

When one gets doing work like this, one wants to be nowhere else in the world, doing nothing else. And yet when it does come to one, one feels so sickeningly unworthy of it.

Such work night after night showed that the men who came for discussion fell into two groups—different in deeds outwardly and in thoughts inwardly—those whose education had been mainly Western in character, the effendis, with their knowledge of English and their red tarbushes, and those whose education, coming from Quranic schools and the Al Azhar mosque, had been mediæval and traditional—the sheikhs with their pure Arabic speech, their turbans and their robes.

Our missionary instructions to work for "educated Moslems" did not discriminate between these two classes of educated men [Gairdner says], although it was thought by most people (including vaguely ourselves, perhaps) that they meant the Quran-educated sheikhs.

III

But now in the spring of 1903 there came a day when the friends bicycled out together, talking furiously, deeply, and resolved to give themselves to a work for students that should touch not only the robed sheikh but the Government student and young Government employé with his longing to be up to date and his beginnings (this was 1903) of national aspiration. Thornton and Gairdner must get quarters to house their two families, with room also for meetings and lectures on the premises, and this house must be in the line of march from Central Cairo to the Government colleges.

Quarters must be found then, and found they were in a house known to all Cairo as Beit Arabi Pasha.

> This house lies between the two tram lines [Thornton wrote], so that notices put up on either side will be seen by every young man who goes to the Ministries and every student as he goes over the bridge. It used to be inhabited by Arabi Pasha[1] before 1882, and it was there that he hatched many of his plots, so that it is an historic place.

"The house is an old-fashioned sort of place [said Gairdner], with two sets of rooms separated by a marble flagged salon. The Thorntons and ourselves are going

[1] Some years later Gairdner had a conversation with the former owner of the house: "I shall not easily forget my interview with him, now an old grey-bearded man, under the stars on the deck of a house-boat on the Nile by Cairo. As we sat together in the dim light the old agitator was gradually drawn into giving me his view of the Arabi revolt. How it was for the good of the country. How he had tried one way and God had chosen another, and he was content. By that easiest of transitions in the East, his talk passed into theology, in which he proved himself a Moslem of the Moslems, holding unmitigated the harshest view of predestination. I ventured to repeat to him earnestly several times the great verse in our Holy Book: 'God, Who willeth that all men should be saved, and come to the knowledge of the truth.'"

to make our home there, each family in one half of the house. The contract is for three years, so you see the greatness of the call to be amiable for a very prolonged time."

The ground-floor rooms of Beit Arabi Pasha, opening on to a small courtyard, were all devoted to the new work for students, and one of them, though dark and not well ventilated, proved large enough for lecture purposes.

They took holiday by turns that year. First, Thornton with a horde of workmen laboured at preparing the historic house for another great chapter in its history, while Gairdner spent one of the most idyllic holidays of his life in camp at Nelson's Aboukir. He swam, he explored Canopus, he took parties out in a *felucca* with a sail "like the wing of a swallow," he built Edinburgh Castle on the sands with a family of children who were his friends, he extracted music in that astonishing way of his from a baby organ and from the other members of the camp, he led uproarious impromptu acting, and he read Exodus and Henry Drummond and Theocritus with his wife.

> Theocritus, and what a setting! The witchery of the Egyptian light and blue; waving palms; sleeping azure; nibbling goats and shy glances of herd boy and girl. Daphnis reading an Idyll to his nymph—a true pastoral if ever there was one.

The entry on his birthday during that holiday is noteworthy, for he and Thornton were on the verge of a great new departure in their ministry:

> Thirty years old to-day—the age mentioned of the Lord Jesus. May my ministry truly begin this year. Rose early and had a time alone overlooking the calm blue waters of the bay. I cannot write here what passed. Why should I? If it does not come out otherwise than on paper, it is not worth the writing here.

The Gairdners returned to Cairo to take over from Douglas Thornton the mêlée of preparations and furniture removal at Beit Arabi Pasha :

> An odd week of jailorship, locking and unlocking cells, running hither and thither, urging on, criticizing, bargaining and paying and the rest. Architecturally, ahem !—we made slight improvements in the back staircase which we covered over and white-washed.
>
> To keep up our tone and stop our minds running perpetually on house-affairs M. and I have taken to reading Shakespeare his plays, at meals !

Reading was only one remove from acting, and history has it that when over the breakfast table he " demonstrated " with brandished bread-knife the degree of fierceness that should be put into certain mouth-filling epithets, the door opened, and the Egyptian cook entered to find the young couple beginning life in their new home with a scene that bid fair to end in murder !

IV

Just before Christmas 1903 Thornton and Gairdner made their venture.

> A double series of meetings was planned for the new premises ; one of these was English and Arabic, to suit the young English-speaking effendis ; and the second was in Arabic only, and specially for Azhar men. The audience were invited, either then and there or at the following meeting, to express their opinions on the various topics. . . . Like all young men when debating together, they said exactly what they meant, and thus we were able to learn their thoughts in a perfectly new way. In the case of the religious meetings this could only lead (in Egypt) to one result —controversy, sometimes of a peculiarly " animated " nature.

Henceforward life was fast and furious.

" We are on terms of delightful freedom with many of

these students," Gairdner wrote, "the best and most helpful element of modern Egypt."

But the work was exacting to the last degree.

> To conduct a difficult dispute [Gairdner said] with masters in the art of disputing, in a difficult imperfectly-known language, and in circumstances highly trying to the temper, is perhaps the severest task to which any missionary can be called, especially when he knows that his failure will be the sign for hilarious triumph on the part of his opponents, and perhaps secret dismay on the part of the Christians present. Often the meeting would break up in disorder.
>
> The enemy got his hand in in the shape of a serpent of a sheikh who with silken insolence made an absurd speech, most provocative [he wrote of one meeting]. Instantly the whole place was ablaze.

An Egyptian friend and helper of those days (now the Rev. Girgis Bishai) keeps some very vivid pictures of those Cairo nocturnes :

> One night in a meeting of sheikhs there was a dispute about the Divinity of Christ. Mr. Gairdner spoke, and a sheikh interrupted him with "Inta qalîl el adab" ("You are very ill-bred").[1] If he had said that to another Moslem there would have been blows. The *qasees*[2] said in a very low voice, "Am I very ill-bred?" He put his hand over his eyes a moment and prayed, and then spoke with great kindness to the sheikh. The man said, "Till that moment I had not believed in your religion, but I believe in it now, because I saw a highborn Englishman take an insult from me in silence. There must be something within him to cause that."
>
> Another night [says the same narrator], at a meeting of effendis, the men divided themselves into two bands

[1] The translation gives no idea of the inflammatory nature of the sentence to Arabic ears.

[2] Priest, the invariable title of our clergy in Egypt.

to break up the meeting. One band broke the lamps and the furniture in our room. The other band went to the police-station and said the *Qasees* Gairdner and I, had spoken against the Prophet, blasphemed their religion and torn their new clothes. They brought some constables back with them to the meeting room. These said, "You must come with us to the police-station." "Why?" "Because you have struck these effendis and torn their clothes." "But it is neither true nor probable. See, we are only two and they are many, and look at the wreckage they have made of our room." "You must come along." So they took the *qasees* and myself to the police-station with a crowd of effendis following and some of them drunken.

The *mamur* asked the effendis what was their complaint against us. They said we had blasphemed their religion and torn their clothes. What was my relief when the other Moslems who had followed us said there was not a word of truth in the accusation. They said, "These men are drunken. Not an impolite word has been said about our religion, and instead of their tearing our clothes some effendis have smashed up their room." The *mamur* took their witness and ordered the plaintiffs to spend the night in the cells. Then Mr. Gairdner said, "Oh no, please let them go home. We came from our country to set at liberty the captives, and I don't want anyone locked up for my sake." The *mamur* was much interested in these words and kept us for a talk. He said, "What do you mean by saying you came here to set captives at liberty?" Mr. Gairdner replied, "We did not come to break into your prisons, but to set free those who are captives of Satan, bound in the chains of sin." Thereupon the *mamur* sent for coffee and listened with a good will, and Mr. Gairdner was pleased that on that evening, when the students would not listen, he had found an audience after all in the police-station.

One can see Gairdner's humour playing over the march to the police-station, so much less terrifying to him than to the brave Egyptian at his side, and the little inward chuckle with which he secured his unexpected audience.

One of the disturbers of the peace, now a Christian, records another evening which, for all his high seriousness, Gairdner must have taken with a twinkle. Had a crony of the right sort been present at the climax he would no doubt have winked at him, for he always viewed his own doings under a lambent flicker of humour. The disturber says:

> Gairdner was the second speaker. His subject was the Divinity of Christ, and when he said, "Behold then, in Christ, God Incarnate," I was furious. I soon had the room in excitement and we broke the chairs and the lamps. In the midst of it I heard Gairdner say very quietly, "The real leader is that little short man"—meaning me. He had a Coptic friend with him, a good man, now a teacher in a Coptic school, who said, "Hadn't I better go for the police?" I shall never forget how Gairdner turned round to him and called him by his name in a tone that held both friendship and horror. "Ayyâd!" he said, "what do we want the police here for? Don't you know, Ayyâd, that we are here for the sake of the Azhar men, and if necessary I'm quite ready to take a beating from them?"
>
> My friend Ali er Raḥmân overheard that, and he said at once, "If you came here for our sakes, let us see if you mean what you say. Now, it says in your book that if you are struck on one cheek, you should turn the other. But you won't follow that." This he said working himself up into a passion and sure that no man so proud as an Englishman would carry it out.
>
> Instantly Gairdner strode into the middle of the room, clasped his hands behind his back and said with a charming smile, "Come on then, friend, strike as much as you like!" None of us could: we were too

much surprised at such behaviour in an Englishman—and he looked so friendly. We stood in silence. Then he broke into a little laugh, and so did we, and he said, " Now let's drink coffee together," and sent for coffee and for Mr. Thornton to come and drink it with us.

V

Was Gairdner an evangelist? He would probably have answered with a note of wistfulness, No. If that term be taken (as it has sometimes been taken) to mean one who year in year out makes only the one great appeal to men to accept forgiveness and justification by faith, then Gairdner was not an evangelist. He was too respectful to the human soul to bludgeon men, though his rapier thrusts at conscience could be keen enough. " That's the best I can do for an evangelistic address," he said shyly to his wife, after speaking in a great united meeting, little guessing how home-thrusting, how poignant, had been his God-filled message. For whatever phrases men might miss from his preaching, none with ears to hear could miss Christ and Him crucified. Only, as with his Master, his appeal was to those with ears to hear, and again as with his Master his preaching was a test of the capacity for spiritual response in his hearers. He could never be a demagogue, but the deeper a man's spiritual capacity the more did he find in Gairdner's preaching, which came from the depths of his own life and called to the deeps in other men.

But if to be a shepherd of individual Moslem souls is to be an evangelist, there have been few like Gairdner. The result of the campaign of witness organized in Beit Arabi Pasha was to set him in a cure of souls in Egypt.

VI

His friend Sheikh Bûlus er Rimâwi (formerly Sheikh Mahmûd) has a tale to tell of long individual shepherding—reiterated personal invitations; special friendliness and coffee-drinkings after some outrageous act; messages by Egyptian friends that "Gairdner longs to see you"; direct intimations that Thornton and he were pouring out their souls for him in prayer late into the night; books lent; lessons given and taken, the one teaching Quran, the other Gospel; a gift of a New Testament:

> Before I left, Gairdner said, "I want to give you this book, but you must promise me you'll read the Sermon on the Mount." I promised him and went home in some curiosity to find out what he was so anxious for me to read. He had written messages from himself to me in the margin—thus where it said, "Pray for them that despitefully use you," he had said, "I continually pray for you." I was deeply touched.
>
> When hard letters came from my father I took them to Gairdner. It was strange how I always had to go to him. He was a magician. We answered them together because he understood.

After months of hesitation, came a culminating day when Mahmûd had to make his decision between acceptance of his father's plan to send him to Stamboul to become a Muslim judge and acceptance of Christ:

> Mr. Gairdner called Mr. Thornton, and then we three prayed together. Perhaps only about three times in my life have I prayed with the certainty of faith, and that was one. Mr. Gairdner said, "I will say the words, and you shall say them after me." He said, "O Lord, what shall I do? Enlighten my eyes that I may perceive the best course, the best for soul, the best for conscience." And even while I was speaking my heart was filled with a great glow of love and I saw shining on the wall opposite me the word *Al Masîh* (Christ).
>
> Then Mr. Gairdner said, "Now we won't talk to one another. You go away and get God's guidance without talking to any human being, and I shall stay here and pray for you."

I went back to the Azhar (university mosque) and took my daily ration of bread. Then I went to the lodgings which I shared with several others. I took out my father's letters and spread them before me. I took the Quran and Injil and I read them in turns. When the others came in, I was in a muse ; they asked me to a party in another room. I said, " No! my thoughts are burdened to-night. Leave me." The two sides of the question kept surging in upon me. How could I face poverty, as I must, if I were a Christian ? But how could I deny Christ ? Why not follow Christ secretly and outwardly comply ? But Thornton and Gairdner said that was only laughing at Christ.

At last I prayed exactly as a man does who is speaking to his fellow. I said to Christ, as though He were at the other side of my bed, " Guide me Thou, O Christ, *if Thou art Lord*."

It was night, and I slept after that. Perhaps I slept an hour, but it seems to me as if I saw in sleep the faces of Thornton and Gairdner and another that I knew was the Face of Christ.

Suddenly I awoke, hearing a voice say, " Mahmûd, rise up, there is light for thee. Fear not." I thought my comrade, Sheikh Ahmad, had called to me, but he was sleeping. Then a man in white passed me and swished me with his robe, saying again, "Mahmûd, rise up, there is light for thee. Fear not." It happened a third time, and I was left trembling all over. At last I said, " O Christ, Thou art my Lord."

My one thought was to meet Thornton and Gairdner. When I went to them, Gairdner said, " Now you who were Saul are Paul (Bûlus)," and kissed my forehead. Afterwards I learned from them that that night they had taken no supper but had stayed till three o'clock praying for me—till about the time of my vision.

Loneliness came on me terribly on the night after my baptism. That is always a hard time, when all the calls of the old life sound in a man's ears and he has not yet rooted himself in the new. I could not sleep that night. At eleven o'clock Mr. Gairdner saw a light under my door and called out, "Bûlus!" "I can't sleep," I said. He came in and saw me miserable and said, "I'll stay with you a little while." Then he began to read to me out of missionary papers about some boys in Uganda who had suffered everything for Christ. He read in English and told me in Arabic what he read. I saw that others had left all for Christ. At twelve o'clock he said, "Now you had better sleep." The war was not over in my soul and I said, "I can't." Then he said, "Very well, I have a proposal. You lie down on your bed and shut your eyes, and I will sit on this chair beside you and go on reading to you. I promise to stay with you till you sleep." I did what he asked. At first I could not keep my eyes shut, but every time I opened them he put his hand gently over them until at last I slept and he crept away.

Others, too, remember that individual shepherding.

He would come on his bicycle every day for a fortnight [one says], and stay two hours to teach me. When we came to the chief points of dispute between the two religions, he would not teach me till we had prayed together. "In prayer, things are explained," he told me. And he taught me to keep silence awhile before entering into prayer. I felt he loved me for myself, not because I might become a Christian only, and in this I found he was like Christ. And he loved our children and always played with them.

It was anxious shepherding. "Do not think that *moral* transformation is quickly reached," Gairdner wrote. "I feel that if we can set up a new standard of integrity, of truth, in these men, that alone is a work of even national importance."

The Eastern mind moves theologically much more quickly that it does ethically. Only gradually does the infinitely high standard of Christian holiness make itself felt, and if it is not seen in those Christians with whom the catechumen has to deal, it will not be deeply felt at all. And as the new ideals grapple with the old habits, through what travail, what struggles, what anguish, what tears is the Kingdom of God won! And alas! sometimes after all these have been freely lavished, the travail is in vain, the strain proves too severe. Some fearful temptation of Satan, or the call of the blood, of the family, of the old social environment proves irresistible, and one beholds a man on whom one's very life has been poured out slip back.

One such wrote him a bitter and insulting letter. Gairdner glanced through it, saw its tenor, and laid it aside. Because he loved the boy, he literally shrank from the cruelty in his letter, and read it at last when he came out of church on Good Friday, "because it seemed a good day to let the nails go in."

VII

They hurt him often, that little company of some few score souls among whom "not many wise, not many noble" were called; they hurt him because his love for them gave them the power to hurt. But they were also his joy and pride, and very often his dear amusement. Old Philibbus, a peasant who sold his little land, his tools, his donkey, and came to Cairo to learn of Christ, stood at his baptism "clad in a white linen robe and a white turban and shod with sandals," Gairdner says.

He stood alone save for alien god-parents, no single relative or friend was there. His own wife "was angry and would not come in." Utterly alone, therefore, he descended into the water, and I had the privilege of baptizing him in the threefold Name.

Afterwards in the vestry I looked forth, and lo! the landscape was glowing—the brilliant hues of the Egyptian spring pervaded everything. I said,

"Philibbus, how seems the world to you to-day?" He replied, "I never saw it before: it is as though I have lived my life till to-day down a well."

A poor old Egyptian fellah with £12 a year showing signs of a changed life! You may say that is small enough game in all conscience. Upon my soul I am sometimes tempted to think so myself. But there are other times when with a judgment illumined by more eternal light one sees and knows and feels that such results are worthy of whatever sacrifice they entail. After all, this and no other is what Christ came to do.

When a whole family came forward together for Baptism, Gairdner wrote:

The two little girls were in high glee at the thought of Baptism, which with the delightful naturalness of children they evidently considered "fun." I declare when I saw those glancing merry eyes, the childlike pleasure in the white robes, and the prospect of the great ceremony, I rejoiced at the pure humanity of the thing. "Of such is the Kingdom." "Are you afraid?" I whispered to the first as she looked down into the dark pool. "No," she replied, and walked down the steps bright-eyed and was immersed. The second was younger and seemed a little afraid, so she was half-sprinkled, half immersed; and so sweet did her little bright eyes seem that it was absolutely impossible to refrain from giving her a kiss as the little dripping form was handed up to the arms of the sponsors. It was a family ceremony. The playfulness and the solemnity did not clash, rather they blended into a rich and beautiful whole where the natural had at last become the spiritual and the spiritual is thoroughly natural.

"He wearied himself out for those who had become Christians," says his friend and co-worker, the Rev. Girgis Bishai, of whom the same testimony might be given, "for every one of them."

There was A., the boy at the oculist's, who stole some spectacles and was sentenced to three months—a severe sentence. He was imprisoned up at the Citadel, and it was a very hot month and visiting hours were in the middle of the day. The *qasees* said to me, "Let us go and visit him," and I said, "I would like to, but my body won't stand the fatigue of bicycling through the midday heat." He said, "Then never mind." But he went off by himself and the boy repented deeply, and when he came out the *qasees* persuaded his master to give him another trial, and he is there still, doing well.

"Gairdner was a man who might have stood before kings," said one of these his sons, "but he used to sit on the ground and play with our children and let them climb on his back. 'A door of shelter was he.'"

To them no apologia for his life was needed. Gairdner himself when asked to make one said:

> If the efforts to evangelize Islam had not resulted in a single conversion, they would have been worth while; for they represent Christianity as a religion that is not afraid, a religion with a message of love and goodwill evinced in deeds of love and goodwill.

CHAPTER IX

APOLOGETICS

1903—1907

May I not write in such a style as this?
In such a method too and yet not miss
My end—thy good? . . .
. . . Let truth be free
To make her sallies upon thee and me
Which way it pleases God.

John Bunyan, "The Author's Apology."

I

"It is to Islam that I go—not to any particular phase of it. My ideal is to become a master in Arabic (an awful aim), and perhaps to help in creating a Christian literature in that tongue; and thus to get at the heart of the problem of Islam."

So Gairdner had written before setting out for Cairo in 1899, and now, with the beginning of their work for students, the literature idea sprang fully-armed to the birth in both Thornton and himself.

> *June 1st*, 1903.—D. M. T. and I quite fixed that we shall try to work among effendis *and perhaps by means of a paper in Arabic and English.*

In their usual complementary fashion they were pushed on to their enterprise by different processes of thought. Thornton saw with his quick, vivid observation that printed paper was beginning to count in the life of the Near East as a means of spreading ideas among more than the scholarly few, and that the age of tracts that had passed with the nineteenth century from Britain was dawning in Egypt and her neighbour lands. Accordingly he made experiments with these tools and the use of them.

> Assuming that the human animal is friendly when it is pleased [Gairdner says], a party was organized on Easter Monday (a universal holiday) to go to several places which are always thronged with tens of thousands of holiday-makers, and there to distribute pamphlets, not controversial, but of general moral interest.

The success of that Bank Holiday outing at once caused Thornton to see visions, and he wrote :

> If we had had ten thousand instead of two thousand, we could have used them well. . . . Only one tract was seen to be torn up, and several said to me, " This is a moral tract, but haven't you one about Christ also ? " or words to that effect. The fact that numbers are now coming to our depôt and asking for more for their friends is a further indication of the good that is being done. I feel that in the next few years we shall have an immense opportunity before us, if only we can take it.

He made street leaflets advertising the lectures at Beit Arabi Pasha and had them given away to the young men who streamed past the house every morning on their way to Government schools or offices. In all this Thornton took the lead and Gairdner was his appreciative seconder. " I'm no good at giving tracts," Gairdner would say ; but none the less, when Egyptian volunteers failed to arrive for the distribution of those notices, he stood in the street and gave them away himself. " I got rid of every one. Alone I did it," he told his wife in triumph.

From another angle it was he who took the lead. He was now becoming familiar with certain Moslem objections which he must always meet when he would fain present one of the truths he lived by, and he wearied of the endless defensive controversy :

> For one and a half hours we went at it, very unprofitably as one would think . . . at such times the preaching of the Gospel seems impossible. When one is set upon with questions and objections, silence and evasion are impossible, and answering is useless and unprofitable—so one is in a dilemma.

It seemed to him that much of this defensive work might be done by literature. If there were but little books dealing singly with the main difficulties, they might be handed to Moslem friends who reached the inevitable objection-point, and they might be distributed over the countryside and do their preparatory work in opening minds. Still more might there be books of narrative quite free from argument, yet understanding and anticipating and meeting the Moslem's difficulties as he heard the Christian story. But when Gairdner looked for such books he found that the literature by which the Christian Church had set forth her living truth to Moslems was a curiously arid, machine-made literature. It was as though the compilers, holy men though they were, had been caught into the argumentative machinery of the schoolmen, and had expended all their vital strength in meeting Moslem arguments with juster arguments. The objector himself might be left on the field prostrate but cursing. The books were starved of personality and of appeal to aught save logic and justice. Moreover he saw, and it was one of his most fruitful perceptions, that the converts made by this literature were often born in its image—with the spirit of disputation rather than of worship and of love, and apt to hammer rather than to woo and win.

Gairdner believed (for was he not nightly battered with anti-Christian arguments ?) that there must needs be an apologetic literature, unafraid of controversial points. Silence, he felt, was tantamount to denial of the truth he knew and lived. But the literature must be humanized and written for fellow-men, not only for the defeat of argufiers. Moreover, to Gairdner, stories, history, drama, music, poetry, pictures, all that could bear the impress of the Spirit of Christ, was a reasonable part of the Christian apologetic to the whole man. So his vision of the content of the literature grew side by side with Thornton's for its circulation, and both were enthralled and inspired at the thought of harnessing that great instrument, the Arabic language, to the service of Christ. Gairdner endorsed with all his being Thornton's flaming pronouncement on this task :

> I do not hesitate to say, or fear to be contradicted, when I assert that *next to the English language*, *Arabic is read and reverenced over the widest area* of the earth's surface, and as to the actual number of those that speak Arabic there are at least fifty millions of souls, and no non-Christian language is spreading at anything like the same rate. . . . The first point brought home to us missionaries in Cairo has been the providential position of Cairo, and opportunity in Cairo for a great *literary campaign for Christ.*

So they saw their calling, and the task before them had for its preliminary steps the persuasion of their comrades in Egypt that they two (who seemed burdened enough with works) should become editors and publishers, and next the persuasion of the Society at home to allow two young men not only to enter on this apostolate but also to shoulder the burden of raising money with which to carry it out.

II

Gairdner and his wife went home for their first furlough in May of 1904, having made an assignation with Douglas Thornton (who would rush home for his " summer holiday ") to meet and lay their plans before their Society. They wanted official leave to make in Cairo a " literature department " of their mission, and to publish an apologetic magazine. Both of them were to make furious inquiries about the cost of printing, the quality of paper, the borrowing of blocks, the experience of Indian missionaries in publishing, and a dozen other points.

It was the only full six-months' furlough that Gairdner took in eighteen years, and he needed it after the sheer fag of mastering Arabic and the strain of handling audiences when they came " in numbers thirsting for the wordy fray, and eyes burned fiercely and the hot Arabic streamed forth in eternal disputation." He was tired and arrived in England in a sort of dream :

> Did not realize where I was till I heard a *blackbird* trilling in a copse near Canterbury. Praised God for this.

Then all the old joy in his country and her beauty came upon him. He never in his life possessed a foot of land, but he possessed the world in love, and his uncovetous, disinterested joy in earth goes some way to explaining the strange promise that her inheritors shall be the meek. Coming back to English twilight evenings, he now wrote:

> The sentinel elms stood round the field, the sky was delicately flushed with pink—all nature quiet as a nun. If the heart is utterly at peace with God it is also entirely one with nature in these beautiful moods. My disobediences destroy both of these onenesses. Yet to-night in the peace of the Son, I could say, Father, Thou art ever with me, and *all that Thou hast is mine*.

His prayer of that furlough, after narrow and intensive work at Arabic verbs and Islamic arguments, was for the release and freshening of his spirit :

> I am trusting Thee to get me out of *ruts*. To free my soul that its whole power may go into moving forward ; into cloudless communion ; into love ; into effort.

He took delightedly the ways that offered for escape from " ruts " : " a perfect orgy of music for which

I took my wife up to London" ; the Greek play at Bradfield (a photograph of the open-air theatre hung in his Cairo study ever after) ; "an airless, moonless, starless night" at Oban when "a man played the dulcimer divinely, a self-taught man with music in his soul, therefore my brother" ; and, above all, an almost startling expansion of horizon when the classically trained man first began to see, through the eyes of H. G. Wells, a new world of physical and sociological questionings. The greatness of the occasion he described in one of the longest sentences that even Temple Gairdner wrote :

> It was a great day in my mental history when in the little parlour of a lonely inn in the heart of the Moor of Rannoch, when the evening had closed in wet and abominably cold and it was with fullness of joy indescribable that one stretched one's limbs after the day's walk up Glen Etive before the blazing fire, replete and complete with Scotch "high-tea," I picked up as idly as one ever picked up a book in one's life, *there* of all imaginable places, and *then* of all incongruous times, a cast-off, dirty, sixpenny edition of *Anticipations* by H. G. Wells . . . a volume that turned my mind inside-out and set me on a course of thinking and reading which at least gave one a coherent idea of the physical constitution of the world one lived in, and introduced one to the real problems in sociology which the physical study of the world forces upon the mind.

In intimate human joys the furlough was a rich one. There was the presentation to Sir William Gairdner of his first grandson, and an idyllic holiday in a Forfarshire cottage with a sister and her family, when they buried the sleeping baby in bracken in the woods or fetched the household water from the spring to the tune of "What are the wild wives saying ?" ; there was a crowded visit to Oxford and a dash into Devonshire :

> He got to know that I was in sore perplexity and great trouble [a friend writes] ; my future was all

very dark. He wrote me, "I'm coming down to stay with you," and came from Scotland to Exeter, just to cheer me up. And his exquisite courtesy was shown by the fact that he would not intrude, so he said, and therefore stayed in the house of a mutual friend. In those days, by music, walks, and prayer such as I had never known before, he lightened the whole cloud. . . . His life and prayer seemed of the same pattern. It was not methodical, it was often ejaculatory, staccatoed, explosive, absolutely unorthodox, but it was genuine. To pray with Gairdner was to learn how a man who lived with God could talk very naturally with Him.

And there were in that furlough moments of solitude when the spiritual tide could be felt to be flowing in and lifting the whole life, as on a visit to Rossall, notable indeed for midnight music with old friends, but still more for what he felt to happen in the secret springs of his being :

After greeting my host I went out alone to the sea wall. I hardly know how I shall say what befell. A glorious wind was blowing in from the west across the Irish Sea, driving along with it warm thin rain. As I faced it my soul suddenly leaped forth—I felt what a cramped-up, stuffy life the life of my ψυχή had often been—and I shouted against the wind, yes, *shouted* in prayer to the God of that wind to blow with the rushing west wind of His Spirit into mine and make it as healthful and free and *blowy* as that gale from the sea. No one was there to hear and I shouted praise in a sort of madness. It was splendid !

Ten years fell off me on that sea-wall. There *is* a secret for eternal youth—the eternal renewing of the regenerate heart—the daily becoming "as a little child" ; that is the secret.

The business of persuading the Church Missionary Society that two young men in Cairo with a great evangelistic work on their shoulders might be allowed to add the burden, financial, organisational, and creative, of a literature venture proceeded slowly. On Gairdner's first visit to his Society as a returned missionary nothing of moment took place :

> To C.M.S. House after visiting the ancient Roman Catholic chapel in Ely Place and prayer there. Sat in Committee and spoke for a few minutes. Useless, I think.

Then D. M. Thornton came to England with this burden on his mind, and he and Gairdner asked to see their friend the Secretary for Egypt in a long untroubled talk before the decisive committee met in London. He invited them to his home in Surrey, and they wandered about with him on Epsom Downs the whole of a long summer day and its lingering evening, pouring out their views and aims.

> The long twilight seemed a blend of the yellow moonlight and the fading sunset light [Gairdner said]. The air was sweet with the smell of hay. All breathed of peace, and thank God I did not find in my heart any voice that refused to harmonize with that peace. With regard to the work, I feel myself at leisure to give myself utterly to it. Glorify Thy Name.

He would be a stout fellow who could resist the blandishments and the reasoning of a Thornton *and* a Gairdner at their most persuasive, especially when his own desires for Egypt were akin to theirs, and next day at the Committee all ran smoothly for the two Egyptians. "The Society decided," Thornton says, "to develop literary and publishing work in Arabic, with Cairo as a centre, especially endorsing the scheme for an Anglo-Arabic magazine as an evangelistic agency among Moslems."

> That walk on Epsom Downs with Douglas Thornton has become proverbial in the Egypt Mission [Gairdner wrote later to his friend the London

Secretary]. The atmosphere of the racecourse is supposed to have made you amenable to sporting enterprises, so that whenever a big scheme is proposed here, the proposer is advised to go home and talk it over with you on Epsom Downs.

The Committee's decision meant of course the beginning of labours. "We have talked over the paper and are going to get out a pamphlet which will be the basis of an appeal for funds," Gairdner told his wife. The appeal, signed by both Thornton and Gairdner, was issued before they left England, under the title *Christian Literature in Arabic-speaking Lands*. They put their case, especially for the new magazine for educated Moslems, and they asked for money for a "Cairo Literature Fund."

This done, Gairdner returned to Egypt. As he stood on the outward boat "looking over the lovely moonlit seas in prayer to God," he felt the refreshment of his furlough and was able to believe himself "at last on a fairer way." "Prayed to be calm, pure, fresh, fragrant, open, spacious, natural as that beautiful sea."

III

"Our programme," Thornton said, "was the pursuance of our former work of meetings and interviews, together with the superintendence of the circulation of the Bible and Arabic and English literature from our Bookshop, strengthened and aided by the Anglo-Arabic magazine."

They were inexperienced in all the work of publication; and in the complicated enterprise of launching a bilingual paper under the shifty, unstable business conditions of Cairo they made the mistakes of inexperience and suffered for them. Gairdner referred afterwards to "the initial maelstrom" as a "nightmare time."

Many late nights [his journal says], for it is in the evening that D. M. T. and I get those indispensable discussions on which the future of the magazine depends. . . . My name for it, *Orient and Occident*, was at first much decried as being too big-sounding. But others liked it and it will probably be adopted.

A week of tremendously hard but most interesting work in connection with the paper yclept *Orient and Occident*, which will, I should think, be known as *O. & O.* We have had some committees, and D. M. T. and I after midnight planned out the first number to a word. A hitch occurred yesterday, however—the Ahram press suddenly threw up the job.

Anxieties about the arrival of paper: arrival of insufficient: fresh estimate to rectify mistake: cable home for further supply: varying hopes and fears: late night consultations. D. M. T. has had an awful time of it, but has ended off the week well and heartily. I must say that I admire him more and more and also love him.

To-day he took a holiday in the desert, and I on my part, after a morning's work, suddenly had a perfect afflatus of music and played and sang Wagner with voice and my patent drawing-room orchestra till I was in the first or second heaven. Didn't want exercise. *The Meistersingers is* spring air.

After all these travails the first weekly number of *Orient and Occident* appeared on January 5th, 1905.

At first, weary hours had to be spent at the printer's office:

The fair result [says Gairdner] was only effected by continual personal pressure of a vigorous description; our long-suffering wives got quite used to lonely meals. Now things are facilitated by the change of spirit in the workmen at the press. The Arabic compositor upon whom all depends really works with goodwill now. And as for the machine man, Hamûda, on whom we rely for pushing through the work, he has had a strange experience. He hurt his hand one day in the machine and Mr. Thornton sent him down to our hospital. There the Christian mode of prayer affected him greatly. . . . One night he had a dream. He thought he saw Christ come to him—tall, white-skinned (as Hamûda told me afterwards), with head, neck and shoulders swathed (oriental fashion) with wrappings. The Figure came to him and said, "Do not fear, Hamûda, for no harm shall happen to your hand." Then It touched his hand and Hamûda at once awoke. "I was not excited," he told me, "but full of fear. . . . I said, 'You Muslims have a care of this teaching, for these people have the truth with them.'"

When Hamûda went back to the press it was to witness in the teeth of contradiction to the truth he had heard. I see him in the press nearly every day, and a glad face he wears.

The circulation of the paper very slowly climbed to about 3,000, in those days very large for an Arabic periodical. It was edited with a kind of passion. "To Thornton," Gairdner says, "it was a proposition so obvious as not to require demonstration that a subscriber to his paper thereby became a sort of parishioner." The two editors themselves and their ideas and enthusiasms were lavished on the paper. Their readers might become intimates if they so would. The old Gordon admiration is there. Gairdner had just made friends with Ibrahîm Fauzi Pasha, who passed through the siege by Gordon's side and saw him fall. "He adores the name and memory of Gordon and spent an afternoon with us pouring out anecdotes." "We know things about that last month," *O. & O.* says, "that make us turn our faces away, even as one can hardly bear to look at Christ in Gethsemane." And a new enthusiasm appears in the paper, a fruit of the recent readings in H. G. Wells. Gairdner's friend, Dr. W. F. Hume, of the Geological Survey, remembers the birth of this new interest :

Gairdner had been visiting the Wadi Hôf and remarked to Mr. Cunningham (then helping in the

Cairo Geological Museum) that that deep ravine must have been produced by a mighty convulsion of nature. To this remark Cunningham replied that, on the contrary, it had been produced by the activities of an age-long erosion. At the same time he suggested that Gairdner should meet me, and wide and searching were the questions he put as to the current geological views of earth-structure. This profound interest in my own special subject of study drew us together.

Gairdner became a fossil-hunter and was, after his wont, breathlessly interested : " The great mountain rotting away before one's very eyes ! And yet a month ago I should have noticed nothing of this and talked about the everlasting hills. Everlasting ! The thing has one foot in the grave ! A matter of a few million years and it is all over."

The natural result of the new fervour was that *Orient and Occident* for the time being had a distinctly geological flavour and the erosion of *wadis* in the Mokattam Hills found its way into Gairdner's articles on " Evolution and Religion."

Later there came weary years when *O. & O.* lost its first fine careless rapture and only maintained its existence through a patience that cost more than the ardours of the earliest days. During the last five years of Gairdner's life the beloved magazine showed steady signs of improvement. He remarked on this to a fellow-editor with great content, and was met with the reply : " But I don't think it has ever risen above its source." " Perhaps not," he said reluctantly ; " you see, in those days we were both young and fresh and both of us were putting our whole strength into it."

Orient and Occident, when this book is written, has readers in fourteen Moslem countries. Its position in the Near East is almost startling. It has won for itself a respect in the moral sphere greater than is given to any other paper, and that by its freedom from mere verbiage ; by its reverent care for truth ; by joint Eastern and

Western editorial work rigidly maintaining a hig standard in translation ; by a policy of outspoken fearless ness as to its Christian character ; and by abstentio from axe-grinding on behalf of any person, policy nationality, society or party whatsoever.

IV

To sum up Gairdner's contribution to Christian literature for Moslems is anything but easy, for the list of titles in the appendix to this book shows that it was many-sided. Let it suffice, in this chapter on his work as an apologist, to look at what he did in the controversy of long centuries between the doctors of Islam and Christendom. No one could think of Gairdner as a controversialist for choice. He was far too richly human. "We need the *song* note in our message to the Moslems," he said at the beginning of the Beit Arabi Pasha days ; "not the dry cracked note of disputation, but the song note of joyous witness, tender invitation," and much of his writing answered to these words. But neither was he of the school that thinks all argument to be unnecessary. He recalled the controversies recorded in the Fourth Gospel, in the Acts and the Epistles, and could not claim exemption for the Church to-day.

What he did in his books on directly controversial points was to humanize the tone and temper in which the argument is conducted. Like Raymond Lull or John Bunyan, he used in his earlier books the dialogue with attached narrative. But this sort of argument by invented dialogue can be exquisitely irritating; it requires the most scrupulous and delicate fairness on the part of him who moves the puppets, and great imaginative sympathy with those he is defeating.

Gairdner's books are courteous with no sham courtesy, and they are the books of a man who *enjoyed* sharing a joke or a story with a group of Eastern friends :

> Yesterday I was returning along the Pyramids road in the evening when I heard the pattering of donkeys'

little feet and a loud voice reading—not the Quran but *Arabian Nights.* Two donkeys pattering along and two swains cross-legged thereon. By their side stalked a solemn camel surmounted by the usual taciturn driver. I begged leave to join this pilgrimage and to listen to the story: so on paced this odd quartette, their backs to the glow: the pattering donkeys, the stalking camel and, oh bathos! a Beeston-Humber bicycle surmounted by a figure in untidy khaki.

His books are good-natured and they play fair. He also expects his Muslim reader to play fair, appealing always to that reader's best mind. Moreover, he pays him the compliment of real indignation (which he expects his reader to share) at what is underhand and mean. This kind of severity has respect at the heart of it. It implies that the reader can share the author's white indignation at deliberate falseness or deliberate foulness. It came (as similar passages in the Bible come) from moral passion in him, passion in the literal sense, for, as his friend Dr. Zwemer has pointed out, it was impossible for Gairdner to be merely interesting and interested when faced with moral issues. He cared and suffered.

"This reckless tampering with ethical values must be put down at any cost," he would say, "and the criticisms thus wrung from us must not and shall not be set down as bigotry." The occasional sharp note of indignation in his writing is literally a *cri de cœur.*

But it is not the main or the dominant note of his work. He is an apologist more often than a scourge of the Lord. "He was a philosopher on fire," says Maurice Richmond, "and when a philosopher is on fire he does not burn, he glows."

"With his instinct for fundamentals he mined and tunnelled his way into the heart of Islamic theology and thought." He worked on all the main points of the age-long controversy between the two faiths, and the chief mark of his work is his refusal to regard any one of these doctrines as an abstract question. They belong to the life of the human spirit, and to abstract them is to wrong ourselves as well as the truth.

After teaching an Egyptian peasant he wrote:

> It is rare indeed anywhere to find a person who sees moral import in the doctrine of the Trinity, who realizes how it bears on the whole question of approach to God and our life in Him. But to see an ignorant Moslem gripping it almost untaught was enough to set the angels singing.

That is his authentic note. " Contact with Unitarian Deistic Islam," he said, " forces the Christian Church to work out again her theology *experientally*." And so the " Mohammedan question " may possibly be as life from the dead to the Christian Church itself. . . .

There speaks the essential Gairdner, the apologist of life. To this attitude he came in those strenuous years while he laboured at Islamics, and faced audiences of sheikhs with Thornton.

V

These were among the happiest years of Gairdner's life. He was young, he had a doughty comrade at his side, he had an exacting task and a call for creative thought, and he had the constant background of the loyalty and devotion of his home life and the joy of his babies.

Already he and his wife were beginning to make those great Christmases for which their home was known in Egypt. In 1904 there was only one babe to make Christmas for. Yet the presence of the one (on whose birth-night his father had played carols in memory of a greater Birth-night) gave its own zest to Christmas in the house, and the young parents threaded their way among toy-laden stalls and made the purchase of a " *very* large " toy horse.

By 1906 John Oswald Hugh had joined William in the Cairo nursery, and Christmas ceremonies take shape.

Gairdner, who seemed to live in a radiant glow throughout the season of the feast, was a mighty inventor (born ritualist that he was) of little tender family rites for Christmas. In 1906 all this was scarce begun:

> A procession was made, led by Paterfamilias, his locks crowned with a wreath of lifelike artificial holly, and the said procession reached the nursery quarters where the two sweet little men were sleeping the sleep of the Holy Innocents. Little Billie's little sock was there, pinned up over the rail of the mosquito-curtain. Into this sock two chocolate fish with skins of silver paper were slipped, and a lovely tramcar was put at the head of the crib, with other delights. Then next door, to the little Raphael-cherub and Reynolds-angel whose still minuter sock received two more silver fish. . . .
>
> Then the festive procession, led by the faun with the garland, went back to the drawing-room, where we serenaded Mrs. Thornton with some of her favourite carols, beginning with "God rest you merry, gentlemen"—a true *waits* carol with its heavy unvaried pom-pom of a four-crotchet time, suggesting irresistibly old "willains" with red noses and comforters and rather bowed legs, with battered hats, standing in the snow and roaring the four crotchets like—well, just as old "willains" with comforters do roar or did roar or would roar. . . . Our Christmas party is becoming quite an institution. We made the staid ladies play dumb-crambo.

The grave young editor and apologist had a purely boyish side, and his friends' memories of the Gairdner of those years are gay with a very youthful gaiety.

> I remember Dr. Pain's coming into the dressing-room (at the hospital) convulsed with mirth: "The *qasees* sent a special messenger yesterday requesting me to supply him with a lotion to prevent his hair falling out" (those thick rather uncontrollable curls through

which in moments of excitement he would run ruffling hand), "and to-day he sends in haste asking for something to prevent its growing so fast!"

The fact that I lived about six miles from Bletchley [Miss Warburton says] always made him associate me with Bletchley Junction. I remember after a heavy storm of rain when the sides of the streets had turned into rivers and lakes, as we were walking near the Helouan station we came to a river which looked as if it could not be passed. With a cry of "Bletchley!" he seized me by the hand, and with a flying leap we cleared the obstacle, to the amazement of other pedestrians.

A purely boyish postscript from a letter of those days reveals more of the scourge of manners than the apologist:

> I ran down a boy on another bike, going as hard as I could, on purpose, because I saw him callously run down a child. I did not come off quite scatheless, nor did the bike, but it was a glorious feeling, ramming him like a torpedo!

"Our children were never in any awe of him," says a friend, "but claimed him at once as a beloved playfellow full of whimsical jokes and fanciful names for them."

"He fought the dragon," one more witness says, "like another St. George. But he fought him *gaily*, even in his very den."

CHAPTER X

SEVERANCE

1906—1907

Certainly to live on the eternal side of things does give one a purchase over events.—*Letter of W. H. T. Gairdner.*

I

When two men of the build of Thornton and Gairdner give themselves unreservedly to making friendships, the inevitable happens—the contacts made open up new avenues for work and friendship ; vista upon vista greets the eye, call upon call dins the ear. Unless their mission is an impossible failure, your Thornton and your Gairdner will call for recruits.

They were now living in the days of such opening vistas, nor were these only the result of their personal effort. In 1906, through the energy of Dr. Zwemer of Arabia, the first conference of missionaries to Moslems in all lands was summoned to meet in Cairo. Sixty-two missionaries from twenty-nine societies arrived and held their meetings at Beit Arabi Pasha, adding one more chapter to the story of that notable house. Thornton and Gairdner as hosts were breathlessly busy, and those days were, as Gairdner says, " entirely relished by Thornton." As for himself, leading hymns on the inevitable baby organ, he was too much a student ever to feel at ease about the scrappiness of the mental fare at conferences, though he came to see their value for creating a common mind.

But whatever its failures as a studious body, this Conference had some noteworthy results. A new picture opened out before those who were present, of the common life of that far-flung Islam which they encountered in the many lands of their service. And with it came a new understanding of the need for common life and brotherhood among Christ's missionaries. To Douglas Thornton vistas opened up—a central training class in Cairo for Christians who had come out of Islam; new specialized preparation for missionaries from the West; a central Literature Committee for all lands. Given the men, what might not now be done? And at home the Conference and its messages began a sorely-needed awakening movement in that Church of the West which, having flung herself against the Moslem in the Crusades, had then forgotten him for centuries. Even now the Church of Thornton and Gairdner, in issuing in 1906 its list of topics for discussion at the Pan-Anglican Conference (planned for 1908), included no mention of Islam, the religion of about 210,000,000 persons and the religion most consciously defiant of Christianity.

Such indifference the Cairo Conference of 1906 aimed at breaking down by its published "Appeal to the Churches," and the appeal came home in time to save the Pan-Anglican Conference from complete forgetfulness. Douglas Thornton was invited to speak on the presentation of Christianity to Moslems.

II

Meanwhile in Cairo, Thornton and Gairdner found a rapidly changing scene. Egypt began to feel the birth-throes of nationalism: there was a grim "incident" at Denshwai; a great force passed from the land with the retirement of Lord Cromer; Mustapha Pasha, the first Nationalist leader, won his people's confidence only to die at the age of thirty-four. Turkey, too, woke up one morning to find that she now possessed a constitution. All these events touched Egypt's life and therefore the life of men who loved her as Thornton and Gairdner did.

The evident sorrow of Cairo at Mustapha Pasha's death moved Gairdner much:

> Within a few hours after his death the news was all over the capital, and that although all the daily papers had gone to press before it was even known that he was dangerously ill. Yet not all Cairo only but all Egypt had the news even on the night of his death.
>
> Next morning I found the court of his house completely covered in by a black tenting. The monotonous wailing of the women, its rhythm marked by the low, dull thud of the tambourine, sounded faintly from within. Many were already in tears, especially young men of the effendi class. The man next me kept crying out "A hundred pities for thee, O Mustapha!" . . . Then the coffin, borne aloft by bearers and covered with the red Egyptian flag, appeared, swaying slightly in the doorway. The whole of the vast assembly in the court beneath burst into tears as by one impulse. For the first time one knew the meaning of the Biblical phrase, "They lifted up their voices and wept."
>
> Neither on that day nor at subsequent great meetings when thousands of Moslems were gathered together to hear orations to his memory did I hear insulting or revengeful or violent words. Tears, not curses, were the manifestation of the public emotion, and tears, one felt, are purifying things. . . . The students, the schoolboys, the younger Government officials—it is they who have made this man their idol and hero, and wept for him as the young weep for their heroes.

Thornton and Gairdner kept, of course, entirely out of the swirls of current politics, but they felt no other attitude possible to them as Christians than that of broad sympathy with any true, unselfish national aspiration. The meetings at Beit Arabi Pasha were slightly smaller through the inevitable anti-foreign feeling that goes with the rise of nationalism; but the student acquaintance of Thornton and Gairdner daily waxed larger. They made a point of attending meetings organized by societies of young Egyptians, Coptic and Moslem, religious and secular, and Gairdner found himself invited to speak, and did speak, at a meeting of 2,000 young Nationalists in memory of Mustapha Pasha Kamil. More widening vistas! Gairdner was now dreaming of work like that of the Student Movement, carried on by students themselves within Egyptian colleges, the missionary only playing at the most the part of the Student Movement "Travelling Secretary."

And Thornton was concentrating on the enlistment of the Coptic Church[1] in work for Islam:

> Did he see [Gairdner says] that our own individual efforts in evangelizing the masses must always be limited by our small numbers and resources? It was only a call to seek indirect methods . . . to make friends with Coptic clergy and laity, old men and youths, all in Cairo who were susceptible of being influenced to have meetings for Moslems. He actually assisted at such meetings in one, if not two Coptic Churches—an unprecedented event.

More vistas! Thornton planned a houseboat on which he should take out young Copts (who would, of course, be encouraged in loyalty to their Mother Church), and also converts from Islam, training them all in divinity and in Islamics and evangelizing with them all the waterside villages.

And while new vistas were thus opening up, the daily pressure of training and shepherding inquirers and new Christians abated not one whit and the magazine and literature production took its daily toll of strength. A memorandum from Gairdner, too, explains the difficulties of carrying on all this work in rented premises, with

[1] Egyptian Christians in 1906 were estimated at about 600,000 members of the ancient Coptic Church (the remnant of the National Church of Egypt before the Moslem invasion swept over the land), and about 30,000 Presbyterians drawn by the teaching of American missionaries from the neglected elements of this Coptic Church.

uncertain landlords and the constant strain of house-hunting and removal.

> Last summer [he wrote in November 1906] only the providence of God prevented seven institutions and three households being homeless at the same time! . . . This year, with the barest legal notice, the C.M.S. was summarily turned out of the central premises which it had used for a book depôt and preaching-room and spiritual centre for fifteen years . . . well known throughout Cairo and up and down Egypt. The labour of moving many thousands of books came at a time of very great pressure of work. The move has spelt temporary ruin to the book depôt work." He begged that the Society might buy its own headquarters in the city—which thing came to pass some six years later.
>
> The pressure of many duties [Gairdner confessed] has rendered it impossible to do half or a quarter of the following-up work that is demanded—seeking out men individually, visiting them, talking with them. The opening has been made, but to follow it up we need reinforcements, we want *men*; when we consider what Moslem work means, the importance of Cairo as the centre of Islam, is it not certain that the two workers who are all that are at present free to do the evangelistic work amongst educated Moslems must be reinforced, and that at once? It takes nearly five years before one is really fit to embark on work among this class of men.

But the Church at home was not then able in any effective way to see "the importance of Cairo as the centre of Islam" or to realize that she was wasting the life-power of the magnificent leaders she had put there, through her failure to understrap them with common business help. They had no shorthand-typist, no accountant, and no group of disciples learning Arabic. "We are fewer missionaries now than we were three and a half years ago," wrote Thornton in 1906, "while the work has doubled all round. Surely it is a short-sighted policy not to back us up by a strong reinforcement of men this autumn."

And when no word came of any recruit, Thornton went home on a so-called furlough in which he worked himself relentlessly to print on the Church at home some sense of the challenge of Islam, the glove thrown down to the champions of Christendom and by them left to lie unheeded.

"So convinced was he," says Gairdner, "of the need of preaching to the Home Church the 'new crusade,' that he had literally to be torn away from England when the end of furlough arrived. For the first time he felt no elation in going abroad." He wanted to work on not only at sounding a call on behalf of Islam, but at raising money to buy a permanent building from which to work in Cairo. "With an unwonted reluctance he returned to Egypt to face the prospect of working out a 'literature idea' in utterly unsuitable premises."

There had been no rest in that furlough and he was unwell in one way or another in the months that followed it. "His face became drawn and aged," his comrade says. "His physical energy seemed to have suffered a shock. More than once he said, 'I feel an old man . . .'—and he was thirty-four. It was saddening to watch."

III

In June 1907 Sir William Gairdner died. It was not a sorrow without preparation, for his family had long known that any of the heart attacks from which he suffered might take him from them. "He and I," said Temple, "have been so long knowing each other in the 'unseen, eternal' way, that I believe when God takes him I shall be able to follow him in thought and mind to the unseen eternal world, and so be comforted with the only real comfort."

Moreover, father and son had taken their farewell of

one another; knowing the hazards that might prevent their meeting again on earth, they had written farewell letters against the day that might come at any time:

> How *much* more of my life [said Temple] have I been absent from you than present! And yet I dare to say that there are not many sons who know their father better than I do mine, though there may be many whose love is nearer what it should be. The thought that we are in perfect accord and understanding has for me, largely *if not quite*, conquered the death of absence and invisibility. O absence, where is thy sting? O invisibility, where is thy victory? Thanks be to God who giveth us the victory through our Lord Jesus Christ.

Yet when the time came it was hard enough.

> He has been like air and sun and fresh water, things that are with us every day and make life what it is, so that it could not be imagined without them. And in spite of all the warnings of these seven years, one has never been able to conceive of life without that dear face and voice somehow entering into it. . . . How great he seems! . . . How many times, I wonder, has he written to me, after the fulfilling of some hope, the overtaking of some horizon, that he must now sound his Nunc Dimittis—his cup being absolutely full, his measure of human wishes being completely satisfied.

"Satisfied" was the word which Lady Gairdner chose as her husband's epitaph. "'Satisfied' was meant, I feel sure, to be written on our hearts as well as on his tombstone," Temple said.

The news had reached Egypt just before the summer holiday and at the slackest season in regard to *Orient and Occident*. Gairdner therefore spent his holiday in a short visit to Scotland to comfort his mother, staying with her at Colinton and "incessantly" playing Brahms's *Song of Destiny*. Then he left his wife and babies for a longer spell of home air and hastened back alone to Egypt to be ready for the autumn's work.

IV

He was met at Port Said by a telegram to say that Douglas Thornton was ill with typhoid. Most of his colleagues were still away, and it was strangely and beautifully arranged that Temple Gairdner and Douglas and Elaine Thornton were once again thrown into the old triple intimacy of their first years in Egypt.

"As the news ran through our mission circle that Douglas Thornton was to leave us, we all felt the comfort of Temple Gairdner's presence," says the nursing sister in charge of the case. It became apparent on September 7th that the sick man could not weather the pneumonia that had supervened on typhoid. "And then," says Gairdner, "if anyone had asked me, 'Knowest thou that the Lord will take away thy master from thy head to-day?' I should have said, 'Yea, I know it; hold ye your peace.'"

There was a vigil at the bedside from seven on Saturday evening till five on Sunday morning, September 8th. Thornton's mind was wandering, though he knew and welcomed the presence of friends who entered the room during the long night-watch.

> I sat down at the right side of the bed, Mrs. Thornton at her place on the left. And he looked from the one to the other, from the wife who was his inseparable partner in life to the friend who was his inseparable partner in work, till almost the very end. For those ten hours I just sat and drank in his face . . . There was something awfully impressive in his voice. It was partly the indistinctness and hollowness of desperate illness, but the effect was at times one of terrible impassioned earnestness, especially when he imagined himself preaching. He would then throw up his right arm, and his voice had the ring of one who pleads with souls.

In such hours all disguises fall off. You see *into* a man, for he is as a man writing a diary and not knowing he is doing so. Not one word did he say but it was about his life-work and the Kingdom of God. The work was not the feature of his life, it *was* his life. I tell you that this revelation of faithfulness and consecration has smashed me into bits. I cannot think of it without streaming tears.

Through that holy night they sang hymns, even the *Te Deum*, and they read Scriptures or rested their friend by speaking the Name of Jesus into his ear. At 2 a.m. Temple Gairdner said, " I think he will need some food for his journey." " We had the whole service from ' Ye that do truly,' and so he had his viaticum. It was an inexpressible joy and privilege to give him the Holy Communion."

We crossed his hands on his breast, and there they remained, and remain.

The dawn was struggling through the shutters. It was the dawn of Sunday morning . . . and the pure, God-consecrated soul had quietly withdrawn itself. The face of our baby son asleep has as much of the Boanerges about it as had his then—with a very humble quiet look, just like a child. It was awfully touching when one remembered

> . . . that Arthur who with lance in rest
> Shot through the lists at Camelot and charged.

" I can still see," says the nursing sister, " the tall strong young form of Temple Gairdner walking back with the widow to her home."

It was a morning glorious, without clouds [he said], the light that makes the whole world a mystery just before sunrise. The streets were silent. All was bright with a brightness of entire peace. " Breathless with adoration." And with reason. It was the morning, and almost the hour of the Resurrection.

And that tireless spirit was then entering upon his first real holiday.

As the sun of that same day was slanting from the west they buried Douglas Thornton at Old Cairo. "It was cooler, and his last resting-place seemed pure, airy, peaceful—what he would himself have liked. As we moved up the path we sang, and the singing sounded sweet."

The Arabic words then sung were like our "Sow in the morn thy seed." "He loved that hymn," says Gairdner, "because he lived it. A conflict of ideas thronged one as we sang it down that graveyard path—were we indeed bringing our sheaves with joy? Yes! And we were sowing our seed with joy too. Oh, the wonder of these Christian paradoxes!"

Forty days later, after the custom of the East, the Coptic Church held a memorial service for their friend the English priest, the Bishop of Khartoum presiding as representative of the Patriarch. "The addresses were all beautiful. I think that the service marks a distinct stage in the relations of our two Churches," said Gairdner, who shook hands with every one of the crowded congregation in token of gratitude.

V

As Gairdner and his wife (who had at once rejoined him from Scotland) travelled back from seeing Mrs. Thornton to her homeward boat, he had time to realize his own position—his working life cut in twain, his responsibility, which had already seemed too great, now doubled. He was reading the Psalms for the day, and looking at the impossible life before him, he took to himself in utter simplicity the words, "Thou hast promised to help me,"[1] and was strengthened.

"You do not, could not exaggerate what this has meant to me," he wrote to Tissington Tatlow, "but I

[1] Psalm lxxi. 2 (Prayer Book version).

hasten to tell you that . . . I have been feeling nothing short of new power, spiritual and even physical. Thornton has died that we may live more."

With a sister he looked it all fully in the face. One week after Douglas Thornton's death he said to her :

> All this week I have been comparing this stroke from the Hand of God with that last conversation we had that Sunday night in the attic. . . . And now I cannot help believing (which is a much bigger thing than feeling, though I do that too) that I have entered on the new stage of life for which I have been pining for the last, long thirsty years.
>
> With regard to my work here, it depended, not to put too fine a point on it, wholly on D. M. T. . . . Even had I been in full spiritual health, we should still have stood in the relation of the Leader and the Helper —and a very good distribution too, not nearly so common as it ought to be. Ah, but there was more in it than that. I really depended on him, because of my own entire lack of vision. As I told you, I needed a Vision of God and a Vision of the Kingdom.
>
> My partnership was not what it might and should have been. It was a tame following in his rear. . . . I often thought of retiring, but then I knew I was really useful here, essential, if you like, to D. M. T. himself.
>
> On the first of January I took as my year's mottoes :
>
> Thou hast left thy first love.
> Repent and do the first works.
> The last more than the first.
> The last shall be first.
>
> I felt something would happen. I did not know what it would be. I sometimes thought of M.'s being taken away, or one of the children, or my power of music. I said to God that I was willing for any of these things, if only I could have those two gifts, the Vision of God and the Passion for the Kingdom.
>
> And now this is it. I never looked for this—it

would have seemed to me the *coup de grâce* of my career. And yet this is what God has sent!

Yet in the same hour I began to feel a gradual, sure infusion of what *felt* like power in myself. . . .

As I thought of it, I felt that if I denied this to be the thing I had been asking for, nothing else would ever come. In naked faith, therefore, I believed it was. I had asked for those two Visions. Well, on that wondrous, awful, sweet, sorrowful Saturday night I must have had both. The room was one of absolute peace—Heaven's ante-room: sin was entirely excluded. It was a night wholly given to the holiest thoughts, actions and aspirations that man is capable of. That was the Vision of God.

And Douglas in delirium gave me the other. . . . I saw a man whose passion was the Kingdom, who in delirium, in death, thought of that and that alone. It was the Vision of the Kingdom.

If then God has given me both, thought I, He will give me also the double portion of his spirit—the passion, intrinsic, spontaneous, own, for God and for the Kingdom. I closed with the thought. What else could I do?

Nothing else can save my career from being a miserable failure—shown up, riddled and tattered, by the removal of what kept it decent (Thornton's enterprise)—and your brother from what I should feel to be disgrace.

Now you know what you have to pray for. An appalling responsibility rests on me from now onward—the responsibility for making good *his* career, my own, and possibly his successor's too. The weight of this I can but trust will resemble the weight of the atmosphere on our frames—absolutely crushing, yet unnoticed through the reaction of a force working from within.

To carry on what has been begun—to develop it—to do so not slavishly but in the spirit of his own spontaneity and initiative—and to do all this for some years alone, with the added weight of a " colleague " who will be really a pupil to be made or marred by me (perhaps) : that is what is before me.

Forty years of this (perhaps) in this country——! God !

That last word must be, is, all that makes the thing thinkable in thought now, practicable in deed, to-morrow.

With that he turned again to the work and wrote in *Orient and Occident* :

We announce to you that, God helping us, this magazine will go straight forward from this moment. No alterations will be made in our plans. No changes, except for the better as God leads us, will be made in the magazine itself. The lines laid down by Mr. Thornton and myself at the first will be followed. Others will come out from England shortly to fill up the gap, and meanwhile, I myself, with God's strength, will carry on the work just as before. Death has been triumphed over by Jesus Christ, and it shall not, therefore, be permitted to interrupt His work or that of His servant. Even as Christ is not dead, but liveth, so Mr. Thornton's life is laid down but not lost. It works mightily among us still.

His friends were often half-touched and half-amused at the self-estimate of the man who had put more original thought into Moslem apologetic than any missionary since Gustav Pfander, but who regarded himself as a " tame follower " of Thornton. To his own eyes his varied works were always in some sense a " filling in the lines of that air-drawn temple " of which Thornton left him the plan. He seemed quite unaware how completely and inevitably any work to which he put his hand became in very fact his own, marked with the unconscious stamp of his mind and love. That autumn as he shouldered two men's burdens, all his Egyptian fellow-workers felt a power in him, and at the end of the year he wrote of his

"Egyptian fellow-missionaries": "How much earnestness and faithfulness they exhibit! How teachable they are! A new spirit seems to have come into our midst."

VI

And in January of 1908, after the year of sorrow and of triumph, was granted an idyll of peculiar charm. Gairdner had thirteen days and a night of "pure holiday" (though he confessed afterwards to having preached in a Coptic church, visited a Coptic bishop in one place, a priest in another, American missionaries in a third, and so forth[1]) with his sister Ailsa in Upper Egypt. He was writing a "geological article" for *Orient and Occident* and interviewing Egyptian colleagues until the moment of departure, but next morning he awoke in the train to find himself far from Cairo and on one of the great holidays of his life, so entrancing an experience and so fully savoured that it has to find special mention in his *Life*:

> A mile or two beyond us rose the pink precipitous cliffs of a long range of hills [Miss Gairdner wrote]. It was in these that we saw first the amazing delicate tinting of everything in Upper Egypt. "Pink" I called them, because the sunlight was still young and pink; they themselves are so tender and neutral in shade that every emotion of light is reflected and reciprocated by and through them. Here Temple left the land of Nod to appreciate with joy the land of Egypt! At the sight of the hills up he jumped and down came another window-screen, and instantly expatiations on all the geological phenomena before us began to flow enthusiastically from his lips. Many

[1] An Egyptian friend says of his visit to Nikheila at that time: "He collected hymn-tunes from that part of the country and wrote them down, so that they might never be lost. The people never forgot his visit, and when he died they wrote to me about him, although it was twenty years since they had seen him. One of the letters said, 'He was the one really good man I saw in my life.'"

great things he talked of that morning. I enjoyed it thoroughly, but whiles when things touched a scale of vastness beyond the sense of grasp I was reminded of the sensations brought about by thinking too hard when one was little on the words "for ever and ever."

It was a very new thing for Gairdner to live a hotel life as a tourist; there was little enough of that in his career and his Franciscan soul was troubled at the experience:

> When finally we reached the swing-doors of the hotel, two little boys in white *kouftans* and turbans and red sashes and shoes sprang out, with the ubiquitous feather brush to dust our boots. Temple could not stand this; he never could bring himself to tolerate the subservience of the native servants and the way they had to jump about pandering to the wants of the luxurious pleasure-seekers of another race. It remained a joke more or less all the time, and he used to talk and "daff" a little with the Soudanese waiter at table, to make himself feel happier.

But questions of luxury apart, Gairdner enjoyed that holiday with supreme zest.

> In all my eight years here [he told his mother] I had never before been more than ten miles south of Cairo. It was very much a new world.
>
> The Luxor landscape is made of great *geometrically simple lines.* Everything is horizontal and perpendicular—like the Egyptian architecture that grew up in that setting—entirely different from the Gothic complexity of our Scottish scenery.
>
> Then, how suitably! it is also a water-colour landscape. All the tints were suggestions of colouring rather than definitions—infinitely satisfying, infinitely varied. All this added to a pure, dustless air, a pervading, diffusive silence broken only by the shouts of boatmen on the river, the chunking of their oars, the curious melody of their snatches of song. The

quite celestial white-spreading wings of the Nile-boats, like so many albatrosses moving gracefully along—albatrosses in the air, swans in the water. And the colour of the river? Impossible to describe it. Pearl-coloured (Ailie's word) . . . it was pearl-blue and pearl-grey at the same moment and rested the eyes.

My heart is in Upper Egypt—in Luxor and Assuan! I was built for doing nothing and having holidays and gracefully and ineffectually scratching the surface of many interesting subjects. . . . I watched the hours run away through the sand-glass with huge grudge, especially the last day, when we came by boat from Assuan to Luxor all one silver-shining day.

CHAPTER XI

A SIGNIFICANT YEAR

1908–1909

But he was beloved of his God: also, he had a good heart of his own, or else he could never have done it.—*John Bunyan.*

I

In the summer of 1908 Gairdner's second furlough was due. Four months was all that he could allow himself, and into that time many works were crowded, for he had accepted from Douglas Thornton the legacy of that "last crusade" of his for the education of the Anglican Church to care for Islam. Alas, that this burden should be laid on men who come back from the spiritual drain of work in Moslem lands! Gairdner made the speeches that Thornton was to have made at the Pan-Anglican Congress on the Moslem question and the relations of the Anglican Communion to the Eastern Churches. His was a fresh voice in that assembly of the elders, as he challenged Christian theologians to look at their faith in the light of the great denials of Islam.

> Christendom, as represented by some writers, scarcely realizes its heritage, scarcely realizes that Christ has once and for all differentiated between physical and moral power. Who can tell what moral results shall accrue, both in East and West, when we shall have allowed the Cross to dominate our philosophy and theology as well as devotional life! Who shall gauge the debt we may yet have to confess to Islam if that great antagonist prove finally to have com-

pelled us to explore unknown depths of the riches of the revelation of the Triune God.

He was always dreaming that the necessity for the Moslem apologetic might inspire some great theologian, some tremendous explorer of the riches of Christ.

The whole experience of the Pan-Anglican Congress warmed and heartened him from the first moment of the service in Westminster Abbey with which it began :

> The bidding prayer, recited by the Dean from the pulpit, was interpunctuated with long pauses of intense silence—a downright unmistakable Church prayer-meeting. A little more of this and we shall get that element of elasticity in our Liturgy which alone is needed to attain perfection!

The great meetings (of course he found his way into the organ-loft at the Albert Hall) and the sense of thought and movement in them he found exhilarating as sea-air.

> There reigned . . . a mature recklessness of faith and hope. It was like the spirit of youth and the dawn. One felt that the Anglican Communion is "looking eastward" and that she has the dew of her youth from the womb of the morning.
>
> You feel that to the Christian there can never be a question of old age and decrepitude, just because the development which God is carrying out is always advancing not from new to old, but from old to new ; is making all things new and consequently keeping all things young, as the flush of sunrise is perpetually running over the face of the world, always making dawn.

He went of course, and with spirit much uplifted, to that last great service at which the Church's missionary offering was carried up by the Bishop of each diocese to the altar of St. Paul's Cathedral.

> Between the kneeling throngs they passed up the nave under the dome, and into the choir, and through

one of the topmost windows there stabbed downwards a burning shaft of light, long, straight, slender, and sharp, cleaving the dim spaces of the dome as clearly as the mystic Ray in Parsifal. It smote the white-clad procession : as it passed under the radiance every figure was for a moment baptized with a sudden splendour ere it entered the dimness of the choir.

When, in the same year at the fifth Lambeth Conference, the Archbishops of Canterbury and York sounded out in their message to the whole Church the call of the non-Christian world, saying, " We are jealous for the honour of the Church of England that it may be among the first messengers of Christ to enter in," Gairdner was full of buoyancy about his Church.

II

But he had to face the fact that his own crusade to rouse her concerning the Moslem world was barely begun. His greatest contribution to it was made through two books, to the writing of which he now turned. First, in retirement at Croydon in the house of relatives of Douglas Thornton, and in the little study which his friend had been wont to use, he wrote that most speaking biography *D. M. Thornton : A Study in Missionary Ideals and Methods*, in its vividness a rare change on the heavy colouring of most missionary " lives." It was written with nearly incredible swiftness, for the whole scheme of it had lived in his mind almost since the day of Thornton's death.

Of this book he wrote to a friend who had reviewed it :

I felt the kindness and grace of what you wrote very much. . . . What most touched me was the effect which you said the book had on yourself, and how you had presented it to God twice, raising it as a " wave offering before the Lord," with the prayer that the book, as the last fruit, so to speak, of D. M. T.'s partnership with me, might speak to the whole missionary body. That was a beautiful act. In that wish you penetrated very deep down into my mind and heart ; for truly my life and his were deeply bound up ; complementary they were to some extent, and that is what constituted the awful bitterness of his loss to me. So, when the loss first took place, it came into my mind that now my task was to take up his work and "make" it. Thus the partnership would go on in death as in life. And when I thought of this first task, the book, it came to me all in a minute ; the whole scheme of it was presented to my mind, and remained steadily before me till it flowed forth on to paper nine months later. It seemed that this book should be in a very perfect sense our joint production. Oh, may I not fail miserably after such a challenge ! Pray I may rather die. Yes, God must let me either die or win.

"Have you seen my D. M. T. ?" another letter said. "In that book you have my past, present and future."

III

That furlough of four months saw also the writing of part of a second book for the education of the home Church, a further carrying on, as Gairdner would have put it, of Douglas Thornton's "last crusade." It was written to give "study circles" some grasp of the main outlines of Islam, its past story, its present life, and its challenge to those who are Christ's, and it was called *The Reproach of Islam*. While writing it, Gairdner joined the week-end of a new co-operative group named the United Council for Missionary Education (now so well known for its careful, varied publication work). This missionary party went to a hotel at Baslow, where they found that the room allotted by the management for their meetings had a polished floor, a small stage and a piano. As the hours went on it became obvious that another group in the hotel—a theatrical company "resting"—were not a little annoyed with the missionaries (probably because of their possession of these de-ights) and took some pains to make their annoyance clear.

"If one of us was walking singly," says a member of the missionary group, "one of their men would race down a passage with a woman on each arm, and barge into us, knocking us against the wall." This was a situation that appealed to Gairdner; he had succeeded during an Austrian summer holiday in thawing and merging various glowering and suspicious hotel cliques, through the influence of a piano which he caused to be borne up the valley from the nearest town on an ox-waggon. He brought the piano to bear in Derbyshire also, and his playing on Sunday evening drew some of the theatrical party to the open door. Suddenly, with that flashing movement of his, he leapt up from the piano and invited them in. "I don't expect you know who we are," he said. "We're all missionaries; and I'm a missionary in Egypt and very much interested in Coptic music." Forthwith he flashed back to the piano and began a "demonstration" of those curious haunting tunes that he had collected in the East. The company was thawed, and he begged them now to sing in their turn. They were doubtful: their accompanist was away; their music was "very difficult." At last they let him play for them; music flowed all the evening, and at the end he rose and thanked them in the name of the missionaries, and said quite simply, "We generally have prayer before we part. May we say 'Our Father' together?" And so they went their ways well content.

The Reproach of Islam[1] is Gairdner's most-read book. Every page of it bears the mark of his own style—a style as far as that of St. Paul from being "faultily faultless, icily regular, splendidly null." Rather does it often rush and surge as though it poured itself spontaneously from the man's eager brain or from his very heart.

[1] First published 1909, with a revised fifth edition in 1920 under the title *The Rebuke of Islam.*

It is sometimes turgid, sometimes flamboyant, and often over-abundant—the style of a man who has more thoughts than time to trim and prune his expression of them—and he was over-fond of exclamations, dots and dashes, and hiatuses at the point where words were no longer capable of expressing the things of his spirit. But when he wrote of music or of people whom he loved, of children, of beautiful places and kindly or noble human scenes, his writing glowed with warmth and colour and often had more than a touch of delicate whimsical beauty. To his colour-loving spirit the dull greyness of committee language (with which his life brought him so much to do) was a burden. Heavy, colourless monsters like *memorandum*, *co-ordination*, *co-option* and the rest he hated, and he and a comrade amused themselves through several long days of conference over a wager of chocolates should a certain member ever complete a speech without the over-driven drudge-word "problem."

When Gairdner wrote of the things of the Spirit his language had a stabbing certainty of touch, a tenderness of perception unattainable except by one who lives the truth he writes.

The Reproach of Islam is notable to his friends because in it he set forth the cause to which he had given his life. "I piled difficulty upon difficulty," he says of this book, "discouragement upon discouragement, until faith almost reeled. I wanted it to reel, that it might reel back on to the arms of God in Christ."

The heart of the book lies in the final climax to his piling up of the odds :

> How colossal seems the sheer mass, how irresistible the momentum of this league of nature, the world and the flesh ! . . . Why must we for ever renounce all the favourable conditions, giving, like the Scottish King at Flodden, *all* the advantages to the opponent ? Why must we strive always up the hill, the wind and the rain for ever driving in our faces ; ever, ever

conceding, never, never receiving the handicap and the odds! . . .

If Islam's forces are indeed nature, the world and the flesh, then Islam has left us one weapon in taking away all the others—it has abandoned to us the Sword of *the Spirit—The Spirit of Jesus is the only asset of the Church.*

That final sentence gives the motive and the keynote of his lifework.

Gairdner used to tell his friends that his books had been a failure. He saw no comrades called by them to shoulder D. M. Thornton's unfinished work until after a dozen years one woman joined him through this call. With that strange denial of outward success that followed him through life (part of his pledged share, perhaps, in the Cup of his Lord), much of the working of his books was kept from him. He did not know, for instance, that a group of students in Sydney were stirred by *The Reproach of Islam* with such results that five of them are now in the Moslem world. "He could never guess," a missionary says, "how that word of his, 'the Spirit of Jesus the only asset of the Church,' has stayed with me and has even made me watch him quite breathlessly at times lest he should fall below the standard he set. I have been sick with dread more than once lest he should not prove equal to it, until by some act of humility on his part I would learn that he was still the same. It was a great illumination to me, that sentence in his book, and made a sort of revolution in my life."

Before he left Britain in that summer of 1908, with one book finished and the next well on its way, Gairdner had the keen joy of the birth of his little daughter Eleanora Mary, and the days at Ochterlony, Forfarshire, with which his furlough ended, were "a happy dream." He was father to his heart's content; and, proud and tender, he escorted his two senior babes to church.

The little fellow strode up the aisle in advance of all, reached the pew at the very end and sat down. It is a splendid oak box-pew, and he sat so as to face all the congregation. As I came up the aisle, I saw the dark oak wainscoting of the pew, and framed in the middle of it a little vision of white with a celestial aureole of gold hair. He looked so beautiful there alone. . . . For full five minutes he held up an open pocket Bible as if he was reading it, never even turning a page or moving a muscle. I generally sat down while singing, so as to let my voice be at the level of their ears, and so, every now and then, my face being near his, I would feel a soft kiss brushed suddenly across my cheek.

IV

From these joys he returned to Egypt at the end of August. " Tuesday is dear D. M. T.'s anniversary " (September 8th, the day of his death), he wrote on arrival. " I do want to learn many lessons. I have written to the Copts to take part in a half-day of prayer. Oh to realize truly that double portion of his spirit ! My friend, my friend ! "

That winter Beit Arabi Pasha renewed its old furious life. The Thorntons' side of the house was occupied by Gairdner's most loyal and devoted friends Rennie MacInnes (now Bishop in Jerusalem) and his wife and children. The Gairdners' side found room (not overmuch room) for R. F. McNeile, a Balliol scholar and Senior Student of Christ Church, who became Gairdner's colleague for the next six years.

Bishop MacInnes has written an impression of his friend :

We were in close daily contact with one another in work. I wish it were within my power to describe what it has meant to me.

To me, the most wonderful feature of our friendship and the most striking evidence of his likeness to Christ was the fact that never once during all those years did I hear him say a word which could not have come from the lips of his Master ; never once did he say a word which could not have been shouted from the housetops. And the marvel is not only that Temple Gairdner could not ever say a word that was disloyal to his Master, but that the other man who was with him could not either. That was Gairdner's strength, the practice of the presence of Christ, and from it there flowed, as a full and even tide, his unconscious, unceasing, yet wholly compelling influence.

Then imagine how the tie was strengthened when such a man as he showed by a hundred signs how much he needed his friends, how much he leaned on them. When he came in to talk, and often to talk by the hour, to detail his plans, to attempt to work out some subject, to discuss how to act in a difficult matter, in such talk he was evidently leaning heavily on others. It was extraordinarily appealing. The strong man who wanted your help! And yet, though you knew you could give him nothing, except a pair of listening ears, and a quiet mind, did that worry you? Did that distress you? Not in the least, for you were already tingling with a new courage, a new inspiration, and all of it simply from sitting and listening to him consulting you!

The Rev. R. F. McNeile arrived in November 1908, and Gairdner wrote:

> Having been accustomed to a suite of three large rooms at Christ Church, he now shares a dining-room with a Second in Greats for a joint study, which room is also a passage for wife, governess, children and servants between the interior of the house and the front door. Also the pantry where milk, knives, spoons and glasses are kept. We think of putting in a third man, if he comes out, by rigging up a cage with a desk inside it, which would swing up to the ceiling by a pulley. As the room is a very high one, it seems unjustifiable not to use its upper area in some such way.

Of his own first impressions R. F. McNeile wrote:

What Beit Arabi stands for—or wants to—is very difficult to say in a few words. It is best shown by reading D. M. Thornton's Life. Gairdner is frightfully overworked and finds it almost impossible to settle down to get anything done—what with papers to write, the *Orient and Occident* to keep going, classes of inquirers to study with and perpetual interruptions by men, women and children on matters great and small, chiefly the latter.

One more picture of Beit Arabi Pasha in those days is left by the Rev. C. G. Mylrea, who came from an Indian mission-station for special Islamic study:

It was a house of unceasing noise, at the junction of two busy streets; the distraction of tramway bells continuously struck and the cracking of *arbagi's* whips like pistol-shots mingled with hoarse street-cries.

Picture a moderate-sized study-dining-room in the Gairdners' quarters filled with chairs and tables, a roll-top desk [Gairdner had now inherited D. M. Thornton's desk] in front of a bookcase in one corner, and the windows at the side open to the clamour below. There might be three or four people working or talking in the room, but at the roll-top desk sat a figure with pen in hand, perfectly serene, withdrawn into himself, working at an Arabic article for *O. & O.*, stopping every now and then as the telephone-bell rang to carry on a conversation in English or Arabic, and then resuming his writing—the finest example I have ever met of concentrated mental power.

Yet, if you ventured to interrupt him, the pen was laid down and without a trace of annoyance Gairdner would give you his whole attention and understanding sympathy.

A man who went straight to the heart of things, a man who mastered whatever he touched.

I remember him once saying that there were two

hobbies from which he was thankful to have been delivered, as they were apt to absorb too much of a man's time—photography and Egyptology [a saying very characteristic of the discipline of his life. He carried on his fossil collection only until he had done all that could be done without too great cost of time. When it would have involved long special expeditions, he left it.] It was only his downright honesty and determination not to take any unfair advantage of India that kept me from asking to be transferred to the Egypt C.M.S. staff. How I should have loved to work with him !

It may have been magnificent that incessant struggle to work against interruptions, clerkless and without so much as a quiet study. But it was not war. The Church had not so many Gairdners among her missionaries that she could afford to leave one of them at the mercy of every call. Mr. Adeney's early saying was justified—"Gairdner is not at all a man to look after himself."

V

Yet at the end of 1909 he could say, "I don't ever remember a more significant year." He and his colleagues had followed up some notable visits made by D. M. Thornton in the last year of his life to Upper Egypt, to salute the Moslem readers of his magazine and to inspire the Copts to witness to their faith.

"What made these visits [of 1908–9] feasible," Gairdner says, "was the call which came to us to undertake services for the English residents. Minia was the last place visited for evangelistic purposes by Mr. Thornton, so it was the first I chose to visit."

On Sunday Gairdner preached either at or just after the Coptic Mass at Minia to the Coptic congregation in his ordinary robes, and immediately afterwards the English residents came into the same church for a Celebration, the Copts having lent their own sanctuary for the purpose. In the days that followed, Gairdner gave lectures every night in the theatre of the town to perhaps a thousand men, nearly half of whom were Moslems. And that audience he had himself collected with the help of some young Coptic gentlemen who were his enthusiastic lieutenants throughout his visit, by visiting every class-room of several schools and every Government office with personal invitations. "He had to travel back by night," says R. F. McNeile, "leaving about 2 a.m., and several young Copts sat up with him till then, talking eagerly the whole time about the work and insisting on paying his first-class fare back to Cairo, a substantial sign of enthusiasm in Egypt."

Of the closing scene of a later visit Gairdner wrote :

> At the end all rose to prayer, and I said, "This last night I will ask you to pray a prayer after me which is the prayer of the publican and sinner : 'God be merciful to *me*, a sinner.'" Immediately there was a roar like distant thunder as the answer uprose from the serried ranks of the audience. I repeated it a second time, and again the response rolled through the building.

A friend who was present says : "For an hour without a note he had addressed a critical crowd of a thousand men, giving them Christ in such a manner as to make every man solemn and no one angry. Afterwards a man said to me in English, 'No one else could have done that : he spoke for an hour and never made a slip.' The Moslem agent of the leading Nationalist paper complained loudly that there was no vote of thanks, and sent an appreciative notice to his Cairo Moslem daily."

VI

Another mark of that significant year was the development of devotional meetings, quiet days and such like, not for the mission staff alone but for any leaders of Christian life in Egypt.

> I heard that someone counted 225 men, chiefly Copts of course [says Mr. McNeile], and, *mirabile*

dictu, a Coptic priest in the chair. You cannot realize what a marvellous event it is. Needless to say the one man responsible for it is Gairdner.

Mr. Gordon Logan has memories of a similar gathering n the summer for the leaders of the Egyptian Presby-erian Church (known in Egypt as the "Evangelical Church"), at which Gairdner had been asked to speak.

As the hour approached he seemed much concerned and asked that someone else might take his place, since he did not feel that he had any message. His address was very brief and to the point, and perhaps the most powerful he ever delivered. He told how God had been showing him his own need, and putting himself alongside the poorest and weakest in that gathering, he asked them to pray for him, and down went his head on the table in front of him. The hush of God and the breath of God came over that meeting. Suddenly a man rose, the most outstanding Moslem convert in Egypt at that time, and in a broken voice told how the words spoken had pierced his heart. If this were true of Mr. Gairdner, how much more true of him. And then followed this leader's confession that self had entered into all his life and work and preaching, and a cry for deliverance that touched every heart. It is doubtful if there was one soul present that did not meet with God that night.

VII

And one more special task of that year was the editing f hymns. Gairdner published his first collection of a undred Oriental tunes for hymns, and with his col-eague Selim Effendi Abd el Ahad he was experimenting uriously in hymn translation. The members of the American Mission in Syria now asked him to join them n the revision of the hymnbook published at the great Mission Press at Beyrout and widely used in Arabic lands. The work interested Gairdner acutely. He had

already written to a friend in Syria his conviction of th
need of such revision :

It is indeed a responsibility forming the musica
taste of the Near East in the Western or harmoni
type of music. I grieve to say that I can't think th
Beyrout book as it stands—which must have had a
incalculably greater influence in this matter than a
other influences put together—rose to the occasion
As a taste-former it is far too mixed to have had an
formative influences that can cause congratulation. A
least that's what I feel.

The tunes are *mostly* of the mediocre grade of tune
current in the West. The nobler type of tune . .
is not much represented. I don't look at this matte
pedantically at all: any tune that will suit the Orienta
voice I vote for, even though it be *Clementine* or *Joh*
Brown's Body ! Only let us choose many nobler tunes
not the sugary or Sankey type.

He keenly enjoyed visiting Syria for these revisio
committees, held at Sidon, and he was enthusiastic abou
the American friends with whom he there worked:

Dr. Ford is the best Arabic scholar in the East (h
was born in the country). I never saw such a sight o
snowy cleanliness as his figure when it entered tha
first morning ; silvery grey hair beautifully parte
and going off in waves, snowy vest gently swept by th
clear snowy beard. I don't think I ever saw a mor
refreshing vision of a man in all my life, and I give yo
details as I noted them while we were revising th
Arabic hymnbook. What grand earnest souls thes
American missionaries are! I felt that their faithfulnes
put me personally to shame. Even to see Dr. Jessu
was a stimulus and a rebuke . . . the intense satis
faction and pleasure which men like Dr. Jessup tak
in Christ and in His religion and work.

My Arabic is Syrianizing quite fast. I was abl
in Sidon to note down a large number of beautif

Eastern melodies. The Sidonians are very music-loving.

VIII

The Gairdner of that year seemed to have an inexhaustible spring of energy within him. Dr. Miller of Hausaland, who visited him for Arabic study, and was introduced by Gairdner to Hausa students in the Azhar mosque who had travelled on foot from Nigeria to Cairo, remembers the springing vigour of those days :

> He walked into the room where I was resting, having found time to come and see me, though he was very tired with a hard day's work. He said, " I must go to sleep," lay down, fell asleep at once, slept for exactly three minutes and then got up. I said, " What's the matter ? " " Oh, nothing. I've had my sleep and I'm quite fit now."

His very recreations were creative that year. " He was a member of a small debating club," says Mr. J. E. Quibell, " which took a pride in not having a name (but semi-authorized vocables like *The Witches' Cauldron* or *The Anarchists* were heard) ; I suppose its object was to knock our little ideas together and see if we could get a spark. It was a great success for a long time. One thing struck me about Gairdner—that he was not handicapped as the clergy often are by the unwillingness of people to speak freely before them. I am sure neither he nor we felt it. We spoke up loud and bold."

> What an enthusiast he was, and how we liked him the more for his enthusiasms [says another Anarchist], even if we laughed sometimes, not ill-naturedly, at the way in which he was carried away by them !

Ever since his first reading of H. G. Wells in 1904, Gairdner had been travailing with the question of social evolution, and he now read the *Anarchists* a paper on roads to social salvation proposed in some current philosophies, under the title of *Queer Roads to Optimism in Nineteenth- and Twentieth-century Thought.* The paper was provocative and (regardless of by-laws excluding religious themes) the *Anarchists* plunged into a discussion as to whether any philosophy that denies or disregards the fact of sin can really account for the world to-day or provide a workable scheme for its improvement. After the meeting an able member of the club wrote to Gairdner of his disappointment that the discussion did not go a stage further. "Of course you accept the scientific point of view—everybody does. But I cannot for the life of me see how in the light of it any view of society is possible that yields a defensible optimism. I was hoping that you would tell us how you yourself square the scientific view of the world with Christian orthodoxy and its view of humanity, which you advocated."

The challenge was accepted with alacrity. Gairdner worked up his correspondence with this friend ("I then took up a very negative and ultra-pessimistic standpoint," that correspondent says) into a modest little paper-covered book called *Science and Faith in Whom?* And the pamphlet, in spite of a disarming preface about the writer's lay status in such matters, meant much to its author.

> Though you might not think it [he says in a letter], it represents to me five years of travail and reading. It shows that the question of *social evolution* is the question of all others which is proving obstinate to those who believe in Christ's revelation of the Father.

This fury of productive work, sustained through days overcrowded with detailed tasks, could never have been achieved but for the unflecked confidence and joy of Gairdner's home life. "In all my memories I see the complement of his life in the picture—Mrs. Gairdner," says one of the friends just quoted. His true place of recreation, where every outside care dropped from him, was his nursery of babes. He was never tired of watching a baby, and his colleagues remember his disappearance from a committee, to be found alone at the cradle of the new-born son of a friend's house, lost in contemplation. His letters are full of vignettes of his own babies :

> As the train flashed up the platform (the day was dull) I caught a brilliant glimpse of lily and rose in literally astonishing contrast to the drab environment. It was the little smiling face of the Babe. When I kissed her, she smelt like the nicest sort of Edinburgh rock—the ginger sort, I think ! . . . She is never still in the short intervals between her marvellous spells of sleep. She is as strong and supple as a baby leopard. Altogether an admirable little sweetling.

> After lunch he insists on going to bed with a toy elephant and bear. He lays them most tenderly on the pillow and covers them with a handkerchief, then puts his head down beside them and goes off to sleep. It is highly absurd and pretty.

But even with a nursery for recreation the strain of that year was an impossible one to maintain. After telling a friend about the various meetings and the baptisms of the year, he said :

> You can imagine that the shepherding of these souls, the ethicising of them, so to speak, the travailing with them that Christ be formed in them, simply took an infinity of time and pains. It was a very busy year for me too in matters literary—really I poured out so much of my capital that I almost felt as if I could be taken away with my work (in a sense) done. I have delivered that which is in me. Now (if I am not taken away) I must have a long period of incubation and quiet work. I can't pour any more out for a long time again.

CHAPTER XII

THE WANDERING SCHOLAR

1910—1911

Her husband's to Aleppo gone.—*Shakespeare.*

I

"I FEEL more and more that there are two or three schemes in the air that centre on Cairo, for none of which anyone on the spot has adequate knowledge." So Gairdner in 1909 to a London Secretary of his Society, with the plea that a certain retired missionary who was an orientalist might be sent out for a spell of scholarly work in Cairo. The scheme for some reason did not prove acceptable, and Gairdner's distress grew as he found the home Society regarding him as an Islamic scholar and looking to him for advice and leadership—" making me an authority without authority," he said.

> It is too mortifying ! That is the worst of writing cheap books that have an enormous circulation guaranteed to them irrespective of their intrinsic value. Dearly do I pay for it ! I am no orientalist nor son of an orientalist, and know only a very *little* more about Islam than any intelligent person in England knows when he has read two or three books thereon. *Never* did man get such a reputation on so shockingly slender an equipment.

In this uncomfortable situation a friend came forward with a plan of which, said Gairdner, " the whole delightfulness falls on me, while the extra burden involved in it falls on Canon MacInnes (the friend in question) and the rest of my colleagues."

Canon MacInnes made his proposition to the C.M.S. headquarters :

> An idea has been in our minds for many weeks that we should ask for leave of absence of at least a year for Mr. Gairdner in order that he may (and it is probably now or never) have a chance, never yet offered, of doing some real study of Islam and Arabic literature, and thus enormously benefiting not only our own mission but every other mission in Egypt, if not also every other mission to Moslems throughout the world.
>
> I cannot describe to you with what anxiety I view this matter nor how urgently we desire to press it upon the C.M.S. Committee.
>
> Here is a man almost unique in the Mohammedan missions of to-day, gifted with the power of grasping a subject, probing it, mastering it, and then passing on the results of his studies to others ; a man who has already a remarkable knowledge of Arabic. So long as he stays in Cairo he must be largely involved in the pastoral work of the mission—Sunday services, meetings, classes for inquirers or converts, visiting, and a host of other things ; he must continue to devote an enormous amount of his time to interviews with people of all sorts, to *Orient and Occident*, to the newly started Y.M.C.A. which could not go forward as it has done but for him. We should of course miss him tremendously, but we are prepared to recommend heartily that he be given leave to absent himself from all this for a year.

Leave of absence was given, and Gairdner wrote to Canon MacInnes :

> To pray daily for you is a daily pleasure, for it is only then that I feel that I am repaying you something for it all. . . . Please add to your kindness also your prayers for me. I am terrified of making a mess of it,

and still more of turning out unworthy of the great scheme when I return. I hate responsibility, and particularly that of the duty of leadership in Moslem work, and yet my own hand is year after year piling up responsibility to do that very thing. Why should my fate be to summon successive circles of x,000 readers by cunning advertisements, to watch me go and do—nothing? I can but humbly implore God for His own honour, to keep me from disappointing His people and disgracing His name by turning out a pure frost—I can think of no other term to express exactly what I mean. *There* is my nightmare, which by your prayers must be turned into a better dream, one that shall not only be better, but may turn out true as well.

II

Before his *Wanderjahr* proper Gairdner attended the World Missionary Conference at Edinburgh, having been entrusted with the writing of a popular report thereof to bring home its significance to the Church at large. Home then he came, leaving an Egypt shocked at the assassination of the first native-born Prime Minister of the country, Butrus Pasha Ghali.

> I so well remember [says a friend] Mr. Gairdner's arriving at Cairo station just in time to board the train as it started, in the highest spirits, and carrying a Bible, an old tie, and a bicycle pump.

At the great conference in Edinburgh (June 13th–23rd, 1910) he had perforce not only to speak for Islam but to grasp the leading ideas of every report and every speaker and the human outlines of every scene for the book which must be written within the next few weeks. The rapid, vivid portraiture of that book was the fruit of nine days of incessant observation. In the midst of it all he took his old friend and governess Miss Calver to a shop for tea and confided to her with a chuckle that he had overheard a Scotch sidesman saying of him :

"That gentleman is going to address the Assembly this evening. He is a holy horror with his long words."

"You were always fond of long words, Temple," she replied.

One of the chief joys of those memorable exhausting days was to feel himself the fellow-worker and lieutenant of his friend of Oxford days, Mr. J. H. Oldham, more than any other single person the moving spirit behind that œcumenical conference; and when the great days were over, Temple Gairdner went with Mr. and Mrs. Oldham, more tired than words can say, for a few days of rumination and slumber on Iona. Gairdner always glowed with delight if the word Iona were but mentioned. "Such holy cleanness," he would say. "You never saw such limpid little waves and such clear-washed little beaches of shells or pebbles and dear little sea-flowers." There he saw his book as a whole, wrote its preface, and returned to his wife and babes at Ayr for the working out of the plan he had seen in the isle of vision. The book seemed to him (and indeed it was) far more than an ordinary Conference report, and he wrote of it to Dr. Mott:

> Have you reflected that in this book, I, and I only, have the chance of *co-ordinating* the massed information and suggestion of that Conference and giving to the world what *I* feel to have been its most important things? Why, it is like having to make the closing address of a conference, and being given a full day's session to do it in!

The greater the speed with which such books appear, the greater their effectiveness. Gairdner began the reading of the masses of reports (not only verbatim reports of the speeches made at the Conference, but the full "findings" of eight Commissions that had sat in preparation for it) on July 6th. Once at least he read seventeen hours in a day, and that in seaside lodgings with small children in and out of the room where he sat with his piled-up papers. The chapters were posted to the printer, generally in the small hours, with the ink scarcely dry, and by September 7th the last proof was read.

> It is 3 a.m. [he wrote to Dr. Mott]. I have been writing the chapter on Commission I, and have just finished it. And yet I can't go to bed without just stretching out a hand across the Atlantic to you, so close have I felt your personality as I pondered on that splendid report, the work of your hands.

Of the book thus furiously produced, *Edinburgh 1910*, Professor D. S. Cairns wrote to Gairdner :

> The way in which you have mastered the immense material and cast it into swift and telling narrative—which is never dull and sometimes rises into pages which are most striking and even brilliant—is quite extraordinary. . . . Peculiarly good is the unity which you have been able to give to the whole. Like the *Reproach*, it shows you are strong in "architecture." But the great thing is that you have grasped the lesson of the whole and bring it home to the imagination of the slowest.

Yet the days at Ayr were remembered by Gairdner less for the fever of intellectual labour and fatigue than for one picture of a child's face :

> I think the vividest and the most poignant recollection of the Ayr time to me is the face of little X. one morning in the hymn at prayers. He had chosen "I want to be like Jesus," his special favourite at that time. Well, the face with which he sang it haunts me still and brings tears to the heart when I think of it. . . . He sang it looking straight at me without any consciousness, either of himself or of me, with his whole soul in his eyes. I shall never forget it.

III

And now began Gairdner's year as a wandering scholar. He had to feel his way step by step as to the best use of his sabbatical year, but the first step at least was clear—"three months spent in Germany for the purpose of learning enough German to give me access to the incomparable German literature on Islamic subjects."

To Germany, then, he went on September 10th, 1910, writing to his wife:

> We are not going to be far from each other. We must try to relearn or learn the *secret* of prayer this year. . . . I need to learn another language beside Arabic and German, the language of Heaven, which once I half-knew and now have almost forgotten. Help me!

He had come to Europe from arduous Cairo days into the pressure of the Edinburgh Conference and the writing of his book. Now before settling down to toil at grammar in Potsdam he went southwards for a walking tour in the Bavarian hills, but still more for the Oberammergau Passion Play. He arrived at the little mountain-sheltered village after a night journey and "spent the rest of the day walking about Oberammergau or the hillsides, studying the German text of the play."

The spirit of the place caught and held him from the moment when on the station platform he saw peasant figures with unshorn locks, their hair allowed to grow because, in the Passion Play, wigs, like artificial light and all artificialities, are forbidden.

The day on which he saw the Play was one of the great days of his life. How not so with its appeal to the dramatic artist in himself, and that appeal made with no jarring note in the beauty of holiness? "Some men can delight in the world, in men and things apart from holiness," he once told his wife; "God has decreed that I cannot. And though the flesh sometimes makes bondage of this decree, it is the supreme mark of His love."

Here at Oberammergau the holiness and the beauty were wedded so as to content him. "The play is the self-expression of a Christian community, representing in action that which is the subject of all their thinking and living," he said.

He went very early to the Eucharist in preparation, and so to the Temple-theatre at eight; and as he went "the floods of morning sunshine made the towering crags glow."

> That peak with its veil of cloud and the sweet pinewood and silver rocks were just visible to me over the foreground of the stage all through the performance, a perpetual refreshment. Perhaps it is because modern drama is not in the open air that it seems to suggest wigs, rouge-pots, gas, machinery.
>
> The Oberammergau play is the Grecian drama become Christian.
>
> To think that all that aristocracy of bearing and tone; that natural grace; those consummate effects of grouping and colour; those most beautiful vocal and orchestral achievements; those deep accents of pathos and tragedy; and above all that spiritual intuition and intellectual grasp combined, without which (permeating the whole community) the play would be an impossibility; to think that these, *all these* things, should be the native fruit of that one little village community whose members in their ordinary lives mind the shop, keep the farm, ply their trade or bring in their hay, that is what seems to me the real miracle of this truly called Miracle Play.

Next morning to hurry back to the plain seemed impossible.

> So I took a walk up the Ammer Valley which brought me right into the heart of the Tyrol. . . .
>
> The floor of the valley was all green and smooth like a lawn, for the second crop of hay had just been cut and gathered into stooks. The rain last week had made everything fresh and radiant. The sweet scent of hay pervaded the air—a holy smell.

He went up the gracious valley and through the forest to the Castle of Hohenschwangau, "haunted truly by the tragic memories of the past and present Kings of Bavaria, their mother, a lady of sorrows, and scenes from the history of Germany, so much of which is tragic."

> I leaned out of one of the casements of the castle facing west. The smell of the autumn woods came up with an overpowering sweetness.

So fortified he settled down to German studies in Potsdam, in the house of Herr Rassow, head of a secondary school, and his kindly wife, a sister-in-law of Harnack.

> Undoubtedly it is a craggy language for early conversational purposes. I read about a dozen pages a day, at present, but shall soon read rather more. . . . I have to look up on an average seven words a page. Thus one looks up 80 a day or 460 a week. After all, the vocabulary is the central difficulty in any or every language. At this rate one would have looked out 2,000 words in a month. In the three months 6,000! [His whimsical arithmetic was not intended to be taken seriously.]
>
> It is jolly to be learning a new language! One makes a sorry figure no doubt, a childish figure. But in this, as in other matters, only those who are willing to become as children can enter into the Kingdom.

Gairdner's most enriching Potsdam experience as regards his own studies was the friendship that he made with two ex-Moslem sheikhs, the elder of whom had been "the half-worshipped head of a pantheistic Sufi monastery in the wilds between Macedonia and Bulgaria."

> *Die beide Mollahs* [he says] are rum 'uns, and no mistake. They are sincere enough men, of that I am convinced. Also they are not Moslems. The question is, however, are they *Christians*? or a something quite patent of their own invention? They look to me more like Oriental heretics of the type that

in the second century used to call themselves Christians, but were more or less impolitely informed by Irenæus and others that they *weren't*. The pantheist can make an equation of *everything* by the simple device of giving every quantity the value of zero, or as *he* would say, of unity. This is, I think, what our two Turkish friends are trying to do. I like the chaps immensely and am really interested. Oriental gnosticism in the twentieth century quite live and real!

Gairdner's third son, Douglas Montagu Temple, was born in November, and that inveterate baby-worshipper longed to be at home. "I do like them so much these first days. . . . Picture the warm bed, and the pathetic little helpless, warm, red, sleeping—or-if-not-blinking, soft, unutterably weak, cuddling, unintelligible little morsel of human flesh." He had to content himself with buying German fairy picture-books and writing a baby-English gloss beside each picture for his nursery party.

On Christmas Eve arrived a weighty letter from Professor D. B. Macdonald which turned the scale in the arguments passing back and forth in Gairdner's mind as to how he should spend the next spell of his *Wanderjahr*, for the German acquisition stage must come to an end.

I can declare that I have done well to put in these three months here [he wrote]. German books have no longer seven seals. They are open, and though it is true that I cannot read fast yet, I can read eight longish fairly difficult pages in an hour. It would have been worth learning German only for the sake of the book I am now reading, Goldziher's *Muhammedanische Studien*. It is a perfect gold-mine.

IV

Professor Macdonald, who now wrote to Gairdner, had seen him in Cairo, and had found him a short-sighted and rather oblivious and brusque acquaintance. But he had heard from Egyptian friends that this man was "willing to sit by the roadside and talk to anybody," and finding him of this mind, the Professor had explained to Gairdner his longing to see " an essential turnover in the training of missionaries for the Moslem field." Gairdner was therefore in consultation with Professor Macdonald over the spending of his *Studienjahr*, and now received a generous offer of personal help in the study of Islamic literature if he came to Hartford. The sequel was a hasty departure for America on the last day of 1910.

> I crossed the Atlantic in order to study Arabic and Islamic theology under Professor D. B. Macdonald, of Hartford Theological Seminary. Hartford term ends in May. I could not afford to lose a single day of the special coaching offered me by Macdonald, hence my hasty exit.

" He arrived one night," says Professor Macdonald, " lugging a big travelling bag and a much bigger paper parcel of Lane's *Arabic Lexicon*."

> From Hartford I write and can report the move a great success. I live with the students, which is a pleasure ; and to study with so good a guide and so enthusiastic a student and teacher as Professor Macdonald is an education in itself.
>
> About sixty students are in residence, and I make one of them despite my years. [" It is my conviction," the President of the College wrote to him after he had left, " that your life among ' the boys ' during those winter and spring months accounts in large measure for the wonderfully fine spirit that has pervaded the student body this year. Every member of the Faculty has felt a difference in the atmosphere."] They have given me a very nice study in a tower over the library. I have shoals of books up from it, to which my professor and I turn during the " lectures," which are *tête-à-tête* in my room, he rocking gracefully in a rocking chair. . . . I live completely immersed in study.

"Things are opening up. I am being stimulated here," he said during the first month. "Macdonald and I get on finely together—and he is familiar with so much Arabic literature and literature on Arabic that he can be giving one points all the time or showing one method. I am sure I shall make my language-study superintendence in Cairo a new thing altogether."

> Gairdner knew Arabic as a language, of course, much better than I did [Professor Macdonald says], but he did not know Moslem theological Arabic, nor the literature of theology in Arabic, nor the books and articles of European scholars on these matters. . . . He adapted himself very thoroughly to his return to school.

At the end of this fruitful term Gairdner could say:

> I have got a perfect framework well fixed up now. I have a bird's-eye view of the entire field; a sense of grasp that I am certain I could never have got elsewhere. And on the whole I have actually read a fair amount—perhaps a thousand pages of Arabic and a fair amount of German, besides an introduction to the science of phonetics.

As for the world outside books, "I am really not seeing much of *America* in seeing Hartford," he told his family. "The scenery is a tame and less picturesque edition of *Old* England. By the way, though, the house in which *Uncle Tom's Cabin* was written is quite near the Seminary." One sight Gairdner saw, neither of New England, nor of the Old, but wonderfully fair to him and never forgotten, Pavlova and her Russian Dancers. "We went to 'rush' seats in the top balcony," says the American friend who was with him, "and had to stand in a queue for about an hour. He was experimenting at the time in doing without food for several days as I remember, but he seemed keener and more enthusiastic than ever. He was talking to me about some religious subject while we waited in the crowd, and gradually the

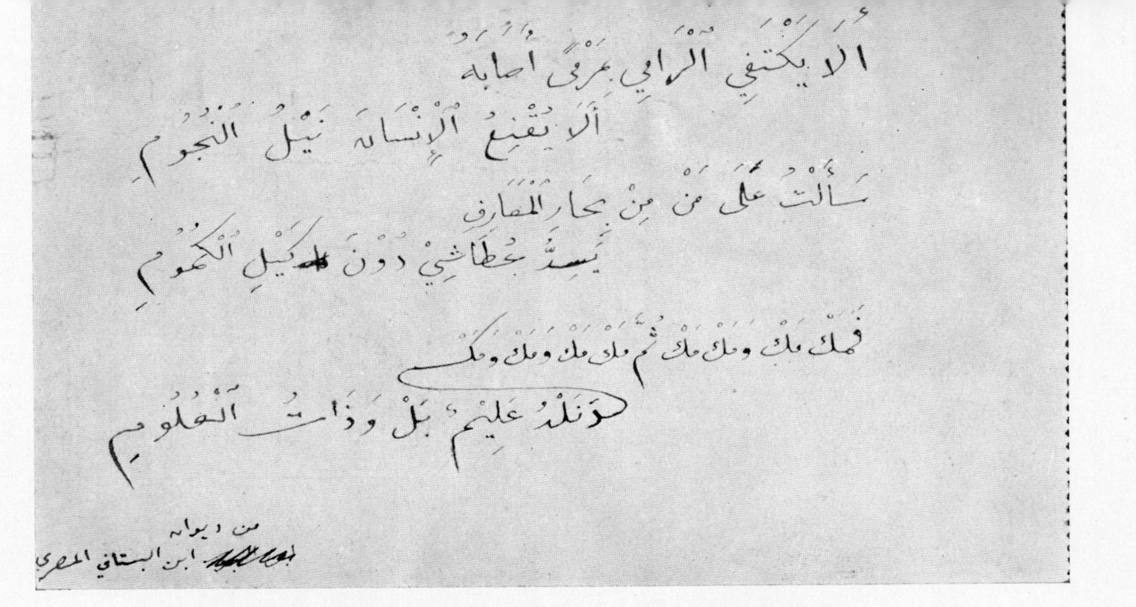

الا يكتفي الرامي بمرمى اصابه
الا يقنع الانسان نيل النجوم
سألت على من من بحار المعارف
يسد عطاشي دون كيل الكموم
فمك مك ومك مك ثم مك مك ومك ومك
دونلد عليم بل وذات العلوم

من ديوانه
ابن البستاني المصري

A SPECIMEN OF GAIRDNER'S ARABIC HANDWRITING.

Complimentary Arabic verses written by W. H. T. Gairdner in honour of Professor D. B. Macdonald.

" Is the marksman not content to have hit his target ?
Will a man not be satisfied to have attained the stars ?
I asked who among the men-that-are-oceans-of-knowledge
Would slake my thirst beyond all measurement,
And it is Mac-Mac-Macdonald who has that unbounded store."

(From *The Poems of the Gardner's Son of Egypt*.)

people round us began to listen, more and more becoming silent, but he went on quite unconscious of any audience except myself. When we finally reached our seats and the dancing began, it was like sitting beside a child at the circus, so bubbling was his pleasure in the beauty of it all."

> The really lovely art of these people [he wrote to his mother]. If this was ballet dancing (I don't even know if it was), then I agree with Father Dolling who preferred the ballet as a thing of truth and genuine beauty to *The Sign of the Cross* ; also with Mr. Chesterton . . . when he said that the tragedy of modern life could be summed up in the fact that Mr. Joseph McCabe—a square-toed atheist lecturer—was not his own ballet-dancer.

Gairdner was received in several hospitable Hartford families, and he was amused at achieving a faint aroma of celebrity through a casual remark that his great-great-grandfather had baptized Robbie Burns. The company present rose and asked to shake him by the hand.

Mrs. Keller, the mistress of a house where he was always made to feel at home, says :

> He was one of us and always will be one of us. We look back to our "Gairdner winter" with peculiar joy. I wish I could inject into this letter a little of the keen love of life and of home and of people, the vivid virility and yet the gentleness of the man as I knew him. It was as if a flash of brilliant light came into our life.

He gloried in the Easter services, in which he helped at the Episcopal Church at Hartford.

> The early service was inspiring to a degree. I felt that the processional entry, the stirring hymn, the exhilaration of both the choir and the crowded congregation, utterly smashed up that *intense* individualism that characterizes early Communions in England.

If something was lost in quietness, greatly more, I think, was gained in joyousness and *philadelphia* and sense of triumph. Not once but many times the sheer rapture of the whole thing thrilled one and well-nigh brought tears to the eyes.

As I went out, the Roman Catholic Cathedral 'scaled'; out came the worshippers by hundreds and because *meeting* that efflux of humanity seemed to symbolize antagonism which I utterly refused to feel I turned and walked along with them for a bit, . . and then thought I would go and wish the priests a happy Easter. I caught a young priest as he was fussing about one of the side-altars. He seemed both surprised and pleased at my greeting, and said he would convey the same to his Bishop.

Having met in New York the secretaries of the Canadian mission-boards, Gairdner promised them that after the Hartford term he would return to Europe by way of Canada, preaching in Toronto and elsewhere. It was a wonderful joy to him to see the world, so keen a pleasure that he searched his heart for fear he who had set out on a life of sacrifice should be growing selfish.

I am terribly alive to the danger I am in of slipping into self-pleasing in all manner of ways, egoism in all its forms: and time and again I have whispered to myself, "Verily I say unto thee, thou *hast* thy reward" I had to read it in church the other day. . . .

You know how I just had to fight out the problem of self-abnegation versus self-fulfilment, and how I felt I had gained a synthesis. The conclusion I came to was, roughly, first that the more one took in the more one had to give out; and secondly, the more one received the more one had to lay down. With regard to the first I can honestly say that I try hard to share all I experience or gain, not only with you but with people in general. And with regard to the second it is all ready to be laid down, at a moment's notice. In a few weeks or months, back to the East again

> and who knows what life of living on capital—no, the interest of the capital stored—must not then be lived for a long time ?

The words were prophetic ; for year upon year that capital must suffice him. But it was a rich store :

> The sail up the Hudson was exquisite; what with the fresh green and the holy smells from the foliage and grass all the way, it was all Paradise. . . . Off the same night to Niagara and there spent an enchanted thirty-six hours. I just heard and saw and did and smelled hard. The Cave of the Winds was the experience of experiences. The moving, circular rainbow surrounding me and advancing as I advanced made me feel like a god ! I thundered like Jove himself and summoned Ganymede and my Eagle. Ha ! 'Twas an immortal moment.

He reached Scotland and allowed himself seventeen days with his wife and children, meeting for the first time his baby son Douglas, born seven months before. " A champion ! "

> Bombarded as I was from every airt the wind blaws with causes and occasions of bliss, what could I do but sit down in the storm-centre of this typhoon of bliss and passively subject myself to it, leaving the gradual realization of it to the coming days ?

Then he flashed away on part three of his wandering scholar's career.

V

" My steps were as usual beautifully determined when the time came. I had a picture-day with Oldham in Strathearn (there is something veritably heavenly about Strathearn), and he convinced me that to complete my experiences in methods of language study and Islamic study I should go again to the Continent and see various leaders in these matters in Holland and Germany."

He spent crowded days at Leyden, Rotterdam,

Hamburg, and Berlin, and wrote an illuminating report to his Society. In Holland he had a three-hours' talk, nearly all in Arabic, with Snouck Hurgronje, " one of the two greatest Islamists in Europe ; he and Goldziher are in a class by themselves."

> He treated me with the utmost simplicity and cordiality. He is not in the least like the adventurous Mecca-breaker that you would expect. And indeed he just is really not that. He and Burton were at opposite poles altogether, and his exploit was as cold a bit of scientific research as Burton's was a piece of personal bravado. For me personally, that talk was momentous, for it resulted in my going (after Hamburg and Berlin) to study with Goldziher at Budapest. It was Snouck Hurgronje who suggested it and made it feasible.

About Hamburg, Gairdner was enthusiastic. " The Colonial Institute (now the University) is leading the world in the study of non-European languages," he told his Society. Here his friend Pastor Enderlin of Nubia rescued him from a miserable hotel and shared a room with him. " I thus secured nearly a week of converse with this admirable man," says Gairdner, " teaching him patience and enabling him to secure merit in Paradise while he suffered and improved my German ! " Ten years later he wrote to Pastor Enderlin : " Do you remember that while we were in that room at Hamburg in 1911 the *Panther* was sent to Morocco ! . . . What a tragic decade has passed ! "

" How eager Gairdner was in those days," says his companion, " in studying phonetics in the phonetic institute of Professor Calzia and with Professor D. Meinhof. He was once so plunged in the pronunciation of the Arabic gutturals that, having forgotten everything else, he began to make exercises with them aloud in the street." The scholars at Hamburg were kind to him. " Meinhof, a giant among linguists, is as simple and unassuming as a little child," he said.

> Both in Leyden and in Hamburg I have been struck by the unassumingness of these great Continental scholars. I have been received as if they were no one in particular and as if I were worthy of honourable attention! Meinhof said to me, "The time has come when missionaries must be less bashful!"

In Hamburg Gairdner wrote his remarkable pamphlet about *The Way of a Mohammedan Mystic*, the fruit of conversations with the Turkish sheikhs at Potsdam. Nor did he neglect the famous Zoo, where he was much taken with the seals and sea-lions climbing on to rocks, and "lumberously splotching" off them again into the water.

> To see a seal getting out of the water [he says] is the only sight in nature which I can remember in which the means seem grotesquely ill-adapted to the end. Yet not once does he complain of Providence, which seems to the human spectator very wonderful!

Berlin came next. "The Berlin Societies," he said, "are going to show us, I hope, how missionary societies if they drop diffidence and are bold in their ideas and demands, may co-operate with non-missionary training institutions, and in doing so mould them to some extent to their own needs. I greatly trust that this will be the case in London, when the School of Oriental Studies comes into being."

Pastor Enderlin recalls how after arduous days at the headquarters of these societies, where he and Gairdner were "simply squeezed with questions," they went off with very tired heads to hear *Die Meistersinger*.

> Gairdner was electrified from head to foot [he says]. In the intervals he always prepared me for the coming music by whistling the leading *motifs*. That night he was all music through and through. Afterwards he wanted to take the tram to his hotel, but missed the tread-board and fell against an iron lamp-post. ["At full speed I had run into an iron electric lamp-post

which I had not seen in the dim light," Gairdner says.] When I sprang horrified to help him and he got on to his feet again, what do you think he said? "That was the shock of the Morocco Question!" It was remarkable how Gairdner with all his work lived in the presence of the vital political events.

VI

From Germany he went to Budapest ("It runs Edinburgh hard," he said) for what was to him the crowning joy of his *Wanderjahr*. Professor Goldziher had invited him to his summering haunt in the suburb of Zuliget.

I could not have dreamed of such a thing; he was too big. I felt that the opportunity was too brilliant to be lost. For a month I enjoyed the extraordinary privilege of personal study and tuition at the hand of Professor Ignaz Goldziher. I continued on the lines so well and truly laid by Professor Macdonald and also opened up others.

The Goldzihers [Gairdner told his wife] are a pair of Hebrew angels. Their generosity and friendliness is simply *absolute*.

There it is and there is no admixture of anything else. The quite beloved Professor treats me as a companion rather than a pupil, and reads Arabic with me not as a task or a duty but more as two people might read Shakespeare together when on a holiday. . . . He appears to think it the most *natural* thing in the world that the greatest Islamist in the world should be *daily* making a gift of his knowledge and experience to a perfect stranger. All I can say is, it is a lesson to me in the inner meaning of hospitality, courtesy and generosity. These are Jews of the stamp of the Greatest of the Sons of Israel; and in His day would have recognized and received Him.

I am at every turn trying to learn Goldziher's attitude and method [Gairdner wrote to Professor Macdonald], and grasp his grasp, so to speak. . . .

Need I tell you that but for your training I should have been totally unable to profit from him in these ways? Goldziher seems to think well of my Arabic and of my general grasp of the subject of Islam—the latter entirely the fruit of your work. One single piece of commendation of my Arabic I value. Once Goldziher spoke of Ihre *Genauigkeit.* Do you know, I really value that very much, because at school and college I was thought incorrigibly *ungenau* as a scholar. It makes one feel as if years had brought some advance. He has said again and again that I do not need to take further lessons, or, in fact, to do anything but go straight ahead on my own feet; for this, he says, I seem to him now amply qualified.

"I suppose I must consider this as the case and attribute any contrary feelings to diffidence or uncourageousness rather than to modesty," he told his wife. . . . "But Christ was before all others courageous, hardy, brave, strong."

VII

And now, laden with his spoils, he turned eastward:

"In chapter the last of the schooldays of a second childhood it was made possible for me by my long-suffering colleagues to get a final month in the East. I wanted to get a fresh insight into Oriental and especially Islamic life and thought, unencumbered by recognition as a missionary." To this end he started for Aleppo, with four days of waiting for a boat at Trieste, during which he "diligently prosecuted Italian." "I have quite attained my end; I find I can read my Caetani. It would be worth while learning to read Italian for that one book."

I arrived at Aleppo at sunset. I abode incognito there, in the house of a Syrian Catholic priest, and disguised, so to speak, as "an Orientalist." I managed to enter on relations of great intimacy and cordiality with the sheikhs there, sitting with them long hours in the college-mosque, fez-cap on head, and minus shoes on feet, conversing on questions congenial to men with the typical education of Islam. In this way I could enter more deeply into the Moslem mind and thought than I had ever been able to do before.

My visit to one sheikh left an altogether peculiar impression. This ancient of days is named the Sheikh el Sînî, which means the Sheikh of or from China. His age was variously reported to me as 103, 117, or 137 years. (If the 103 estimate were true, he could tell us of the Battle of Waterloo, and if the 137, he would be an authority on the whole of the French Revolution.) The old man is a sort of ascetic, and has not and has never had a woman so much as in the house with him—in fact he is a misogynist. . . . I beheld a beaming old spectacled face as of an Oriental Pickwick who might not be more than eighty, . . . his body was straight as a ramrod (erect as an *alif*, as one of us said admiringly). Indeed the only sign of old age that he really evinced during the afternoon was his tendency to pass too quickly from one subject to another, and his dislike for the least hint of contradiction or opposition. I put out my hand to salute him, and he waved his right hand in the direction of mine in an airy way, just touching the tips of my fingers with his, beaming all the time just like a Mr. Pickwick in his old age, and making us sit down in his own place. He was from Chinese Turkestan. Turki therefore was his real language, and his servant might have been a mandarin off a plate. The latter had lately come from Kashgar. Truly Aleppo looks east as much as it looks west.

Before leaving the country, Gairdner finished a collection of Syrian-Arabic tunes corresponding to his Egyptian collection. Then he set his face once more towards the land of Egypt—an Egypt with Kitchener now at the helm.

One of the letters of the last month of his *Wanderjahr* sets a seal on it.

Looking back [he said], the year seems to have been fitted and articulated like a fugue of Bach. I could not have imagined that I should have been able to open so many avenues, to do all, and far more than all, of what I hoped to do. It is this sense of finish that makes me feel it is a work of God.

CHAPTER XIII

THE ARABIST AT WORK

1911–1914

(with excursions into later years)

Your Lord Christ is he that worked, and hath given away what he wrought for to the next poor beggar he meets.—*John Bunyan.*

I

"THE student and the missionary—the two must be more one henceforward than they have been in the past," Gairdner wrote during his *Wanderjahr*. And the professors under whom he studied, finding an Arabist of unusual ability, urged upon him the claims of a scholar's work.

"Goldziher presses me to concentrate on some Islamic subject with a view to making it a sort of life-work and publishing on it something worth doing. And then think of that Cairo life—and Mrs. A and B and C," he told his wife, A, B and C being weaklings of his Cairo flock whose tangled affairs spiritual and temporal cost many an hour of patience.

Professor Macdonald, to whom this was confided, was as anxious as Professor Goldziher that Gairdner should not (in his own phrase) "be reabsorbed into the maelstrom of mission-station life." He would not have him forsake his missionary vocation, but accept within it an apostolate of scholarship, set apart for work that his brethren could not do.

> You are a research missionary [he said]. You have a metaphysical mind that likes to run things back

> and down. You are now ready to walk by yourself and to add to the world's knowledge. . . .
>
> Keep on being a missionary, but remember that you are called to other things than the ordinary cycle of missionary life. And don't measure other missionaries and their minds and studies by yourself and yours. You must teach them and they must take of you. . . .
>
> But *can* you be a research missionary? Could you get along if you were put on half-time?

These were winged words. They met with a response in Gairdner's heart. "But I may be building absurd castles in the air—that Cairo life!" he said.

Yet when he returned to Cairo it was not without some hope of scholarly work. Surely recruits must soon strengthen the mission. He settled hopefully into the new headquarters of the society, a roomy house at 35 Sharia el Falaki, where for the first time in his Egyptian life this man had a study that was not also an eating-room and he laid in all the books and opuscula that he could find of El Ghazzali (the philosopher proposed for his special study) and actually made in that first autumn a translation of one of his books, *A Niche for Lights* (*Mishkát al-Anwár*), with a view to research on its mystical and philosophical ideas.

Then he watched his hopes slowly fade.

> (*At Christmas* 1911:) My reading has suffered eclipse, but I hope to resume.
>
> (*A few months later*:) The thing that has chiefly kept me back from study is just—evangelistic work! The fact is that when I came back I found the Arabic Y.M.C.A., which I had helped to start just before leaving Cairo in 1910, nearly moribund. I threw myself into it as a matter of course and speedily became pretty much involved. It *has* been and *is* worth it, but of course the cost is considerable.

And again (to Professor Macdonald):

We have decided that McNeile should go ahead with his studies and train for becoming the student *par excellence* of our mission, and the man who shall do the most in guiding people through Islamic literature in Arabic. I do not think this will disappoint you, except perhaps that you had for me, and I for myself, a sort of hankering after this student and teaching work.

And by the end of 1912 there is no remaining glimmer of hope :

Take the work of classes for catechumens and converts, and the whole work in general of *building up* what God has already given us. It is an enormously important, necessary, exacting, time-expensive branch of work. It is morally our first duty. It is, moreover, work that no novice can do. . . . It is work, in short, that every week and every day falls on me. It is work which, when it falls upon one, can no more be shouldered off, no more be disclaimed, no more be ignored than the father of a family can ignore the claims of his children because he happens to want leisure for let us say conchology. Personal work. Personal work pressing in on one imperiously every day.

Yet—not the sort of thing we had in mind in 1911 !

With all my heart I could have gone in for the research work, and I feel that I might have done some decent work in it. But I think it is not to be.

The dream was dead. He had made a present of it first to evangelistic shepherding, and secondly to the needs of new missionaries in language study. Into both of these tasks he put his creative life, and so gaily and ardently that neither the little flock with their daily lessons to learn in Christian life and worship nor the missionaries at their grammar classes realized that he had any other wish than to be solving their difficulties. Gaiety touched everything he did ; he was brilliantly happy in his four little children, and the brightness of a boy still hung round the man of forty. He was proud of telling how during his *Wanderjahr* an acquaintance in America had congratulated him on being the *son* of the man who had written *Studies in St. John* a dozen years before.

> I can see him still as he was in 1913 [Miss Lilias Trotter wrote], flying round bare-headed on his bicycle, and ringing wonderful and unforeseen changes on the Arabic Liturgy in the crypt chapel at Sharia Falaki, and giving the most racy lectures that can be imagined in the Arabic Study Centre.

Egyptian friends had the same impression of light-heartedness and vigour :

> Yesterday [Gairdner says] I had a most enjoyable day in a village in the heart of the country. Over twelve years ago I had an amusing scene with a huge burly fellow (a landowner in these parts), who, to show his strength, had raised me from the floor with one arm ; whereat I took him under his hips and swung him over my shoulder. This has never been forgotten, and at the *Omda's* house yesterday the matter came up in the presence of the burly chap himself, now grizzled and a good deal aged.

The *Omda* (village mayor), a gigantic personage, asked for the story of twelve years before (stories die hard in village guest-rooms), saying, " What's this I hear about lifting people ? " Then, hoping to outdo the friend who had been the hero on that occasion, he picked Gairdner up and carried him the length of the long guest-room.

> Even so [Gairdner says], I don't think the company were prepared to see their revered old *Omda* heaved up over *my* shoulder, turban, beard and all, to be trotted up and down the guest-room.
>
> As we stood later in the court to go, the old *Omda*

spread his arms and came flying at me like an aeroplane and hugged me.[1]

II

As a shepherd evangelist Gairdner was helping the early days of the Arabic Y.M.C.A.

"I have had to put in more time than I wanted in helping to organize and run a vigorous work among the youth of Cairo. The moral lapses of young men and schoolboys in this city are frightful, and they find next to nothing to help them. If so many of the Christian Copts have sunk so low, how necessary it is in relation to the Moslem work itself that they should be helped! I am the only non-Egyptian member of the Arabic Y.M.C.A. They receive me completely as one of themselves. I go along in a fez and take part in everything just like one of them. It is an honour."[2]

At the beginning of 1914 came a tempest:

> A most furious storm broke out here [Gairdner wrote], and it was my duty to be "on the bridge" throughout it. An extraordinary outburst of Moslem opposition has taken place, quite unlike any we have before experienced, for it is organized, deliberate, resourceful, supported by the highest in the land, heavily financed. *One* of its planks is the seduction of all known converts from Islam. At that very hour of danger I became aware of some serious weakness in our own ranks. For a fortnight I suffered more than

[1] The first of these jests took place in 1901, the second in 1914, and in 1928 women missionaries reported visiting the village to find the *Omda* on his deathbed and a quite surprisingly open welcome to themselves—until the old sick man told the oft-repeated tale. "And we traced our welcome entirely to Canon Gairdner having paved the way for us."

[2] A little pamphlet of this year on *The Anglican and Coptic Communions in Egypt* shows that Gairdner had lost none of the eagerness of Thornton's days to help and serve the Egyptian National Church. This has remained the official attitude of the C.M.S. in Egypt under the leadership of Bishops MacInnes and Gwynne.

I can tell you—days sick with anxiety and evil news and rumours and restless, dreaming nights. It was like having to repel an assault and throw up the earth-works at the same time. Well, it drove us to our knees.

" Black Holy Week " the mission called that of 1914 when the fact became clear to Gairdner that one of his own men had been seduced and was working for the seduction of the rest.

" At Gairdner's suggestion," his friend Dr. Harpur says, " several of us went out to the desert near the Pyramids to pray. We got into a sheltered cave in a quiet spot (it is a cave used regularly by dervishes for their *dhikr* gatherings), and I remember Gairdner asking Toop to read some verses of Scripture. Some of the words read seemed to me like a picture of Gairdner's dealings with his children in the faith : 'So being affectionately desirous of you, we were willing to have imparted unto you, not the Gospel of God only, but also our own souls, because ye were dear unto us.' "

Then Gairdner spoke with the severity which is only the right of those who have gone all lengths in love and prayer. And this right was surely his, for his wife remembers that he felt so deeply the attack on the Church and the losses it sustained that he said to her (devoted father as he was), " I believe I should have felt it less even if one of our own little ones had been taken ? " In the right of this love he proposed to his comrades that, for the saving of the Church, all calls to repentance having been rejected by the seducer, they should make the terrible spiritual act described by St. Paul :

" In the name of the Lord Jesus Christ, when ye are gathered together, and my spirit, with the power of our Lord Jesus Christ, to deliver such an one unto Satan for the destruction of the flesh, that the spirit may be saved in the day of Jesus Christ."

They agreed with trembling. There in the cave the spiritual transaction took place. The man was laid under a power he could not resist. The Egyptian Church remembers the Gairdner of those days. "Who is weak, and I am not weak?" he cried, a suffering man; then with a sharp note he called them to decision. "Will ye also go away? The way is open. Go your ways if you will." "It was his courage that astonished me," says an Egyptian friend.

> We invoked the divine power [Gairdner said]. There was a rallying, and only one or two fell away. We breathed again and are now praying for and believing for a manifestation of divine power. For over a month I have been "on the bridge." Study, Islamics, phonetics, writing, evangelism and everything else have been so many empty terms to me.

"We're not the first to cope with this," he told a friend in his philosophical way. "The men who *really* had a hard time were the people in the first centuries when there was no Church history. We have only to look up the Early Fathers to see that our troubles have been survived before. Blessed be God for History!" And the same friend recounts her sense that he had more inward consolation than that of historical reflection:

> He never lost sight of Christ. You felt he walked in His presence and was as human as He was. I always remember his talking to me, in the course of an ordinary expedition, about St. John—"The old, old man who could touch his hand and say, 'This hand has handled Him, the Word of Life.'"
>
> I remember feeling that, as St. John had really handled the Lord, so the man who was talking to me had mystically done the same. His mysticism could lift him to heaven.

III

The second rival in Gairdner's life to any work of pure scholarship was the practical necessity for teaching Arabic to missionaries. In this he worked from the year 1912 with a committee drawn from five different missions, but the spade-work of the early years fell on himself.

> I have by an imposed necessity gone off into linguistics—the subject I merely dallied with as relaxation during my *Studienjahr*. All this was settled on the day when the C.S.C.[1] became inevitable, and it was certain that no one excepting myself had so much as begun to think that the conduct of its linguistic side required a little thought !

He had dabbled in phonetics at Hartford with Dr. Worrell, and at the Colonial Institute in Hamburg had " put in a hugely important time seeing their language-study methods of scientific phonetics."

And now, with Dr. Zwemer at his side, full of zeal to inspire young missionaries to the study of Islam, Gairdner revolutionized the teaching of Arabic ; and " his first revolutionary act," said the Rev. R. F. McNeile, " was to gain official consent to teaching the spoken language to the new missionary before the literary form was tackled."

Previously the teaching had been concentrated on the classical language, and the spoken was picked up in a haphazard way.

> I remember the day [Gairdner used to say] when we were studying the usual classical Arabic, and Thornton suddenly said to me, " I say, Gairdner, let's see what there really is in this colloquial ! "

Gairdner accordingly did " see what really was in it "—and discovered that, far from being only a rather slovenly and degraded form of the written tongue, it was a living language following very exact grammatical and phonetic rules of its own. He saw that to teach a missionary the classical language of literature first or only

[1] Cairo Study Centre for training missionaries in Arabic and Islamics, a co-operative work organized by Dr. Zwemer, Rev. W. H. T. Gairdner, Mr. Swan and others, and a direct result of suggestions at the Edinburgh 1910 Conference.

was seriously delaying his contact with anything except the world of books.

> *The* thickest skull [he said of one of his pupils] and the most hopeless pupil of the fifty or sixty we have had. He broke the heads and hearts of all his teachers. Yet he is just the sort that the Cairo Study Centre *saves*. He escapes being returned empty by being *put straight on to the living oral work.*

But for this revolution new tools were necessary and Gairdner had to make them.

> I have to create all my apparatus [he said]. I am giving at present the major portion of my time to matters linguistic—my job being *very* much the heaviest end of the stick in this emprise. In addition to a handbook on Phonetics, etc., I am writing two others, conversation-grammars ; further, I am engaged in training some native teachers to use the new methods, and superintending the new students (Germans some of them) on whose corpus the new experiments are being made. As these persons are eating up my handbooks as fast as I write them, sheet by sheet, you can imagine the charming time I am having.
>
> Truly one needs to have all one's faculties working at their best and not to spend one's time sinning and repenting.

They were impossible and yet glorious days. That to a Gairdner should be left the details of organization and time-tables for students scattered all over the city ; the scolding of the teachers when they failed to keep appointments ; the hundred details in the daily running of a school which had no office but his own over-busy study and no class-room but rooms borrowed from missions in different parts of the town—this, curiously enough, seemed strange to no one, least of all to himself. He was now so used to working without secretarial help that he was fast becoming incapable of using it.

The pages of his books, the examination papers, the

diagrams for his lectures, were "jellied," generally in frantic haste, by Mrs. Gairdner or some friend, and many were the woes and confusions about their distribution to the pupils. Yet through it all a great thing was being evolved.

> The influence of his life in this one field of Arabic teaching alone was perhaps more extensive and lasting than that of any man in the Moslem world [says one of his former pupils].

When the time came for all this linguistic work to pass from its first creative stage in Gairdner's hands to a settled, organized life, American friends came to its help. The American Mission allotted valuable men to the work and the new American University gave it a home.

"They have taken over the linguistic section (of the Cairo Study Centre)," Gairdner said, "and are 'doing it proud' in material. We have fine premises, and the Douglas Thornton Memorial Library has been loaned thither. Everything is now more shipshape."

IV

Of Gairdner the Arabic teacher, scores of men and women now have memories, and the memories of all are vivid. For he was no ordinary teacher. Who could forget that active figure, prancing about the room, covering itself with chalk-dust, expending itself in illustration, urgent, humorous, eager, behaving as though for the moment nothing in the whole world mattered so much as cajoling the right pronunciation of an Arabic consonant out of three newcomers, or inventing some comic scene which impressed for ever the meaning of a new verb?

> I had been told before my first Arabic lesson [says a pupil], that it was well to have an engagement fixed for an hour or two after the lesson began. I went into his study and for about two hours had strange and terrible sounds poured out at me. He was wonderfully patient and so engrossed that time was quite

forgotten. I had to suggest at last that I had an engagement, and gain my release.

You ask what drew me to him [writes another pupil]. His brilliant mind and scholarly mastery of Arabic, his interpretation of Islamic literature and history, his accuracy, his insight, his poetic and dramatic sense, his power to make grammar one of the most absorbingly interesting studies. Yet before friendship came, one persistent impression had to be surmounted. This was the feeling that he was impatient with me, and with others because we were slow in our ways of thinking and learning, slow in expressing ourselves. Gradually this was replaced by the discovery that he took infinite pains to help those who were slow, and did not look down on them but reached out his hand every day *to give them a swinging lift!* Furthermore, I found that when I had really grasped and could make use of some of the fine points he gave us, *he simply glowed with friendship.*

The Rev. Arthur Jeffery, his colleague at the School of Oriental Studies (into which the "Cairo Study Centre" has now grown), says:

Latterly he took very few Arabic classes, and those he did take were without preparation, for he would come into my office to ask what it was that the pupils were reading and to borrow the text, but while reading the text with the class he would throw in a wealth of illustration. He excelled in discovering felicitous translations. I remember reading Qurân with him, and the joy it was to have him start up in excitement and bring forth a new rendering of some obscure phrase where Rodwell and Co. had made a hopeless mess. He was the one first-class mind we had.

As an examiner he could be dreaded or loved. He was gentleness itself with those whom he knew to be timid or slow, but he had his sternnesses. "An Englishman not naturally timid," says Maurice Richmond, "who was working under him for an Arabic examination, felt as soon as he got inside that study door that the hours which he had frittered away were all known and read as in the Day of Judgment. He asked Gairdner whether he had not an extraordinarily clear intuition of what was passing in the minds of those whom he was interviewing. 'Perhaps,' he said, 'sometimes I have.'"

"How he enjoyed the recitations in character which form part of the examinations," says yet another pupil. "We loved him to be one of the examiners on those occasions. His appreciation of any genuine spirit put into them, and his happy laughter even when he heard the same piece repeated for the *n*th time, helped us all through the ordeal. He was intensely considerate in his attitude. We liked best to hear the results from him personally, he was so generous in his praise, and so gentle in mention of deficiencies."

And humour played over it all.

One pupil cherishes the report:

"*Conversation* : speaks no known dialect of Arabic, but is intelligible."

Of another, a mission received the following pregnant report:

> *Etymology* : Good
> *Syntax* : Equally bad.

> At the end of an immensely long examination paper [says the Rev. S. Van R. Trowbridge] was the question for us to answer in Arabic, "Do you love your examiner ?" The thermometer registered 104°, we had been writing all day, but we could not resist his final thrust.

V

Of the technical books which he wrote for this language work, Mr. H. A. R. Gibb, of the London School of Oriental Studies, says :

> There was nothing in Canon Gairdner's work of a lifeless reproduction of other men's thought, and as

little, on the other hand, of that assertiveness which thinks no opinion or method but its own entitled to respect. Behind all his writing the reader is conscious of a deep humanity, eager, persuasive, hearty and full of laughter.

The first edition of his " Conversation Grammar " of *Egyptian Colloquial Arabic* (1917) would have satisfied the ambition of most men, but it was like Gairdner to be dissatisfied until a second edition (1926), completely revised and rewritten, perfected the work. Who but he could have written such a textbook for learning such a language, which not only took the tears out of it but filled it with laughter?

His book on *The Phonetics of Arabic* was published in 1925, but devised in 1912. During the whole of the interval Gairdner had been listening to Arabic and teaching classes in its phonetics. His friend Mr. Grahame Bailey recalls the genesis of the idea. " I remember saying to him, ' Get a complete list of every sound in the language, where it is used and how it varies, and describe and illustrate every one.' We were sitting in a Cairo hotel and he suddenly rushed out into the Square and got hold of a passer-by whom he persuaded to come in, and then and there we sat for a long time studying the sounds."

" Being familiar," says Professor Steventon of Glasgow, " with practically all the best work on Arabic phonetics, I can confidently say that Canon Gairdner's account of the Arabic consonants is easily the best I have read." " It has taken its place as the standard book on the subject," says Mr. H. A. R. Gibb.

This technical work had to be done, but it was not work that by nature his soul loved. " I hope I have written my last stroke on colloquial Arabic for many a long day," he said, after finishing his grammar. But he hoped in vain. His own books were written, but he had yet many and many hours to put in on the ' Reader ' prepared by his friend the Rev. E. E. Elder, and again on a Grammar of the Sudanese Arabic for which his friend Dr. Worsley collected the material. To the last year of his life he was never free from tasks of this kind. It was necessary work and he had the gifts for it, but he longed to be at something freer and more creative in the way of literature. One and only one adventure he allowed himself, escaping from linguistics into the realm of pure scholarship and philosophy. He and Professor Goldziher had seen together in 1911, and both of them for the first time, the mystical-philosophical treatise of Ghazzali called *Mishkât al Anwâr* (*A Niche for Lights*). Gairdner was at once struck by this book, which seemed to him to give a key to the heart of the great man's teaching. He longed for freedom to investigate the manuscripts, but that never came his way. But for several years when his thoughts were at leisure he would put down his comments and ideas on the printed text of this book, slowly working them up into a little treatise. "My one ewe lamb," he called it. It was published in *Der Islam* at the very moment of the outbreak of war, and he wrote to Professor Macdonald :

> I am wae to think of my ewe lamb, the Ghazzali article coming out in the very month of the war and thus falling flat as a pancake, as who should appear on the stage at her début at the precise moment when 'Fire' is cried throughout the auditorium.

Meanwhile his study of his author was maturing, and in 1923, through the suggestion of Professor Margoliouth of Oxford, he revised his translation, which with a new introduction was published by the Royal Asiatic Society.

> It has been accepted for publication and is now actually in the press [he told his friend Professor Massignon of the Collège de France]. In it I grappled afresh with the whole problem. I hope that now at least it is further on towards solution—I feel such a dreadful amateur in these Orientalist questions.

"Don't say you are an amateur in Orientalism," his friend replied. "I think it is a very valuable advance in our knowledge of El Ghazzali"; while to another he wrote: "Gairdner's attempt to guess Ghazzali's deepest thought is highly remarkable."

And Gairdner, with something of the incense of praise coming his way, for once from equal and discriminating minds, searched his heart as to motives.

> Try as I will I cannot feel that the Pauline ambition is really at the bottom of my desire to finish this. What is stimulating me is another cycle of ideas: to get a clean job cleanly cleared off; to show something for my year abroad even if it be a specimen which remains a mere specimen for ever; to express myself and honour the idea of personality; to do something worthy of the family name. I shouldn't call this cycle of ideas ignoble, and yet what is there Christian about them?
>
> I think that tremendously wide minds *can* synthetize the two cycles of ideas. Life is so multiplex and its motives and aspects so multiplex that it is only a genius who can hold everything steady in one glance and see the whole in every part. The majority of people, in sheer desire for consistency, make jetsam of half their cargo in order to simplify the intellectual problem of their lives.

VI

There were reliefs to these labouring days, royal Christmases with the children and idyllic holidays by the Mediterranean, a week in Cyprus, a week in Jerusalem, and in 1914 a furlough.

With tenderest joy he instituted for his children "the shrine" at Christmas-time, a very small crêche for which he chose the toy figures (they were no bigger) himself, and which he would arrange with delight and mystery in the central room of the house. On Christmas Eve his "little varlets" sat down to a decorated tea, and at sunset their father would throw open a window to listen for the Angelus from the Roman Catholic Cathedral. As the bells rang out, the company sat on the floor—"shepherds watching"—and sang the hymn in which the angel spoke his message, upon which the children, tiptoe with excitement and singing the *Adeste Fideles*, processed before their parents into the big dark room lighted only by the shrine. There, standing with the light on their fair hair, their shining eyes fastened on the stable scene, they sang, each child down to the smallest taking a solo verse, "See, amid the winter's snow." The music and the light of it and the mingled freedom and ritual of it were after Gairdner's very heart. He read the Christmas story, prayed with his little "faithful" who had come to Bethlehem, and then gave them an unforgettable evening of dumb-crambo, never in that house *very* dumb.

And at the sea in summer holidays his children were his glory.

> The little fellows think just about as little of jumping into deep water as two little frogs.
>
> The wee girl now frogs it merrily in the swimming-pool. Anything neater than her trig little body with its tiny, light-blue bathing-dress, and her head in a red bathing-cap to keep the hair out of her eyes, you never saw in your life. In she goes and looks for all the world like a little froglet, with all the wee limbs making the orthodox swimming motions so neatly.
>
> As for the wee lily-white mannikin, the dazzling whiteness of his body when we take him in is too lovely! He now has no objection whatever to being ducked.

And another very joyful relief to these grammatical years was the sudden deep friendship that sprang up between Gairdner and the French orientalist Louis Massignon. They first met on March 3rd, 1913. Three days later the acquaintance had passed for ever beyond the sphere of orientalia alone, and became a friendship deep "in Christ":

> That perfectly charming fellow Massignon has turned up and in the first ten seconds I felt drawn to him.
>
> I have quite fallen in love with this man! His conversion at Bagdad was a far deeper affair than a theological one based on his sufistic studies. It was profoundly ethical and spiritual, a truly Augustinian conversion and most remarkable.
>
> He has thought much about Christian theology in relation to Islam, and, like you, sees in the doctrine of the Trinity the great pillar of the faith, nay, of faith itself, faith in the Divine Personality and human personality too. But he is terribly 'sweir' about putting his thoughts into writing, and talks about retiring to a monastery for the contemplative life, which would be a grievous mistake and loss.

Throughout the hard years that followed, Gairdner's correspondence with Professor Massignon was one of the joyful refreshments of his life, and those letters among the very few he kept. "Amice amicissime," Gairdner would begin, or "My very dear Brother," or "Dearest friend ἐν χριστῷ." And the other would respond, "Brotherly yours in the Cross" or "Dear Friend, dear brother in God." They corresponded upon oriental subjects, upon their thoughts on Islam, and then, with the turn of a sentence, one or other friend passed to the love of their lives and their "shy longing for Him alone." Both in things intellectual and things spiritual Gairdner had usually to be the giver in his friendships, and the peculiar refreshment of this friend, given to him when intellectual drudgery was often his lot, was the equality of their brotherhood.

VII

The years contained enough of drudgery with promise of more. For recruits never came to that part of the work which touched Gairdner's life. In 1911 he had written in great joy: "Lloyd, the Dean of Trinity, my old college, is joining us." When the expected sailing-time came it was found necessary to send Mr. Lloyd to India. Gairdner wrote to the Secretary in London. "I believe that this appointment is absolutely right and I do not complain, except that we have been expecting Lloyd so long we have eased off in looking for fresh recruits. It is a young, keen, spiritual, recklessly-devoted University man we want for Cairo."

To Dr. Mott he said:

> We are going ahead at the [Language] Training Centre scheme. I will, however, tell you that although I think we were right in going ahead, I consider the total amount of our scholarship and general equipment quite inadequate to such an enterprise as this. I go further and say that the total weight of the scholarship and equipment in the Moslem world is awfully light. We need not so much many recruits for this Moslem field as a few first-class ones. We have had, I may say, no inquiry at all from really first-class recruits. . . . The last straw was when Lloyd of Trinity, Oxford, who was to have joined us this autumn, was at the eleventh hour sent to Agra, and we find the Cairo mission still weaker than it was *before* Thornton died, though *he* between 1904 and 1907 was complaining of the fatal weakness of the staff. Since 1904 we have only been asking for one such recruit and in 1912 he is still not in sight, for McNeile only takes the place of Thornton. We still have not begun seriously to take in hand the Moslem problem.

Only second to the hardship of the unrecruited mission is the hardship of the secretary at home who has, mail after mail, to read appeals that he cannot answer. In the spring of 1914 the cry from Cairo was still the same: "We are to-day weaker than we were in 1907, and reinforcement is even now not so much as in sight."

And in August 1914 the storm broke on a mission still unrecruited.

CHAPTER XIV

A SECRETARIAT IN WAR-TIME

1914–1919

Oh, Sir, I know not how to be willing you should leave us in our pilgrimage. You have been so faithful and so loving to us, you have fought so stoutly for us, you have been so hearty in counselling of us.—
John Bunyan.

I

"We were surprised how with all his work he lived in the presence of the vital political events," Gairdner's German friends had remarked in 1911, and English friends were often equally surprised. He seemed to spend less time than any man in newspaper reading—he would hurl himself off his bicycle for a few moments at an Egyptian café near his house where Reuter's telegrams were posted up. But somehow he would be mysteriously "there" in public and political happenings. When they looked back from the awful revelation of August 4th, 1914, his friends said that Gairdner all that spring and summer had been a prophet.

A series of articles that spring in *The Student Movement* and a paper for the Cairo Discussion Society showed him alive to the thought-movement of which Nietzsche was the apostle; showed too his consciousness that Christians had strengthened the case for such a movement by "dull anæmic lives whether of individuals or Christian communities; by the want of interests and *joie de vivre*; the arbitrary curtailments or the simple ignorance of whole sections of human interests and experience." In early summer he went home, forespent with anxiety for the Arabic Church members whose loyalty to Christ was tampered with. "During the past month I have had neither heart nor strength nor appetite except for this struggle with darkness that we have been going through," he told his mother.

Now coming to Europe he was conscious, in part intellectually and in part through his sensitiveness to spiritual climate, that an unseen moral struggle was being fought out, and that an assault was being made by the forces of "spiritual wickedness in high places."

T. R. W. Lunt tells how Gairdner joined a week-end party of laymen held at Eastbourne in mid-July.

> Some forty or fifty leading laymen in business, politics, diplomacy, were there. We were discussing education in the Far East, problems of Islam, and so forth. I remember that we had a little difficulty in keeping Gairdner to the programme, and with one consent we agreed during Sunday afternoon to give up the whole of that evening to him and to let him say whatever he wanted. Certainly we all, knowing what happened afterwards, feel that he prophesied then. He began by describing the trend of European philosophy during the last half-century, showing how Nietzsche's teaching had been woven in to make for Germany a new *Weltpolitik*. He talked also about the insurgent nationalities of Europe and especially of Ireland, and indeed he foretold the whole tremendous crash that was to come not much more than a fortnight afterwards. I shall never forget the impression it made on us, and our heavy hearts at the end.

A Sunday later, a friend in charge of a church at Inverness was startled to see "far back in the shade of the gallery a familiar face above *un*familiar and far from Sunday garb. It was Temple Gairdner with a brother at his side. For a week they had been tramping the West Highlands and reached Inverness very much travel-stained. Nothing daunted, they appeared in church, attracting (as I afterwards observed) not a little attention among the douce Highland churchgoers by reason of their faded travel attire. But none of the features of that unlooked-for and unforgettable week-end lingers in the memory so arrestingly as the startling prescience Temple Gairdner showed of the magnitude of the impending disaster of war, from which in thought and talk he could not get away. He had missed, as he said, up and down the land, any real sense—even in the worship and prayers of the Church—of what was so possible and so near."

On the night of the next Saturday (August 1st) Gairdner arrived at his sister's house at Newport, Fifeshire, beside the great Tay Bridge. "My spirit was confused and aghast," he told his wife, for he saw that the doom was now inevitable.

> One circumstance [he said] seemed to bring it through senses and imagination home to the mind. This was the continuous roll of sound made by the trains crossing the Tay Bridge on the Sunday. We knew it must mean the hurrying of trainsful of men and material to some military or naval base. That long-drawn rumble told us that Britain was sleepless.
>
> As I read Sir Edward Grey's speech my whole soul was a pæan. Here were the man and the hour who together would lift England on to a new plane of life and action. And I blessed God in my soul. . . . This crisis is going to bring us good in ways unimagined. I have no doubt, for example, that a practical scheme of Imperial Federation will be a necessary outcome of this war, and that the Irish problem, which on the very eve of this had reached its final stage of intolerable strain and absolute hopelessness, will be incidentally solved.

To Dr. Mott he wrote two days after the declaration of war:

> The important thing is, not the emergence of Britain, nor the emergence of Germany, but the

> emergence of a new order, a new moral equilibrium. Is it too much to hope that the result of this war will be a more successful attempt to graft moral ideas on to social and international relations?

These world-hopes came from a man essentially patriotic. How should a Scot be otherwise? How should the son of Gairdner's passionately loyalist mother be otherwise? He was forty-one, but he decided to enlist and was only stopped by the Archbishop's manifesto calling the clergy to abide by their tasks.

He and his wife therefore determined to leave their children in England and return to their Egyptian post. The time had come to put the two elder little sons to school, and that summer had been one of school-hunting. Gairdner turned loose to hunt for schools was tremendous. He was too brilliant a teacher not to be fascinated by educational questions. The man who had revolutionized the teaching of Arabic in Egypt must see what the Perse school was doing with Latin. He spent hours in the classrooms there, brilliantly happy.

His friend the Rev. F. D. Browne, whose preparatory school at Lambrook in Berkshire was the one chosen that summer, gives a picture of Gairdner's unconventional methods of school-hunting.

> He arrived early one morning, and went from one classroom to another entirely on his own, sat down, listened, and in every case joined in the work going on. His comments to me afterwards were clever in the extreme. He seemed, in the short time at his disposal, to have summed up the good and bad points in every case. The staff were unanimous afterwards as to how nice and helpful he had been to them all! This has never been done here before or since. I do not think it *could* be done by any ordinary person. He invited confidence. Surely in his life's work he must go down to memory as a *great person*. In this little school world we always felt that this was so, and our reason above all others was that he made us feel that *we* were

doing a great work and that the little things of everyday life in a boys' school were great things.

II

Before he left England, Gairdner met his friend Canon MacInnes in London and learned news that altered his life. Canon MacInnes, the Secretary of the Egypt Mission, had been appointed to the Bishopric of Jerusalem, in which diocese Egypt still lay,[1] and Gairdner must now take the secretaryship of the mission with its combined leadership and servitude, its innumerable personal dealings and, alas ! its countless business details. "This I had to do," said Gairdner, to whom (although to have his friend as Bishop was a joy) the task was far from desired or desirable, more especially since no other provision could be made for all his former works.

He returned, then, to a strange new Egypt and an impossible task. But with an easy task in wartime who could have been content ?

Lord Kitchener had departed, martial law had been declared, the Lancashire cotton market was inaccessible, and when the Turkish War began early in November, agitators in Egypt promised the speedy arrival of Turkey across the Suez Canal. Turkish prisoners began to arrive in the capital instead of Turkish victors, but the same agitators gave out that these were "Indian troops dressed up to deceive the public." Who could tell ? One saw a platoon of Turkish prisoners come from the station, it was true ; but the next day one saw a string of ambulances full of British wounded. On the whole, the attitude of the average man in Egypt was fatalistic, but with a very real sense of irritation at the loss of cotton sales and the resultant acres of good cotton left unpicked.

The rich merchant and the *fellah* both felt this pinch, even though the Government devised a scheme for buying

[1] One of Bishop MacInnes's first episcopal acts was to appoint Gairdner to the honorary canonry of St. George's Cathedral, Jerusalem, which he had vacated on becoming Bishop.

in the crop, albeit at a lower price than that of Lancashire. Egypt was a land outwardly quiet but filled with rumours and dim mutterings. There was, as everywhere, a fury of readjustment when 20,000 Australians camped under the Pyramids and war hospitals sprang up everywhere. Members of the mission were called on for all sorts of service, medical or spiritual, and Gairdner was chaplain to a hospital.

The women missionaries of Palestine, too, sent out of that country by their consular authorities, arrived one by one in Egypt, for the most part having had to leave the bulk of their possessions. Some of these uprooted ones had to be sent to England with money matters and passages and special permits from the Residency arranged. Some did yeoman service in Egypt and some studied Arabic, but each arrival brought its interviews and correspondence. There was constant sudden responsibility. "I have been for a very long time indeed without any guidance as to how much money I should be sending to Palestine," Gairdner told his London secretary. "I am totally in the dark as to how far I am to go."

Then the tide that had set inward from Palestine set outward. "With the full concurrence of Bishop MacInnes and Gairdner I have applied for an Army chaplaincy in Egypt," wrote the Rev. R. F. McNeile. He never returned to the Mission. And others went, one by one, to chaplaincies, to hospitals, to soldiers' homes or Church Army huts, and always with the goodwill of the fewer and fewer left-behinds. Was it not the same in every British settlement throughout the world?

Gairdner was all ardour. Of course he demonstrated with maps the strategy of combined operations on various fronts, and he had an astonishing way of getting to the heart of a situation. It was hard to say how it was done; it was like his way of flashing across a room when something interested him at the other side of it. Somehow before you were aware of it he was *there*. An amusing instance of this took place when official Cairo was electrified to hear a thanksgiving for " a measure of success at sea " one Sunday morning at Matins.

Nothing was known " officially " in Cairo till Monday morning of the Battle of Jutland, but Gairdner, having got hold of the news through Arabic telegrams late on Saturday night, insisted that the chaplain must say a thanksgiving, which for most of that official congregation had the effect of " stop-press news."

Gairdner lectured considerably to the troops and enjoyed it—so, it seems, did they.

> I was hunting round for helpers to entertain five or six hundred convalescents in the Military Hospital at Boulac Dacrour [says his friend Brother Douglas Downs]. Temple never once refused, and gave the most interesting lectures. Nothing could equal his charm and good-fellowship. The men felt at once that they had a friend on the platform.
>
> He was expected to lecture at Kantara Camp [says Maurice Richmond], and in answer to a question he sent a brief note of subjects from which to select. It was as follows: Mohammed; Mohammedanism; The History of Egypt, ancient, middle or modern periods ; Modern Novelists and H. G. Wells ; Ancient and Modern Cosmogonies (early systems of Astronomy and the latest) ; The Causes of the War from Cæsar to Kaiser (race movements and European history) ; Some Shakespeare Plays ; R. L. Stevenson ; The Development and Structure of Music ; How the Hieroglyphics were deciphered. Such was the list on that half-sheet of paper, and he asked for half a day's notice before giving a lecture.

He intensely enjoyed a lecturing tour on the Palestine front during the summer of 1918, and next summer just missed a longer tour because, having urged his Arabic congregation to faithfulness through the hot weather, he would not leave them.

> I have had the offer [he told his wife] from the Army to be sent up lecturing right through all Palestine and

to Syria and perhaps as far as Konia in Turkey—and I have had to refuse it! After my pastoral letter I daren't leave St. Mary's.

"One of the things that struck me about Canon Gairdner when I came to live in his house in 1917," says a friend, Miss Isabel Scott Moncrieff, "was what a real sacrifice it must have been for him not to go to the war. When various padres whose work he was quietly doing (I suppose he did about four extra jobs) would come to Cairo clad in khaki, full of adventures, he was generously and genuinely interested in all their tales of the war. Indeed he seemed literally incapable of thinking ungenerously of anyone. A talk he gave one afternoon lingers in my mind. He was speaking about the patience of Christ, and he pointed out the difference between submissive inaction and this 'active patience' that goes steadily working on, running the race that is set before it, because it knows that *on the plane that counts* victory is already won. It was not so much the words he used, as the facts of his life that made this sermon so vivid and so true."

III

And indeed for the impossible task of those years he had need of patience. For in war-time who could hope for missionary recruits? And a recruit when he comes needs five years' Arabic training for all the higher work. One indeed who became a real friend joined him in 1915 ("I like him very much but, oh Manley, he's very far on in the thirties to make a good job of Arabic") but was soon swallowed up in chaplaincy and Church Army duties. "Salisbury Square" keeps in its files an official document describing Gairdner's duties at this time (as apart from the thousand extras due to the war). It makes dull reading, but for all the deadness of official précis it is a record of life that was not dully lived:

> He is Chairman of the Educational Committee and of the Evangelistic Committee. Has also to be in touch with the missionaries themselves and be

available for interviews at any time. From time t time goes down to Menoufia (a province of the Delta and spends some days at mission-stations ; is suppose to go regularly to the Sudan and last year spent a mont there, but has not been this year. There is the correspondence with the parent committee, with missionaries and others, besides all business correspondence and interviews with Government officials ; there i also the preparation for the conferences of the mission writing up of minutes, etc. Arrangements for meetings, special services, etc., have to be made and notice typed and sent off. A great deal of hospitality fall to the Secretary. Egyptian workers have to be visite in addition to the pastoral care of the Cairo congregation. As clergyman in charge of the Cairo Churc arranges services and does much of the preachin (in Arabic). Is also Choirmaster. Tries to kee in touch with this scattered congregation, visiting th sick, etc., and also arranging social afternoons fo the members. Is at present making a complete lis of all the children of the mission. Prayer-cycles o other aids to devotion must be got out for use o members. The organization of special Churc schemes, committees, editing *Church Notes*, settling disputes, making up quarrels, advising in law-suits, classes for inquirers and for confirmandi, special Bibl classes, daily prayers for workers and servants on the premises ; editing *Orient and Occident*, issuing o Arabic tracts, organizing distribution, editing English papers about the mission. And in linguistic matters, is superintendent of Arabic at the Cairo Study Centre, and Chairman of its Committee, lectures twice a week on Arabic, sets papers for examinations. Now and again contributes to *The Moslem World*, and is getting out a booklet on Arabic poetry and metres, and a chart on " Islamic History and Thought."

And yet though the tasks were far too many and some might have said too small, " He could not be enslaved," says Maurice Richmond, at this time a member of his household. "Whether it was through his lifelong love of music, to which he always had recourse, or from some deep fount from which music itself and his strong dramatic sense and love of art took their rise, he kept his zest in life, and the sense of his own spontaneous relatedness to its widely varying forms."

"His house in Cairo," says a war-time padre, "was like an oasis in the desert, full of friendliness and peace. I do not remember much of our conversations, only the sense of encouragement and inspiration derived from him."

The best tonic to a jaded Gairdner was a child, the younger the better! And on October 10th, 1915, came the crowning joy of his family life with the birth of his youngest child, Lilias Margaret Patria. Had he but a baby to come back to Temple Gairdner could stand a great deal of uncongenial toil.

> The adorable little wheezy high-pitched gusts of crying [surely few fathers reach that point of adoration!]. The girning, twitching little bundle trying hard to suck the middle finger of its left hand—most aristocratic filbert nails! Those little gurglish, gerny, wee-creaky sounds, murmurlets which I need not describe. *Salus Patriæ summa lex*, the well-being of Patria must now be our highest law.

In the summer of 1917 he wrote to his mother, "parabling of Patria":

> I will merely say that I have decided (and the decision has been borne out by the Pope of Rome by wireless) that of all little female angelettes from the eldest daughter of Abel (never mind Cain) down to the latest who will only just anticipate the last trump, she is *facile prima*. She gets on an average 937 kisses a day, and each one makes the next more necessary. Never has the word "yes" been so adorably rendered as "yush," spoken with the innocence of all Sir

Joshua's angelicals rolled into one. It is calculated that this one monosyllable must have cost her 4,368 kisses at least.

He enjoyed his babies. He enjoyed swimming adventures on the tricky Egyptian coast (more than once another life was owed to his strength and resolution in the sea). But what did he not enjoy?

> Beauty of sound, beauty of shape or colour or movement, beauty of scent, he loved [says Miss Scott-Moncrieff]. He enjoyed the pleasure of creative work, or the reception of the great work of other minds; he enjoyed children's parties, and mangoes, Charlie Chaplin, treacle tarts, swimming, bores, kedgeree, analysing sensations, geology, charades—one couldn't give a list of all the things he enjoyed. In three dimensions he savoured life and found it good. Mark you, there are twelve manner of fruit on the tree of life, and even in this world he seemed to have savoured most of them.

IV

It is none too easy to be the leader in an evangelical mission where everything is conducted on democratic principles, and the democracy consists entirely of strong-minded individuals, such as find their way to foreign mission-stations! By his relations with his colleagues a mission secretary must be judged.

In this matter Gairdner made his mistakes. It had been said of his father, "He never saw, nor ever could comprehend, even in argument, the working of baser passions or intrigues in any of those around him." And it was owing to a like habit of judging everybody by his own single-mindedness that Canon Gairdner made most of his mistakes in handling men. Perhaps one could hardly wish them unmade. It never occurred to him that a fellow-worker could allow care about position and prestige in the work, or the carving out of an individual lifework, or the securing of a little more than the regulation holiday, to guide his decisions. It was unthinkable and Gairdner did not reckon for it. Then, if the existence of some such weakness were forced upon him, there might be indignant expostulation, a sharp storm of surprise that would have been avoided by a man who calculated more upon the frailty of human nature. But Gairdner's storms could not last long, so far as he himself was concerned. "You and I seem to have had various episodes, but you know I think a lot of you," he would say, and after receiving a note of apology, he wrote :

> DEAR X,
>
> Just a line in haste—splendid ! Well done !—I am very much encouraged. And now, *en avant* ! and you may be very sure that as far as I am concerned everything painful is as though it has never been.
>
> Laus Deo Soli !
>
> When are you coming to see Patria ?

He demanded a great deal of those who were able to give it :

> I was so very keen to hear that you had risen to the occasion and accepted this call willingly. May I not put it to you in the light of a privilege ? It never can be everyone who is called upon to make the sacrifice on these occasions: it must always be one or two. Here is the chance to contribute something *more than life-service*, and you are the one honoured by the request to represent us in the sacrifice.

"Whether it was from his searching and exact study of God in Scripture or from years of deliberate communion with the living Christ," says Maurice Richmond, "or both these influences combined, Gairdner seemed to have within himself a living sense of right and wrong—of sin, seen against the background of God's holiness. One saw the aftermath of days when he had had to choose—to take sides. His continual occupation with the mind of Christ gave him a piercing integrity of judgment."

One friend observed of him : "He always answers what you think, and not what you say." "I felt he was my friend," says a member of the mission, "because I knew that he would put his finger upon the spot that was hurting and, having discovered the trouble, would give the right medicine, which was not always sweet to my taste ! Nevertheless I knew he was right."

His colleagues had much to bear during his secretariat from his unpredictable and unmethodical ways of working ; nor did they always find it easy to remember how much more of detail he was carrying than any one man should.

> He and we knew well that he was not cut out for the administrative part [says one to whom business failures were most irritating], but we welcomed him, knowing what a spiritual lead he would give us. "You will feel for me and I for you," he said as he took up the reins, and in times of exasperation it was a great thing to know that he was conscious of his failings and not cocksure and masterful.

Stories went round of days when, receiving a telegram to announce the arrival of some missionary, he would slip it into his pocket, pursue the task of the moment, and later, when the newcomer appeared, greet him with amazement and of course with no arrangements made for housing.

Yet with all this, when the burden of work now laid on his shoulders is remembered, one is less astonished at these lapses than at the number of detailed personal services that he *did* perform :

> Canon Gairdner met me at the station and circled round my *arabiyya* (cab) on his bicycle like a swallow, quoting Gilbert and Sullivan with a gleaming phiz.

> I remember specially a few minutes of prayer and blessing on the night I left for Omdurman, when he read Ps. 121 and commended me to God and saw me off at the station on the eve of the Mulid en Nebi.

I see him robed in the doctor's long white coat and entering the ward of the infectious hospital when I had been transported there with suspected smallpox. Later during that same exile came careful notes of Holy Week addresses, which he knew I should have liked to hear.

We remember well his wonderful kindness when he was fixing up about our wedding. He seemed to think falling in love was a wonderful thing. He thought it a tremendous thing too, when X asked him if he would take her father's place in the church. He gave me the impression that it was too mystical for words.

I was starting off for England and I did not pretend I was sorry [a colleague says]. He saw me off at the station and heard me say triumphantly, "Thank Goodness I'm off at last." I saw a flicker of surprise and pain go over his face, and when I got to my boat I found a telegram on my berth : "Your labour is not in vain in the Lord." It was more than I deserved.

And there was a regular ministry of little notes, on all sorts of scraps of paper—notes of thanks or congratulation or sympathy.

Thanking he brought to a fine art, and "I hate ingratitude like the very devil" is a true Gairdnerian phrase.

I was once on board ship with a railway official from Cairo [a colleague says]. He told me the Canon came one day and asked his advice about a journey and took his departure. Half an hour later he reappeared in the same office and said, "Oh, when I got home I remembered that I had not thanked you for your trouble. Many thanks !"

The strain under which he was living made itself felt not in any nervous impatience or short temper, but in a sort of compensating mental escape, when his mind became oblivious of the drudgery and fled to its own realms ; or sometimes in a half-pathetic whimsicality.

> I used to feel that there was part of him that came uppermost sometimes that was extraordinarily elusive, almost " Peter Pannish " [says a friend]. At those times you just had to let him go, and then at others he was just on the same plane as oneself, and would be with one as simply as a child, yet with the wisdom of the wise.

Thoroughly bored at luncheon with two fellow-missionaries and never a child in the room, he escaped into whimsicality. He launched into a story of a missionary in India who was in the habit of retiring longer than others for the afternoon siesta and gained the reputation of being a lover of ease, till a fellow-missionary venturing to reprove her found that she spent the whole time in prayer.

> My friend and I uttered some obvious platitudes about not judging by appearances [says one of his companions], when the Canon with a twinkle in his eye remarked, " Unfortunately the lady did not speak the truth." At this our indignation rapidly changed sides, until the Canon finally remarked, " Indeed the story isn't true at all. I've just made it up."

Another escape from the tyranny of things he found in the hours he sometimes snatched in the desert, " and so open and frank and fearless was he," says a comrade of those days, " that he would ask a friend to share his solitude with him and some hours would be spent in self-examination, in mutual confession and prayer. One saw the childlike humility of Gairdner on those days, as he attempted ruthlessly to lay bare his own motives, his pride, his failures, his self-satisfaction, his want of faith. If one tried to put a better construction on one of his confessions he would have none of it. 'I have sinned most grievously. Have mercy upon me, O Lord, for Thy great Name's sake.' "

V

And the shepherding of the "little flock" went on. Gairdner had gone home in 1914, forespent with spiritual agonizing over a traitor whom it had been necessary to suspend from the Church.

> I suppose for the best part of a year [he told a friend] I directed almost all of my prayers against that man. I say "against," because he was still in the Society's employ, still unrepentant, and still unreachable. We had asked God to mend him or end him with the year. Well, on *December 31st* (1914) I got at the facts which a few weeks later brought him down with a crash.
>
> Very shortly after I arrived in Cairo in February 1915 [says Maurice Richmond], Gairdner took me out for a long walk in the desert. He told me that the discovery of the sinuous, deceptive, evil, malignant and underground eating away what it had taken years of Christian work to build up had for the time been felt by him so deeply that he had almost cabled to me not to come and work in Cairo.

The traitor was faced with the facts. "Since then," Gairdner said four months later, "the Lord has been dealing very hardly with him and I believe He has made a new man of him."

"Not long after Easter," Maurice Richmond says, "Gairdner went down to Alexandria to have an interview with X, which he had in the chapel of St. Mark's church. Something said at a Good Friday service on forgiveness and re-creation had come with a 'boom of power' to Gairdner, and he hoped it would be possible to put a term to the period of excommunication which they had been compelled to lay upon X. The journey down to Alexandria simply to see that man and have the interview with him in St. Mark's is an instance of the unreckoning price he was ready to pay for reconciling men with God."

A year later Gairdner could say:

> We simply had to fight a spiritual fight. When the attack passed and we counted our losses, two or three were missing—alas ! ingloriously. Nevertheless, we refused to give up hope of these men. We pursued them with secret prayer. And what I want to tell you is that every single one of these men has separately and individually and in strange and wonderful ways been dealt with by God, been smitten by His discipline, been convicted of his sin, and has come to me beseeching to be received back and to be assured of the pardon and absolution of God.

VI

As secretary of the mission Gairdner lived through war years when work had to be kept going by all sorts of makeshifts and improvisations. There was very little chance of carrying out any creative policy. " Some who were expecting a new colleague to relieve strain have gone on with the strain and without the colleague," he said; " indeed the most serious danger that faces missionary work in the next few years is, in our estimation, not the collapse of missionary financial support, but what we might call neglected dilapidations, over-subjection of missionary staffs to wear and tear without repair, to depletions without reinforcing." Still, he could not work without a thought-out plan, and in 1916 he and his colleagues produced a *Scheme for the Policy of the Mission.* Gairdner, with that love of " getting back to first principles " which his colleagues half-laughed at and wholly respected, urged them all to " hypothetize our evacuating Egypt and then see what the objections are, and from that build up our reasons for staying and the work we stay to do." The common thinking done in the production of this scheme of work (which was printed and officially adopted) clarified many issues and united the thoughts and plans of the mission.

For the work in the Sudan (also under his general care) Gairdner had a great love and wide plans—audaciously vide for days when, as he said, the mission was near to 'ade away from sheer attenuation. "The extreme mportance of the Sudan minutes" was always emphasized by him. "The Egypt Conference feels that there is still a chance of doing in the Sudan what we never did in Egypt, what perhaps we never could have done, viz. to set our impress upon a national education."

And in his visits to the Sudan the old Gordon love returned upon him.

The wife of the Governor-General had asked the school-children of our schools up to the palace, to spend the afternoon. I accompanied the river-steamer which had been sent to convey the children up from Omdurman. We were on the very track of Gordon's "penny steamers," whose evolutions he watched with such anxiety from the roof of that palace. The signal is given and the children file in through the gateway, pass the cloisterlike hall, and go out into the glorious tropical garden behind. Into the grounds through which on that morning the yelling crowd of dervishes had rushed with their spears "to the palace" trotted the little children to spend their happy afternoon on the lawns among the date-palms and tropical trees. And this year completes the thirty-three, the *one generation* which has seen all the changes since the tragedy. And I have eaten in the very room where he walked up and down in the hopeless night; have stepped over the very landing where he came out to meet the Dervish spears.

All his hours of secretarial toil for the Sudan would seem to Gairdner a cheap price for that experience.

CHAPTER XV

ARTIST

1918–1924

This Mr. Standfast was he whom the pilgrims found upon his knees in the enchanted ground.—*John Bunyan.*

I

WITH 1918 came peace for the combatants, but for Egypt, the non-combatant, no peace.

Gairdner was sent for by his Society to renew contacts after the war and had the joy of Christmas holidays with his two schoolboys in England.

> Those golden four weeks [he wrote afterwards to one of the boys concerned]—the afternoon teas with buttered toast and jam ! . . . That wonderful walk to the early service under the frosty stars . . . the bathroom with my beasticles in the cold dark mornings . . . and the journey to Stratford when we first felt we were absolutely alone together !

On his return to Cairo in the spring he found the Nationalist risings under Saad Zaghloul Pasha filling the town with fear and tumult.

> Things were pretty sulphurous here when I arrived on April 15th, and before that they had had an anxious time with noisy and ugly-looking crowds actually passing our house and shots frequently heard. But all missionaries and Egyptian fellow-workers have behaved splendidly.

For the next few years he was to look out anxiously on the seething Near Eastern world. "I cannot

magine," he wrote later to his friend Professor Mas-
ignon, "that you are any more satisfied than I am at
he way outward events have been going, whether in
Anatolia, or Syria, or Palestine or the West, as con-
lucted by the Foreign Offices of the world."

As for his own work he was of course eagerly awaiting relief. The thought of the Literature Department, which he was unable to touch, brought groans. "Such work imperatively needs time and undistractedness," he wrote. "How fatally hampered I am by our short-handedness !"

He came to a friend one day with a haggard face to say that he must "close down" *Orient and Occident*, not because its circulation was failing, but because he could not find time to make it as good as it should be, and the printer's price was to be raised £100.

"Destroy it not, for a blessing is in it," was in effect the reply, and it was saved by a special gift from friends of £100, with the condition that he would carry it on for one more year. The discovery that his friends cared about his magazine was the tonic he needed. The Church had but one Temple Gairdner and one *Orient and Occident*, and it is painful to think that she came within £100 of losing that magazine, the child of so great endeavour.

In this state of struggle it was with thankfulness indeed that Gairdner welcomed his colleague, the Rev. W. W. Cash, D.S.O., who had done distinguished work as Assistant Principal Chaplain during the war, and now came to take over the secretariat of the mission.

The very thought of such relief brought comfort, and Gairdner turned to the reorganization of his magazine (this time he associated a board of editors from other missions with himself) and to arrangements for teaching Arabic to the new American missionaries who swarmed in after the war. But all too soon he found that the expected relief was at best but very partial, glad though Mr. Cash and his comrades would have been to see him free. The new secretary could only slowly disentangle himself from the aftermath of his great work during the war, and when he was freed of that he found himsel secretary of the mission not only in Egypt and the Sudar but in Palestine, with all the delicate negotiations involvec in re-starting the life of a war-ridden country. Palestine inevitably absorbed much of his thought, even when he was in Cairo. He did all that one man could do in his vast field, and left a deep mark on the whole work. But he was not able to relieve Gairdner, whose house was in the same compound with the Society's office, from the daily clamour of telephone calls and small business details and small urgent decisions that must be made by the man on the spot.

Next year, for nine months of the twelve, Gairdner was again secretary of the mission, the only difference being that he was now described as " acting-secretary."

> All sorts of people used to come to ask his help [says his friend the Rev. Girgis Bishai]. I remember finding one day one Moroccan, two Upper Egyptians, two Cairenes, two men from the Delta, two Syrians who were Latin Catholic and one Greek Catholic all waiting to see him.

And Gairdner himself said to his secretary in London :

> My centrality and availability and perhaps a certain plaguy versatility which may be shallow enough, but has proved useful to C.M.S. and must be accepted as a thread in the web of God's providence—these explain many time-consuming yet utterly ineluctable little calls. I am *there*. I am not like Toop monopolized by an institution ; nor like Cash by a gigantic double-secretarial task involving frequent absence ; nor like a succession of recent figures who pass off the scene before they become really available.

It was too true.

" Gairdner became the residuary legatee of works begun and left, of pastorates vacated, and the standing arbiter for little matters that never should have reached him," says Maurice Richmond. "We saw his great creative genius cut to pieces." But Gairdner's friend Dr. Lasbrey, who loves him well, can say, "I don't know that I would have had him otherwise. His life was something like the life of Jesus. . . . He also spent a lot of time in settling the quarrels of catechists and other petty things, little things which He made glorious."

II

Precisely in these disappointing years when he was nominally set free but really still the slave of a hundred details, came two heavenly reliefs to the man whose spirit fed so hungrily on beauty—two glories, one of sorrow and the other of pure joy.

The sorrow, of which Temple Gairdner would yet speak with joy shining from his eyes, was the "spring passing" of his sister Ailsa, beautiful of body and of soul. She died in early March of 1921, and the divine-human beauty of her last days, the haunting poetry of them, made a spiritual springtime for her brother whenever he thought of her, and an escape to his soul from the tyranny of little things.

> Don't you see and feel a perfect atmosphere of warm radiant loveliness, holy beauty, *lux perpetua*, how it rises round her, like an aureole, an *atmosphere* of warm light, like Dante's Virgin and the Paradisal Rose? Is it *not* the Beloved calling to her, "Rise up, my love, my fair one, and come away"? . . . Our sister of spring.

And so he would escape into the Communion of Saints.

And his other relief came through the sudden flowering of the dramatic power and insight that was in the warp and woof of him. It was one of the marks of his mind that if he pondered a scene, he saw it less as a spectacle from outside than through the minds of the chief actors.

And he had taught himself in his holiest meditations to try to see from inside Another's mind.

> How fertile is this looking at Christ's life from its internal side ! I feel sure that the way to progress is reverently to ask God to enable one to *act* Christ in one's imagination (guided by the narrative), and as it were live through those two years, with the eyes shut, in heart and mind.

And now, with a sudden expansion, all this came to the flower. "I suddenly got inspired to dramatize some of the Bible narratives," he said. And his holiday moments and journeys were snatched for this rush of creative work. He first wrote *Joseph and his Brothers, an Old Testament Passion Play.*

> I think back [he told his mother], to that Sunday evening on the French boat off Port Said, when the closing scenes of *Joseph* sprang into being in the mind, and the following day (at sea) when with headlong speed, without intermission from dawn to midnight, they dashed themselves on to paper, and the finale the closing scena, was imagined down to its last detail after the whole ship was quiet for the night, and committed to the *last* sheet of paper under the only remaining available binnacle light, while I sat in the passage by the cabin doors, on the floor.

Then, he being in the vein, or, as some would even dare to say, "in the Spirit," the plays streamed forth. He published them in Arabic in his magazine and in English through the good help of the S.P.C.K.

Passover Night, *The Last Passover Night*, *Saul and Stephen*, and after these :

> I am now bursting with a new drama, the first sketch of which came to me like lightning during the first lesson at Newport one Sunday—the Hezekiah and Sennacherib story. . . . The thinking out of the drama elicited the fact that there is a puzzle in

FACSIMILE OF AIR WRITTEN BY CANON GAIRDNER FOR ARABIC GIRLS' VOICES AT THE END OF HIS PLAY OF "JOSEPH AND HIS BROTHERS."

The last words of Judah in the play are, "The forgiveness of God! The peace of God." The choir responds, "Great, great, is the Truth of God, the forgiveness of God, the peace of God. Amen!"

regard to Hezekiah's character and his relation to Isaiah which the big commentators are simply silent about.

" Isaiah and Hezekiah," that veritable epic, practically forgotten by the Jews though it is so much grander than either of their other two national epics, the Exodus and the Restoration after Babylon. The more I reflect the more moved I am. . . . I wish that some Shakespeare could get hold of my crude materials and make of it—what Shakespeare made of his Holinshed, his Plutarch and the rest.

A friend remembers the writing of this too, when in the first hours of furlough after the stresses of a Cairo year the scenes came " into the eye and prospect of his soul " as he sat " on the third-class deck of a Mediterranean steamer between Alexandria and Brindisi, writing, writing, writing, oblivious to passing meals and dancing sailors and playing children, as hour after hour the characters came to life under his pen. A thread was tied round the manuscript at Brindisi—to his wife for typing, and so to the publisher."

And there were more dreams ahead. Saul, King of Israel, what a theme for tragedy ! He strode the desert, too, planning a drama of Job. It was to be a thing austere and mystical.

III

But Temple Gairdner could not make a play for paper use alone. It burned in him until his friends had shared it. " Readings " were constantly organized.

I remember [says Mr. A. P. Bolland, late of the Sudan Government] a crowded darkened upper chamber in Sharia el Falaki with one shaded reading-lamp illuminating his earnest face as he read his *Saul and Stephen*. And a somewhat similar memory is of an evening at Bishop's House when coming home late one night I heard a voice in the study, and there was Gairdner reading to his beloved Bishop his latest play

—I think it was *King Hezekiah*—and the Bishop, tired with a long and busy day, serenely slumbering by his side.

An Oxford friend keeps a memory of Gairdner reading *King Hezekiah* in a London drawing-room. "He said the banqueting scene was modelled on a 'Trinity drunk,' and gave it with such dramatic abandon that passers-by under the windows, open wide to the summer night, began to stop and gaze up at the house!"

But even to read a play was not enough to a man who was actor to his finger-tips; a play was made to be played. And suddenly it seemed to him that he had found a new thing. His Egyptian friends were undeveloped as regards most forms of art, but like himself they were natural dramatists. Why should not this gift of his and theirs be offered to Christ? Why should not the truth of Christ be *played* into the life of the Egyptian people by a group of dedicated Christian Egyptian players? He learned with eagerness how an Indian missionary would take out a group of boys and by the light of a few bicycle lamps act out with them the Bible stories for a crouching group of villagers. Here was a service that fitted the genius of Egyptian people.

He trained some boys of the C.M.S. School, Old Cairo, to act his play of *Joseph and his Brothers*. It was done at first as a contribution to the life of the school, and the head master said, "The effect on the boys went deeper than I ever had anticipated."

But why not go further and make a true evangelistic effort in the manner of the mystery-plays of the Middle Ages? The idea developed in several minds, and on the last day of 1920 he wrote to his Society in London:

> We have been a good deal led out on this dramatic tack as a possible new method of presenting religious truth in Egypt, and the boys are at present rehearsing the whole drama of *Joseph* in Arabic. . . . By the special wish of Bishop Gwynne, we are going to make it a regular sort of passion-play or religious performance

THE FINAL RECONCILIATION SCENE AT THE END OF "JOSEPH AND HIS BROTHERS."
Played in St. Mary's Church, Cairo, 1922.
(The photograph represents the scene as it was when the air facing p. 256 was sung.)

with no applause, but with prayers, hymns, etc., and *in church.*

We enacted *Joseph* in St. Mary's church [he said] five times, to 1,700 people in all, an extraordinary effect being made. Like an atmosphere about all was the beauty of the heavenly story.

It was indeed an unforgettable scene in the spiritual beauty of St. Mary's church, which hushed the people even before the play began. It was set out with no scenery and therefore no fuss of shifting scenes, on a bare and simple stage, backed by the chancel screen and the great rood-cross. The whole picture was steeped in the brilliant yet mellow light of an Egyptian winter day, and at the greatest moments of the story a touch of song stole down divinely from a hidden choir in the gallery.

The audience was hushed and very still; many, both Moslem and Christian, were moved to tears.

The place vibrated with the spirit of the simplicity and passion which breathed through the play [says Maurice Richmond]. At the close, as the church emptied, and the spell cast by the play gradually lifted, a figure in a black cassock was left kneeling in his own place, his features motionless in prayer. It was the author-producer. The drama in Cairo had been consecrated at last, and steeped in the spirit of prayer. *O si sic omnes!*

That evening a letter reached Gairdner from a member of the audience:

It was a great, rich gift of beauty that you gave to Cairo to-day. For me the best moment came when we reached "Each of you, each is beloved" (said by Joseph in a final reconciliation scene when he gives to each of his brethren the kiss of peace), and for a moment it *was* the Voice of Jesus, and I looked round the faces in the pews, thinking "They are His brethren, and He is coming to kiss each one."

"The only two things which can be put in the same class with this," said a visitor, "are *Parsifal* at Bayreuth, and the *Passion Play* at Oberammergau."

And Gairdner, full of deep contentment, said:

> I thank God and I thank those who helped us by their prayers, that *Joseph* has been a deep success—beyond our dreams. Everything was so novel, so untried, so daring. Naturally almost everybody jibbed at the idea of having it in a church. But afterwards I think the general verdict was '*Never anywhere but in a church.*' It is certainly a wonderful experience when a thing which was conceived within the mind, and there remained for two years, takes shape and colour and visibility and is quietly born into the world of the actual.

That was one of the most exquisite moments of his life, and when the young men of his Arabic congregation came spontaneously to ask him to train them in the play of *Saul and Stephen*, his cup was full. He saw his vision, his inspiration as it seemed to him, passing out into the life of the Church that he loved. Through consecrated acting, in an atmosphere of prayer and reverence, Egypt should *see* the Gospel.

IV

Suddenly at the height of this creative joy came a short, sharp arrest.

There was fear on the part of some representatives of a committee of the Society at home (those days are past and among the leaders to-day reigns a spirit ready to reverence and accept the gifts of God with joy) lest the idea of plays in church should prove too shocking to supporters of the Society and money gifts should be lost. And fear and "common sense" were allowed to rule. Gairdner was told that this method of evangelism was costing too much of his time, and he must confine himself to simple colloquial plays (not in churches) for the peasants at the hospital. "I thought that any of their other evangelistic methods, their schools and hospitals, consumed far *more* time," said an outside observer.

Only those with something of an artist's gift can know what the ruling cost Gairdner when he had at last escaped into his natural world and milieu. It killed his unborn dramas ere their birth. It took the spring and the creative joy out of him and left him in mind appreciably an older man.

But with the heavenly compensation which never fails the man whose life is hid in Christ, that beauty which he now surrendered from the life of his mind was reborn in the life of his spirit.

For his joy was not only torn from him; he surrendered it. A friend remembers meeting Gairdner in the train shortly after the verdict and offering him condolence. "How awfully sorry I felt for you when I heard that your Bible dramas were to be stopped. I know what I should feel if anyone tried to tear poetry out of my life!"

"Oh," said Gairdner very quietly, "it is just part of the price one has to pay for being a member of a Society; there are other sides to it that are compensations."

And the spiritual mastery of his surrender is shown by the fact that he did not, as most artist natures would have done, turn away with a sense of sickening from the limited sphere that was now prescribed to his dramatic work.

He took great pride in the work and workers at Old Cairo Mission Hospital, and for them he now gladly wrote his *Good Samaritan*, a little play so simple as to seem almost artless, and of clear spiritual beauty. This was acted in the common language of daily talk and in the open air. It ends with a procession of pilgrims on the Jericho–Jerusalem road, a singing group of Galileans escorting their Leader to Jerusalem. "The procession is seen, but the figure of Christus will be indistinguishable. For the pilgrims' song" (an Arabic poem by

Gairdner himself) " I have taken a Hebrew melody from Bruch's *Kol Nidrei.*"

> I remember [says a Cairo resident] I noticed a grizzled, bearded old *fellah* with a handsome careworn face, sitting at the back among a lot of his fellows. I was told he was a Moslem patient of the hospital. Presently I noticed that he had disappeared. Soon after, the procession of palm-bearers passed, praising our Lord, and there at the tail of it I saw my old man carrying his branch. I think it was the most moving experience I ever had.

CHAPTER XVI

IN CO-OPERATION

1921–1928

I have noticed that there is generally a nemesis about any concealment policy. "The truth will thee deliver, it is no drede."—*From a letter of Temple Gairdner on co-operative enterprises.*

I

"In the year 1921," Gairdner said, "I rose up in wrath and gathered my colleagues about me, and declared that we could not and should not go on like this any longer: in fact, that we must get on or get out."

The cause of this outburst was the condition of the Arabic Anglican Church. Gairdner saw that the future of the Kingdom of Christ in Moslem lands rested less on missionaries than on a Church of the children of those lands which should be "a home for Christ's converts from Islam" and a spear-head in evangelization. Of what urgency, therefore, was the training of such a Church! And through years of strain, that training had been neglected or carried through in hand-to-mouth fashion. Now, in 1921, he challenged the mission with this duty.

> We decided to have one real shot at getting *on*: to take stock of our members, quasi-members, adherents, see who was who, have a campaign of explaining what the Anglican Church is, what it stands for in Egypt, what is its order, liturgy, aim, spirit: regularize, take hold, take stock, rekindle, and finally ordain the first Egyptian pastor, as a first step towards building up a really indigenous non-foreign Church.

But why a branch of the Anglican Church?

The Church Missionary Society in Egypt has always tried to be a mission of help to the Coptic Church, and Gairdner would gladly have seen it solely this, winning back Moslems to the ancient national Church, and baptizing them into her membership.

But practical experience showed that the Coptic Church had still too great a heritage of fear from days of persecution. She was yet so far from being a home for converts from Islam that her bishops or priests would sometimes pass on Moslems won to Christ by the good life of a Coptic family to the Anglican Mission for Baptism, not themselves wishing to incur the danger of Moslem retaliations. It was decided therefore to retain the Anglican life and order as a home for converts against that day, of which Gairdner never wholly despaired (though appearances were hard against it), "when there shall emerge a reformed Orthodox Coptic Church, showing at last those two lost 'notes' of a Church—evangelical militancy and Catholicity."

And if there were to be such an Anglican body in Egypt (though Gairdner never dreamed that this would be Egypt's final way of life and worship), "the grand aim," he told his colleagues, "should be to raise a truly militant, evangelical and therefore evangelistic Church, however small, a truly Catholic Church with power to absorb and unify the most diverse elements, and gifted with historical order and reverent, inspiring and liturgical services."

To build such a Church out of mutually mistrustful elements, Egyptian, Palestinian, European, welding them into a common life and love, was work for a leader. Judged by numbers it was a very small task, but into it entered all the problems that beset Church life in a diocese of mixed nationalities, of confusing and difficult ecclesiastical relations with other Communions both of East and West and in a diocese that lives its life under the hostile shadow of Islam.

For leadership in this task the mission saw but one man

(whom they hoped to have released from the secretariat in Palestine for the purpose). "It was unanimously felt that the Rev. W. W. Cash, and he alone, is the worker with the requisite gift and vocation to be the clerical-missionary-superintendent of the new scheme and policy." And this was endorsed by the Society at home in 1922.

II

Gairdner now turned creatively to what he called "much necessary, indispensable and important inter-mission work." He believed in co-operation. "You know on the field we must rub along with all whose *hearts*, not necessarily their heads, are set in the same direction. That is a fundamental law with me," he said; but he sometimes groaned because his central position made him in those days invariably the man picked out to represent his Society in such works.

And half pathetically he said to a secretary at home:

> When you and X twitted me a bit about the way *Joseph* had "interrupted my proper duties," I said nothing, but wondered if either of you remembered the colossal inroads into my time, all that autumn, of Council and Nile Mission Press and other inter-mission work.

The great thing now a-building was the Egypt Inter-Mission Council. "After prolonged negotiations, the tale of hours spent in which I should not like to compute," he said, "this Council was at last formed. Our hazards, crises, despairs and hopes were distantly comparable to the Irish negotiations."

Nothing caused Gairdner to girn and groan so much as the sight of some little group in a committee determined to listen, to learn all, but never to commit themselves or their society or to make a positive contribution. Such an attitude (and committee workers in all countries have met it) seemed to him a negation of Christianity, each man looking to his own (society's) things rather than to the things of others.

"Gairdner counted more than any other one man in inter-mission work," says Mr. George Swan, the Secretary of the Council. And this although his superficial manner as an acquaintance was not good, but rather the reverse.

My earlier impressions [says his much-admired Dr. C. R. Watson] were that he was so absorbed with his own views and ideas as to be indifferent to the views and feelings of others. I know whole groups who were frankly afraid of him. Approaching him as I happened to do through some of these circles, I found him in reality extremely considerate and the very opposite of what I feared. I know of more than one occasion when he straightway sought out the man whom he heard to have been offended and, with a humility which often seemed to me more than was due, he tried to clear away the misunderstanding. The Gairdner I knew was brilliant intellectually but also humble and tender-hearted beyond measure.

He had [says Mr. Swan] a real catholicity of heart. Most of us have so few real friends. He had many, he was unstinted in his friendship, reliable, transparently sincere, a real friend. And that Nathanael-like quality of Gairdner, the unmasking of guards, the sense that you have to do with a perfectly honest man, is in the long run the quality that makes co-operation possible.

III

The unity of the Church of Christ was one of the passions of Gairdner's life.

In Egypt he found all the traditional hostilities of centuries, in a land where a man's religious communion is also his social and legal community, and too often a sort of armed camp against the possible aggressions of any other communion and community.

During his early days in Cairo, Gairdner wrote :

It takes faith, believing in Christ, His Church and ministry, here in this Moslem city. But on my word, it takes *more* faith to believe in these when one thinks of the Church itself as it exists here—sect upon sect, each more intolerant than its neighbour, each practically excommunicating the others in the name of the One Lord—and that in the face of an Islam which loathes all alike. It makes one feel passionately careless of ecclesiastical or doctrinal niceties and simply desirous to do something to promote spirituality and righteousness here in Egypt. "The Church of Christ"—shades of Paul, of John, of Athanasius! O Lord, how long? And why is it that this grotesque travesty mocks these names and Thee and tempts us to feel that all is and has been empty?"

It was natural that this Gairdner should from the beginning have been one of the leaders of a "Fellowship of Unity" organized in 1921:

Equally with Richmond the cause was absolutely a part of him, part of his missionary outlook and ideals, of his daily thinking [says Raymond Whitwell, who was for some time secretary of the fellowship]. He was the specialist in regard to the Coptic Church, with an intimate personal knowledge of its reform leaders, and a firsthand acquaintance with its internal politics.

He worked and prayed vehemently for the Coptic Church [says one of his Coptic friends, Abadir Effendi Hakim]. I last saw him during his last summer holiday on earth. He made an appointment with some of his friends for the cause of Coptic reform, and in spite of a night of high fever he received them (he being in bed), and after fervent prayer gave them his best of thoughts and love.

At one meeting of the Fellowship of Unity at a time of great crisis in the Church [Mr. Whitwell says], he spoke for some time on Coptic affairs, and the Committee listened almost spellbound. Later, when he found he had delayed at the Committee so long as to make him late for a dinner engagement, to the distress of his wife, his "dash it all!" was very heartfelt. He was never more human than at such moments!

His last visit to the School of Oriental Studies must surely have been on February 17th, 1928, when at great cost to himself, both in preparation of material and delivery, he gave a Friday lecture on the Coptic Church. The attendance was less than a dozen, and quite half belonged to his own Society, but he gave of his very best. His voice was very weak, and as he stood in the corner of the lecture-room it was with difficulty he could carry through. But the subject was a lifelong interest to him, and his interpretation of the patriarchate controversy was an illumination. He told how the reformers, with unscrupulous and moneyed opponents in high places, yet believed in their cause, because "we are the only ones who can pray about our plans."

At the conferences of the Fellowship of Unity, many-minded and many-tongued, Gairdner was a familiar figure. He often acted as Arabic-English interpreter, either for the whole conference or sitting beside some individual member. Maurice Richmond remembers him "simply eviscerating" a long pamphlet by Archbishop Nicola in modern Greek and preparing a masterly digest of it; and Mrs. Gairdner recalls her husband's sudden astonishing request to her to go to a Greek lawyer's office and sing hymn-tunes to him! Gairdner had been charged, in collaboration with his friend Maître Zahos, a Greek avocat in Cairo, to select tunes and words of hymns of identical meaning and metre in Greek, Arabic, French and English, which could be sung simultaneously in four languages. "He was very exceptionally sympathetic to our Greek people," says Maître Zahos, "and he had a great esteem for them and worked with them in the putting into Greek language of many English hymns, for he desired that in the meetings of the Fellowship our divine language should be heard."

It was in the committee work of the movement and in

two or three group discussions held between Anglicans and Presbyterians (Egyptian and American) that much of his closest work was done. "Sloppiness" of thought he hated, and he had no use for any synthesis reached by ignoring half the facts. He saw "the intense importance of denominational distinctions," even while working for unity, "because they enshrine fragments of truth which are necessary to the perfect whole."

"I believe his greatest contribution to the Fellowship of Unity is that he *refused to stop thinking*," says Maurice Richmond. He also refused to stop hoping. In this matter, as in the Moslem question, had not the Church, if she chose to draw upon them, all the resources of the Spirit of God?

> Unity, when it comes [he said[1]] must be something richer, grander, more comprehensive than anything which we can see at present. It is something into which and up to which we must grow, something of which and for which we must become worthy. We need to have sufficient faith in God to believe that He can bring us to something higher and more Christlike than anything to which we at present see a way.

IV

The year 1923 dealt Gairdner the greatest blow of his working life since the death of Douglas Thornton.

It began with brightness. He was especially happy in some "Parents' Conferences" (with inimitable dramatic illustrations of different sorts of child discipline or undiscipline) held in several centres of Arabic Church life, and was dreaming of an exhibition of educational toys, at which he would undoubtedly have been showman-in-chief! And it was a joy to him that his new friend and colleague, Mr. S. A. Morrison, had shouldered evangelistic work in direct apostolic succession to Thornton. None responded so quickly as Gairdner to

[1] Quoting from one of the commissions of the Edinburgh 1910 Conference.

any joyful stimulus. "There are many things which make work in the Egypt Mission exceptionally delightful," he now wrote: "a Bishop great in himself and in co-operation; splendid colleagues; peace, harmony and *philadelphia* in the Mission; fine workers in other missions and abundant co-operation; great Egyptian fellow-workers, . . . and lastly an ideal home. What lack I yet? Nothing in point of blessings."

And now too he saw hope of returning at last to Arabic literature.

His annual reports for the past years had made monotonous reading on the subject:

> "I confess it moves on at a snail's pace."

The marvel was that it had moved at all. But at last he saw hopes of better things, for a colleague already knowing some Arabic was to join him for this very work. He envisaged a new sort of apologetic through literature. What was now needed was a literature which took account of the scientific life, and the Biblical research and criticism of the West, as they would be seen through Moslem eyes in Arabic newspapers. He suggested "Tracts for the Times" meeting new situations. And he planned a wider and more human literature of story, drama, poetry and picture. He made a memorandum outlining all this, which was to be undertaken when his new colleague came. And in his wife's absence in England he spent his summer holiday (unwisely of course) at Old Cairo ministering in the little church and burying himself in some of the literature tasks, for which he could never find the time in that central city house of his. He sent his literature colleague a list of these holiday tasks, winding up whimsically:

> When September comes shall I not revert to be the mere drudge of the casual daily calls? Oh, let me use this last ten days. . . . Sometimes I feel so disgusted that I seriously wonder what I am doing in Egypt: except that it is easier to get people to make

guttural noises for me here than in England in connection with some wretched phonetic book. Well, perhaps that's sufficient reason.

I sometimes think my real function in life is not to preach or teach at all, but simply to listen to music, to make some myself, to watch drama and read books and do a very little writing myself, and to write amusing letters to the children.

Life is odd.

Clearly here was a man in need of the summer holiday that he had not taken. He welcomed his new comrade with zest, but he was a tired man that autumn, and in October he had news of the deaths within thirteen days of one another of Lady Gairdner and his youngest brother.

For Gairdner death was only incidental in the pilgrimage of the souls he loved. "To essential Christianity," he said, "it is only a mode of life."

I think that in Elysium all is understood. And in bliss are their eyes still gazing at CLEARNESS, like Arran on a still, clear evening after rain: they see clearly, and are seen clearly.

Yet quietly as he accepted and surmounted this sorrow, it was a hard preparation for the blow that fell at the beginning of November, a blow that sent Gairdner reeling, when Mr. Cash, the leader-to-be of the whole scheme of Arabic Church development, wrote very sadly to say that owing to his wife's health return to Egypt was impossible.

Cash dealt us and himself too, poor chap, I doubt not, a staggering blow. To me its dreadfulness did not consist in the loss of another, and the best, of our small men's staff, but in the thought that this retirement seemed to land us in bankruptcy. Neither need I labour what this means to me personally ; how it is dislocating my life and work.

Gairdner was then a tired man and his well-known buoyancy for once seemed to fail him. "I lost my normal sleep after getting Cash's news," he said. At first fearing that the secretariat might once again be laid on him, he wrote long, almost frantic letters pointing out how much of the secretarial work was really a layman's task. Could not the Society find some godly, retired Indian civilian who would take up this type of work? Then, to his wondering admiration, his friend Dr. Lasbrey, with the burden of a great work already upon him, volunteered to take the secretaryship also.

> He once told me [Gairdner said] that his decision to take the burden of the secretaryship, with *all* that that meant to him and his wife and children, was largely in order to set me free from an unsuitable task to tackle certain essential work. I can never forget that. It seems a wonderful thing for a man to have had done for him by another.

Henceforth he was less heavy-hearted, for nothing cheered him like affection, but a second burden was yet on his mind. Had not the Committee decided "that Mr. Cash and he alone was the worker of the requisite gift and vocation" to carry through the plans for Egyptian Church development? And, failing him, there was none else but Gairdner. Yet Gairdner was even then launching, as he told his son, "an enormously extended scheme of literature development, of which X and I were to be the equal and sole leaders." To lead the new life of the Arabic Church would mean "my virtual defection from literature, a cruel disappointment. I have felt this keenly and painfully."

The decision lay between his usefulness to the Church's whole work in the Moslem world if he became an apostle by literature and the need of him to guide the life and growth of the little Egyptian Church in its most formative years. It was a hard enough decision to himself, it must have been harder to his Society at home when the following letter was sent (of course without reference to Gairdner) by the Bishop and twelve leaders of Cairo life :

> We are impressed by Gairdner's exceptional and outstanding ability and power to contribute to the whole Moslem missionary problem. . . . We feel it would be a thousand pities if his own deep, spiritual and intellectual gifts became the permanent victim of his physical endurance and of his selfless loyalty to the Society with which he has identified his life. . . . We feel sure that you will agree with us that any society employing a worker of the calibre of Canon Gairdner is responsible to the whole Church for the uses to which he is assigned.

And Dr. Garfield Williams also, after visiting Cairo, was, like Esaias, very bold, and said :

> The chief immediate task of the C.M.S. in Cairo is to make it possible for Gairdner to be used where and in the way he can count most for the Kingdom. And I want to say that that is a tremendous responsibility for our Society, for, like most really great men, he is intensely humble and as simple as a child. He will never " play for his own hand " or strive in any way to give himself the chance that ought to be his. It is the Society that must guard his genius and care for him.

Gladly would a Society so urged have done all in its power. But the die had been cast, not in 1923 but in all the long preceding years, when the Church at home had failed to send out young men of promise to the Moslem world. There was now no other Arabic-speaking priest in sight, able for the guidance of the new Church life. In such a case Gairdner elected for a third time to let the dream of an apostolate by literature go. He had renounced it once for the teaching of Arabic, once for the duties of secretary and acting-secretary. This third time for a worthier cause than either, even the life of the Arabic branch of his Church. The little living

Church claimed and held him ; and no work for her is small.

He made his decision, but he told his son that it "consumed much nerve-energy." "It took longer than usual to recover one's elasticity." These are unwonted phrases from that buoyant nature. He was fifty and had had too little of real furlough and holiday in his life, and he still lived close to a telephone in the central house of the mission.

"My desire is to get Gairdner out of 35 Sharia el Falaki, where he becomes a sort of addendum to the C.M.S. office, and is at the mercy of any worrying person or thing," Dr. Garfield Williams had written. And Mr. Cash, as his last great personal service before he left the mission, was carrying through a plan whereby this desire might be accomplished and a move made to more peaceful quarters.

V

Canon and Mrs. Gairdner had made of the house at 35 Sharia el Falaki a wonderful home, the home of their children, and the home of the whole mission, the scene of much music-making and of Christmas revels, when with some of his best fooling, and his best was inimitable, Gairdner acted Charlie Chaplin, or burlesqued *Hamlet*, or set the company to fantastic "musical chairs" in improvised costume.

> Number thirty-five Sharia el Falaki has been razed to the ground [says Maurice Richmond]. The house, the garden and the chapel have given place to speculative blocks. But why is it that, for a number of us, to pass that place is still to pause and slacken speed and look and think ? It is because we know that there we were allowed to share a life that was being lived on such a plane that it is one of our dearest possessions to recall. Now it was music or drama—*Joseph* or Charlie Chaplin. Now it was the *obiter dicta* of a philosopher or a scholar or a historian, and now—yes, always—it was fellowship with those who

were personally and intimately interested in the recesses of many lives. In that home life one had got behind the Fall on to the plane of actually redeemed life, where the purest mirth and joy and music are possible, without masking out any of life.

It cost Gairdner little, when the time came, to leave hat house of joy, for half its glory had already gone for him with the going of the children.

"I miss you all dreadfully. I do not seem to be more than half alive without you all," he told them. And to a friend he said : "After our children all went home the Falaki premises ceased to have any meaning for me personally. Still, I love the *memory* of them."

VI

In 1924 Dr. Mott held conferences in Egypt at Heluan and at Jerusalem on the Mount of Olives, and Gairdner, with an unwonted sense of strain, threw himself into the preparations for these.

> What personal satisfaction it will be to me to see you again, and work with you once more, I need not describe to you [he wrote to Dr. Mott]. I must use this personal motive to lever up my enthusiasm for the enterprise itself, for I will not disguise from you how few are they upon whom the burden of these big special stunts falls in Egypt, and how overloaded those few already are with very full programmes of highly responsible work.

Since at these conferences Gairdner made his last ppearance before the leaders of the missionary world, it is well to ask in what direction, amid all the racket of his Cairo life, his general policy had been shaping.

In 1922 he had been called to speak at the Missionary Conference of the Scottish Churches. It had been a memorable time. Before setting out for the Conference he had knelt down and asked the blessing of his old riend, Colonel Oldham. Then at Glasgow he knit up many ancient friendships, and not least that with Dr. Donald Fraser. When he came to speak to a packed audience in his own Scottish city, he delivered his soul of a burden. He spoke on *Brotherhood, Islam's or Christ's.*

> The brotherhood which Christ brought to earth is infinite and unlimited, *but Christians have limited and particularized it.* The brotherhood of Islam is finite and limited, but such as it is Mohammedans have universalized it. Not until the perfect thing is once more available and offered to Mohammedans can Islam's imperfect thing pass away.

This was the burden of his speech and of his soul. Christ's brotherhood was virtually denied by His brethren and yet nothing short of Christ's brotherhood could claim the Moslem world. He spoke as a prophet, and then was gone. "When the time came to part," says a friend, "as usual he said 'No, we never say good-bye,' and just walked away."

And now in 1924 at Dr. Mott's conferences it was seen that after the troubled months of 1923 he had found his poise and made his synthesis.

Not necessarily by a literature apostolate could he best win Islam. What was most needed for her redemption was the living exemplification of Christian brotherhood. A Church that lived it, a Church that was no chilly barracks but a home where newborn souls could grow and thrive, that was the paramount need. He wrote a paper and he spoke on "the Egyptian Church as a Home for Christ's Converts from Islam," and he said later to his comrade, "If I die before you, promise me that you will give what I said then as my last message to the Egyptian Church. It is far the most important thing I ever wrote."

Now, then, would Gairdner give himself body and soul to the building of the Church.

> It is sometimes said [he had written long before] that little mission churches will be as islands in the

sea of Islam—but let us not be enslaved by dreary metaphors. Let us rather say that such churches will be centres of life and heat and light, serving and saving the Islamic peoples round them.

At these conferences, too, he shouldered his last co-operative task in Christian literature. Through American initiative and gifts a survey had been made which revealed Christian efforts at literature throughout the Moslem world as so insufficient, so dislocated, so lacking in imaginative and creative power, that Gairdner was stirred to action in spite of what he described as "that disinclination of the natural man after he has passed two score years to be jerked out of his ordinary ruts."

He wrote to Dr. Mott before the conferences :

> With regard to the programme I believe the nucleus of it ought to be that literature report, the consideration of which *alone* would make some sort of united conference worth while. At Jerusalem especially, this must be paramount.

And when a Central Committee for Literature for Moslems was mooted, and proceeded while coming into existence to make all the mistakes of inexperience, Gairdner followed its fortunes with eagerness, rejoicing in every triumph of love and unity, and suffering (no lesser word will do) at every manifestation of the spirit of suspicion or separateness. Only those who knew him very intimately in those days realized the burden of dull fatigue under which he forced himself to long days of counsel on this central work, and that in spite of the knowledge that it must steal much of the time of the only literature colleague his society had sent him.

His comrades who came from a distance had the impression not of fatigue but of the strength and buoyancy of the man who turned a board-room into a sanctuary when he played a baby organ. "He seemed full of purity and joy," one said.

And finally, because at Heluan and Jerusalem he was for the last time daily linked in work with Dr. Mott, let a word be said of the noble friendship between these two.

Of Gairdner, Dr. Mott wrote :

> One of the most difficult things to find in this world is a man who will give wholly detached and courageously unselfish advice. This I never sought from Gairdner in vain. I came to trust to the limit his spiritual intuition. Moreover, he was in a class by himself in planning and conducting the devotions of a conference. At Heluan and the Mount of Olives in 1924 I looked to him for the conduct of the music, and his leadership was inspired.
>
> He was one of the greatest of intercessors, and in the difficult task of presiding, involving countless instantaneous decisions, it was of incalculable help to me to remind myself of his presence.

Thus one friend. And what J. R. Mott meant to Temple Gairdner is shown by a letter written during the closing hours of that Jerusalem Conference :

> FRIEND,
>
> . . . I feel I must just send you a message ere we part. My mind has been going back to 1894, just thirty years ago, when I first heard you speak, and it strengthens my faith to do so, for in exactly the same way as you helped me then I find you helping me now. All these thirty years then you have " continued," like Daniel, in that deep life in Christ for which you pled to us—in 1924 as in 1894. Surely the best way I can repay you my very heavy debt of gratitude is *this* time at least, to practise the " sinking of those shafts apart from men. . . ."
>
> To-day again I have been deeply touched by seeing you in the chair. You were probably the most tired of us all, yet you could not afford to relax one moment. And yet not for one moment did that huge Christian

courtesy of yours relax, and when *we* were getting a bit rattled, you preserved your poise and calm. To watch this all to-day has moved me very much. . . .

Your friend in the love of Christ,

W. H. T. GAIRDNER.

One last memory of Gairdner at Jerusalem in 1924 has been kept by Mr. Gordon Logan :

A little camp on the Mount among the olive trees, with a carpet of blood-red poppies under foot. In the very early hours of each morning before the dawn, on the brow of the hill overlooking the city, a solitary figure with folded arms, and head bowed in prayer and meditation. Motionless he stands until the city beneath him is bathed in the light of the rising sun and life begins to stir around. It was thus I saw him for the last time on earth and, remembering him, one ever thinks of the life that was his, above and beyond all the outward activities of service, the life that is hid with Christ in God.

CHAPTER XVII

THE CHURCHMAN

1924–1928

(With excursions backwards)

"I saw the Church triumphant. Why not triumphing more visibly? Because she has not been militant. She is only beginning. . . . Oh, let me be a soldier!"—*W. H. T. Gairdner at the age of nineteen.*

I

It was deeply in Gairdner's heart to care for Christ's Church above all else. Even as a boy not yet twenty, at Student Conferences where other men of that day and group were seeing the world in terms of "fields" and "missions," he saw always the one Society, the Church Universal.

He took great joy of his Anglican heritage and wrote of the "genius of the Anglican Liturgy, rich and simple, restrained and emotional." But into some aspects of his Church's life he never entered. "I remember," says a relative, "when I once said chaffingly, 'Temple, are you High Church or Low Church or Broad Church?' he seemed almost to choke at the idea of being tied down under a label. This I thought very typical." "What I do want to be is *Deep* Church," he told his wife. "Because his faith was founded in the central truths," a friend says, "he would not be a party Christian."

He ministered in a succession of churches in Egypt, poor enough places at first, where he would deal mightily with a baby organ, a hymnbook more than half of which was second-rate in both words and music, a Prayer Book translation that troubled him by combining formality with *lack* of euphony and stateliness, and a people not by nature musical. Not the most promising materials for one who said: "I believe that the alliance of the beauty of holiness and the holiness of beauty is—well, in short, a holy alliance."

In his earliest days in the mission the Society had no property of its own in the city, and worship had to be in hired rooms. The church then was an upper room, over the boys' school, in the heart of the city. Naturally, too, in those early ministrations he was absorbed in the battle with Arabic.

> And yet I am not discouraged. For I am putting down all these drawbacks and discouraging circumstances to the weakness which we share with Christ and through which God is able to conquer and show His glory.
>
> But the glory—where is it? when shall we see it? I know not, but I have lived this day in faith, and in faith will I close it.

His next "church," and that in which, having gained his footing in Arabic, he was able more freely to pour out his spirit's life, was a crypt or basement, the large, dark, central room under the house at Sharia el Falaki.

Of this Miss Lilias Trotter wrote when she wintered in Cairo in 1915 (one saint testifying of another):

> That little crypt-like C.M.S. church within a stone's-throw, where Canon Gairdner has charge, is full, and the atmosphere spiritually is scintillating with light and life. The Liturgy is swept in strange, sweet, unlooked-for cadences, all blended by the strong impassioned touch of the one who leads us. Now and again the service simply breaks through into the place of adoration at the Feet of the Master.

Canon Gairdner's third church was a deep joy to him. Bishop MacInnes lent to the Arabic congregation the beautiful Church of St. Mary, next to his house at Kasr-el-Doubara. Gairdner used to bicycle there at first. Then it occurred to him that as the way to church lay through public gardens surrounded by Government offices (all in full work on Sunday), it would be a kind of witness to the community at large, and would perhaps recall some Christian officials to thoughts of their Church life, if he walked in cassock and "mortar-board." It was the first apparition of that particular kind in the many-costumed Cairo streets, and a beggar-woman called after him, "Why do you wear a tray on your head?"

Of his work at St. Mary's he wrote in 1921:

> For the sake of our school-girls, and of the children of the Cairo Arabic community, and for the sake of three- or four-score dear little urchins from the Cairo Waifs' Shelter (many of them Mohammedans), the service is, once a month, specially suited and adapted for children, when the literary language is dropped in the sermon, and the instruction is given in broadest colloquial Arabic, pure and simple. In this and in many other ways liturgical "research work" goes on at St. Mary's, with the aim of making every service a spiritually beautiful whole, from the first note of the opening hymn right through to the Blessing. In a land where Christian services are attended with not a little of uncouthness and irreverence, this is one little contribution to the Christian life of Egypt which the Church Missionary Society as an Anglican Mission makes or is fain to make.

He dearly loved this church, with flickering leaf shadows on the windows and the unfussy restfulness of bare stone and rough-cast pillars; and it was a wrench to him to leave its spiritual beauty.

The last church of his ministry was far more centrally placed for his Arabic congregation, widely scattered through the northern suburbs.

This Church of the Saviour at Boulac is a solid semi-

Byzantine building with a raised apse-sanctuary of some nobility and a western music-gallery. When Temple Gairdner first visited it, the fat plaster cherubs and plaques of opulent fruit used as decoration irresistibly suggested some City church with the Mayor and Corporation attending in robes of office. These decorations seemed quite irreconcilable with an oriental congregation whose glories were to be poverty and evangelism, and he stipulated for their removal and the retention of purer, simpler lines.

The smooth, plastered completeness of the new church appealed to the urban tastes of his congregation, and they felt it to be their home, his and theirs. But he welcomed them to it with stern warnings. It was "a house that they had not built"—then "beware!"[1] Either must that church be a lighthouse in the city and the surrounding slum, or its candlestick would be removed from its place in the hand of the Risen Christ. He grew terrible in his sternness. And because it was Gairdner speaking, his people knew that he was sternest with himself. When his friend, S. A. Morrison, established a boys' club in one of the alleys of the slum (and each teeming alley could fill such a club), Gairdner, the leader of twenty-five years' standing, would himself go once a week to teach simple arithmetic to the slum urchins.

He longed that his church should be much prayed in on weekdays, and should become rich in holy and common or communal associations, so that a passer-by from the great city might in that church find the barrier thinner than elsewhere between him and the spiritual world. And this was granted him.

> I can never forget [says his friend and sacristan, Miss Christina Barclay] the impression my first Sunday in Egypt left on me. From the moment Canon Gairdner came in in his cassock to give us the number of the first hymn, or explain anything that needed explaining in the service that was to follow, one felt that here was

[1] He was preaching from Deut. vi. 10–12.

the beginning of a tremendously purposeful act of drawing nearer to God through worship. And each prayer, or versicle, or psalm, that followed seemed to be said or sung not because it was the next thing printed in the Prayer Book, but because it was the one and only thing that we wanted to say to God at the moment; until, as the service closed, often with the singing of the Nunc Dimittis or the 150th Psalm, one could only thankfully feel "the whole earth is full of Thy glory, glory be to Thee, O Lord Most High."

All this cost Canon Gairdner a travail of preparation and thought, and looking back one sees that his pains-taking preparation was probably the secret of it all. Sunday, which began with him at sunset on Saturday, was kept as a day of seclusion (unless he had sick ones to visit), and prayer, and often fasting, and as one caught glimpses of that and of the constant renunciations which all his life he must have been making, one understood the reason for the heavenly atmosphere of that church.

A priest from the Jerusalem Diocese wrote after visiting the Church of the Saviour, while Canon Gairdner lay ill:

> I was specially struck by the atmosphere at the Boulac church. I try, when praying for people, to bring them into the presence of Christ, and after a shorter or longer period I feel an assurance that contact has been established. But in your church it was effected almost instantaneously, which means, I suppose, that those who worship there had learnt to pray. Possibly the training of that congregation was the Canon's greatest work.

II

It was a training in worship that he gave his people, but it was also a training in a full Church life. He would not have an isolated congregational existence.

> We are working steadily also [Gairdner said] at drawing our Arabic community into closer and more organic connection with the English half of the diocese. This is necessary from every point of view if the diocesan movement is to be a true one and the Bishop is to be the Shepherd of one flock and not of two, as discrete as two kernels only held together by one hard shell.

To this end he magnified the office of Arabic Church Councils ; he pushed on to the ordination of the Rev. Girgis Bishai to the priesthood (" I remember the radiant joy on Temple Gairdner's face that day," says a Government official). And he was urgent concerning the establishment of a " permanent diaconate " of men still supporting themselves by lay employment, a use which has never dropped out in the Coptic Church. And in all this building of Church life he used as a point of unity the office of the Bishop. He built up in the Arabic Church a deep and affectionate loyalty to this Father-in-God, who was never referred to without some title of affection—" Our beloved Bishop." And in spite of the cleavage of nationality this was not difficult to do, for he was set under a friend and Father-in-God, " great in himself," as Gairdner said, and great in humility.

And of Gairdner as the builder of the Church in that diocese Bishop Gwynne testifies:

> From the first he was an inspiration to me. He was so single-eyed and sincere—so humble about his own opinion and so ready to adopt another if it seemed better than his own—that when he was at his best there was no man who showed me more clearly what " the will of the Lord was." He looked at questions from the Godward side. He would come in to discuss a point in our work (*diocising* the Arabic work, he called it—his word) on which my mind was a blank, and as he thought his thoughts aloud the obvious right policy took shape. He was my *wakeel* or Archdeacon for

the Arabic congregations, and used to magnify my office for the sake of discipline.

He was cleverer, abler, knew more than I, yet he served me; and his tenderness, patience and absolute loyalty caused deep affection and emotion. Though he was never seen in the gatherings of the mighty, he was one of the biggest men in the Church of England.

Canon Gairdner was the leader in drawing up for the Arabic branch of the Church a statement of "Working Principles," announcing her primary mission to the surrounding Moslem world and her sisterly care for other Communions. At the request of the Archbishop of Canterbury, Bishop Gore, early in 1925, scrutinized these "principles" lest anything should appear that might be wounding to other Christian Communions.

I remember well [says Bishop Gore] my impression of Gairdner—of his whole-hearted and simple Christianity and of his wise statesmanship, which in his case at least—what is not common—did not seem to detract from his courage in action.

And after the scrutiny he wrote to the Archbishop saying:

Not the most sensitive Anglo-Catholic can find in the document anything disparaging to the claims of the Orthodox Church, and it is to me a great consolation to find that Bishop Gwynne and Canon Gairdner and I could reach such cordial agreement.

III

Certain Gairdnerian uses in church all his friends remember. He was, he said, "continually wounded" at the thought of a certain sentence in a letter of R. L. Stevenson, which speaks of "a man as big as a house, and far bigger than *a church where no man warms his hands*."

Church for Gairdner was the gate of heaven; his everence was awful; but it was also a very human place where a man might warm his hands. He was prostrate before the altar one day, before a Communion, when a little boy of the congregation casually stumped up within a few feet of his praying form, and passed into the clergy vestry (entered from the sanctuary) where he had left a toy. Someone apologized afterwards to Gairdner, who, smiling, said, "I thought the little fellow seemed so much at home in his Father's house." He was himself perfectly natural there.

> When I went into the vestry one Sunday morning [says Bishop MacInnes], I found Gairdner standing simply wrapt in silent prayer. He heard nothing, saw nothing. When I had nearly finished robing, he became conscious that I was there, opened his eyes and moved over to where I stood. Then, with a smile of keen enjoyment, he repeated some absurd joke that had become proverbial at our recent conference, and without another word went back to his place, closed his eyes, bent his head, stood motionless and so remained sunk in the most complete joy of communion.

And this holy freedom and naturalness was a constant note.

> I remember [says an Egyptian friend] once at Ashmoun (in the Delta), when we were beginning service, we could hear all sorts of sounds from the village—donkeys, cocks, geese, the mill thud-thudding, the children calling. "Listen!" he said. "We must all sing well. All Nature is praising God with us to-day."
>
> One very hot summer day, as we began service there was a little movement in the air. He came into church, and before anything else, he said, "Let us sing hymn No. —— as praise and thanksgiving for this fresh breeze." It seemed so natural and happy.

This element of spontaneousness, the shout of triumph with which he cried, " Lift up your hearts," or the " Our Father," which rose like a pæan after the Communion, or the pauses for silence between Confession and Absolution—these things seemed to those used to the dignified detachment of most Britons in Church, distinctly " queer."

A self-respecting Britisher does not hope for any *notable* answer to the prayer, " O Lord, open Thou our lips," but Gairdner did (" What an opportunity for a ' sanctified shout ' ! " he said when the " Hallelujah " Chorus was sung at an Easter service in America), and when " his mouth showed forth praise," the less imaginative of his friends might say that he was " overdoing the dramatic." He was not being dramatic in the sense that he was acting a part, he was merely being natural—and never too natural for Orientals, to whom the expression of worship also comes naturally.

At the Confession he was manifestly a penitent for his own and his people's sins, bowed low, often prostrate. To his people this meant a great deal.

> Those silent seconds or even minutes at the end of the Confession [one says] bowed to the ground, did give a sense of the burden of sin to his pure soul. He was like St. John, who, when he saw the All-Holy, fell at His feet.
>
> And then for the Absolution he would come out of the reading-desk or rise from before the altar and stand facing us on the chancel step to give us the good news. " *He* pardoneth and absolveth " he would say with tremendous emphasis, as of one to whom it had just come afresh in those moments of penitence.

In shepherding men who had come out of Islam, he felt the need of something to take the place of the short, sharp rallying-cries of that faith. He determined to make a far greater thing of the recitation of the Apostles' Creed, and instead of turning eastwards in a reading-

A DERVISH DIRGE.

A dervish dirge heard one night as a funeral passed the house, noted down and harmonized (with four harmonies for a four-verse hymn) by Temple Gairdner, and sung on Good Friday.

desk, he stepped out to the middle of the chancel and stood there exactly as the Imâm in the mosque stands before the long row of worshippers.

During his visit to America he saw the collection taken in a far more impressive way than is usual in England, and this he brought back to Cairo for the Arabic Church.

> The alms [he said] are taken while the congregation *sits*. Then the minister advances with the great alms-dish, the four churchwardens walk up the whole length of the aisle, *and as they reach the chancel the entire congregation rises to its feet.* The minister raises the alms high above the altar, and the organ and entire congregation crash out into the Doxology, while the four churchwardens stand where they are. Lord ! it has given me a thrill up my spine every Sunday. That rising of the congregation to its feet at that time is a thing to dream of. How dramatic and how *true !*

> Admission to the catechumenate [Gairdner wrote] is by a solemn service in church ; and it was deeply significant and interesting to me, in helping to draw up a draft form of service for that occasion, to discover that many of the prayers used to this day in the Coptic Baptismal Service were really part of an old office for the admission of catechumens ! Now this at once carries us back to a very ancient time indeed, for there can have been little or no paganism in Egypt after A.D. 400, yet these prayers envisage in the most living way a state of society where paganism was still at least common if not the rule ! . . . To-day these prayers are still recited and *only* recited at the baptism of little brown Coptic babies ! They are fossils of a past that once lived. It was a joy to bring some of these old prayers into a nobler and more living use by introducing them into an office for real catechumens, men who in renouncing Islam for Christ are often exposing themselves to nearly as much perse-

cution as those their unknown brethren of those far-off days.

He was glorious on Palm Sunday, when his Egyptian babes entered in procession with palm branches, and at great moments throughout the service, *Hosannas* and *Glorias*, every child (led by the Canon with his palm branch in his hand) must shake its palm till the church was filled with a distinctive rustling sound like the voice of dry reeds in a strong wind.

"He loved the Church's fasts as well as her feasts," says one of his friends, and fasting entered deep into his own life.

> To me [says his friend Aziz Effendi Habashi], nothing in the whole world is like his Good Friday services. The whole story of the Passion taken from the four Gospels was read aloud [1] in a harmony composed by the Canon. Prayers were offered and hymns were sung at each of the seven words uttered by our Lord on the Cross. I was always careful to occupy one of the last seats, to avoid being seen when I was weeping.
>
> In the matter of spiritual healing [Gairdner said] we are trying to work out the *congregational* aspect. We want to have such a dynamic congregational life, as part of the Body of the living Christ, that those "greater works" shall we do "because He is gone to the Father." We have formed a special prayer-circle for praying for the sick, and, as the congregation's representative, I not infrequently use imposition of hands or unction. It is certainly notable that two or three desperate cases for which we have thus worked have recovered. We desire to go all lengths in this matter that are Christ's lengths, in His will for the Church by the Spirit.

Temple Gairdner was perfectly fearless about praying for the sick and very sure of the power of "dynamic

[1] This is the custom of the Russian Orthodox Church at the Matins of Good Friday.

prayer" in desperate cases of illness, as in all desperate cases. But living in the East, he feared that a revival of this old "power" of the Church's endless life, if it were an individualistic, charismatic revival, would only draw crowds round some one person or place. He dreaded all noise and advertisement. One note of our work must be, "See thou tell it to no man," he said.

IV

It was for music that his church was known to the widest circle. He was for ever working at it, aiming always at a beautiful austerity, the bell-clear voices of a carefully taught girls' choir in one part being better in his eyes than a slipshod four-part rendering of "the harmonic mush which the average missionary produces."

He poured his life into this. He wrote a chant for the Te Deum; he collected Oriental tunes; he studied plainsong.

(*To his friend and organist, Miss Margaret McNeile*:)

There is really a good deal of promise in the choir this year. I am striking out a new line too—short psalms most carefully pointed and sung by the choir alone to Gregorians at some effective point in the service. To-day we are going to have Psalm 150, as a sort of Gradual between the Epistle and Gospel. *How* suitable for All Saints' Day and its Epistle!

(*To his wife after a Good Friday service*:) We introduced this year little chanted comments on the lessons, just a sentence or two sung after each by the choir. And one of the great moments in the service was (to me) the childlike artlessness of the voices in the question, "Behold the fire and the wood, but where is the lamb?" after the first lesson, just as it might have been a choir of our own babies: and then the weighty fortissimo of the reply: "Behold the Lamb of God."

CHAPTER XVIII

THE BOULAC HOME AND PASTORATE

1924–1928

Then said the Shepherds, This is a comfortable company. You are welcome to us; for we have for the feeble as well as for the strong. Our Prince has an eye to what is done to the least of these. Come in, Mr. Feeble-mind; come in, Mr. Ready-to-halt; come in, Mr. Despondency, and Mrs. Much-afraid, his daughter.—*John Bunyan.*

I

"It may be," says Maurice Richmond, "that the divinest thing that Gairdner ever could have created was what he did create, a welded group of Egyptians, and Syrians, and Europeans, in one Church, in whose lives his spirit and the Christ to Whom he pointed had become a precious and integral possession."

And since in this pastoral task his home was central as well as his Church, a word must be said of his last home in Egypt. It was part of the buildings grouped round the German Consulate of Cairo, entrusted to the C.M.S. by the trustees appointed to administer the property under the Peace Treaty.

The site is unsavoury but central, not far from Cairo Station, and the chief centres of the city's life. The compound, which has an imposing and solid air, is built between a railway-siding used for the unloading of timber and building materials and a dense rookery of tumble-down, mud-brick houses known as the worst criminal quarter in Cairo. Here, beside the church and removed at last from the telephone of the central office, Canon and Mrs. Gairdner made an unforgettable home. Their four elder children visited it, but for the most part it was a childless household. Yet never could it have been taken for the home of childless people. The great news of the day, when one entered, was of the latest letter from some boy or girl. And the letters sent home to sons or daughters were letters of real sharing in all the interests of life—books or games or art or human nature—and without that fear that holds most of us back from laying bare our love.

> (*To a schoolboy weary of living in lodgings:*) Be sure that mother and I *do* know and feel the trial which separation and lodgings mean. We do, we do. You must look on it as part of your contribution to the work of Christ, because that is what has caused it, really. And you always have *Oxford*. I would say, I'd rather be in "digs" at Oxford than in a nice house at Mudmarsh-cum-Slocum. Do you agree? And finally, you always have your father and mother's heart and love—all of it. Live richly—in "digs"! It reminds me of a piece of rich embroidery worked on coarse commonplace canvas. The *embroidery's* the thing.
>
> (*Or to a boy and girl together:*) This is just to mention that I love you both extremely. This fact you may have forgotten slightly, and as it is sure to come in useful in the terminal examinations (paper of General Facts) you ought to get it up most carefully. I should recommend your recalling it for fifteen seconds as you dress in the morning—no! as you take your tub—and again fifteen seconds after hopping into bed.

And with the absence of his own children, all this fatherliness of the man seemed to find wider channels. At the new home at Boulac he was (to his own amusement) chaplain or abbot to a large community of women missionaries (a Mission High School for Girls stands in the same compound), and quaint as he found his solitude amid so much femininity, he accepted as much as they were willing to accord to him of fatherly position *con amore*.

A temporary member of the compound says :

> My own father had just died, and I felt that Canon Gairdner more than anyone else came into fatherly relationship with me.
>
> I remember his writing me a note of great regret because he and the *Sitt* happened to be out for my last Saturday evening prayers in their house. That he should write so was essentially the expression of the family feeling of that compound. He lived in a vast world of his own, and to that extent his was a lonely life. But in striking contrast came that amazing humility with which he pinned himself down to the most trifling and worrisome details for the sake of other people. It was the difference between the Great Man and the Great Christian Man.

The home at Boulac became central as a place of prayer, but also as *par excellence* the playtime centre. If he had a ministry of prayer, he had also a ministry of play.

> The night when I had started for Europe with our eldest little girl, Canon Gairdner came in and had a romp with the younger children because he knew my wife would be feeling " down " that evening [says a member of the mission].

" It was his own intense enjoyment of everything that made him such good company," a friend writes. " People laughed at him, as one does at the vagaries of a child, but bucked up and enjoyed themselves more than they could have risen to without his infectious example."

He had a way of bicycling in the afternoon with a tennis racquet over his handle-bars, even on days when there was no chance of using it. " It makes one feel as if one had had a game," he told his wife. And when the game was more than imaginary he would urge himself and the others to their utmost efforts, whatever the heat, and was supremely happy if they reached their " top form."

He loved a long-drawn-out rally [says Raymond Whitwell] and if it ended in a brilliant "kill" by himself or his partner or an amusing mis-hit, I have seen him throw himself flat on his back on the court in his excitement, or fling hat or racquet high in air.

The gift of laughter that he gave to Cairo, relieving dull or strained committees, cheering a conference by volleys between himself and his beloved Bishop, refreshing a friend with his affectionate chuckle, enlivening an American evening by a rendering of "Britons very, very seldom shall be slaves," or convulsing an Egyptian party by making a grave senior in mission employ accept a glass of (faked) liqueur—all these things were a real contribution to Cairo life, and gave an impression of inward joy and spring in himself, concerning which the Rev. F. R. Barry says :

I had several long walks by night with him in the desert, and I think I shall never forget the inexhaustible interests of his mind and the radiant spirit, which seemed to illuminate everything he said. I remember coming back from the Pyramids in the middle of the night—for, characteristically, he had taken no account of time—bounding along while he rushed forward at about six miles an hour discoursing about everything in heaven and earth from Æschylean Tragedy to the Coptic Church. It all seemed to well up from some inexhaustible inner spring.

Professor Erdman Harris, an American friend who knew him in these Boulac days, has written :

The door swung open and in breezed a slender, lithe, athletic figure clothed in loose but becoming linen, with a black silk sash around his waist, after the manner of a troubadour. His hair was wavy and brown, his eye eager, his face clean-shaven, aglow with good-humour. I had never met anyone so thoroughly approachable, who was so willing to lay before you the treasures of a well-stocked mind as he. . . .

Other things impressed me about the Canon : his riding a bicycle around the town when the President of our College drove a car ; his dressing up in all sorts of ridiculous costumes in order to give the meetings of the Shakespeare Club a little more " atmosphere " ; his appreciation of the beautiful (he used to stand for minutes at a time before some of the etchings we received as wedding presents) ; his amazing ability to play the piano ; his genius in the direction of choruses and choirs ; the simplicity and hospitality of the home that he and Mrs. Gairdner built up together ; his Christlike treatment of every Egyptian, high or low ; his sympathetic understanding of the American temperament.

Time and again my wife and I would come home from some affair or party or dinner or meeting at Boulac and reaffirm our belief that he was the greatest living testimony of the joyfulness of Christianity.

II

The enjoyments which above all others he shared with his friends (" in such a spendthrift way," one says) during these last years were music, of course, but also now Shakespeare and Italian pictures.

He could always be made happy when tired, if someone mentioned the name of Shakespeare. He would tramp the desert discussing favourite characters : Hamlet, and how the learned with their " problems " had buried the real humanity of him (he wrote a paper digging out, as he felt, the true living Hamlet from under the dust of scholarship) ; Falstaff and the tragic end of his relations with Prince Hal (" I'd rather be Falstaff than Hal. The former was false ; but Hal had what Plato calls ' the lie in his soul ' "). These themes he never wearied of.

And there were Shakespeare evenings, acting-readings or reading-actings. For he was actor through and through. Writing of an evening of impromptu scenes, a visitor says :

> The Canon was so beautifully serious in his nonsense—he skated over the floor in his pretence of Sam Weller until you could feel the cold wind against which he had buttoned up his coat. The rest of us enjoyed our own performances and those of others. He *lived* his ; just there was the touch of genius.

And some of his work was fine and finished, the acting of a man who had pondered the plays. The parts supremely his were comic parts with a touch of pensiveness or grace in their buffoonery. His Caliban was a half-wistful clod of earth ; and he never did more finished work than as the Clown in *Twelfth Night*, half-poet, half-buffoon.

The other golden joy of those years was in pictures. It was a delight to him that an artist-missionary lived in the same compound, and she found no more responsive and no shrewder critic of her work, while to him it was sheer delight to know that Arabic books were through her work becoming beautiful.

"The Canon said," writes this artist friend, Miss Elsie Anna Wood, "that he could not draw anything at all. Yet he looked at drawings with the insight and understanding of one who did nothing else."

And in 1925, when after twenty-five years in Egypt he needed some great renewing and enriching of experience, came an Italian holiday and the revelation of Florence and above all of Botticelli. The members of the compound coming to his house for prayers would find him gloating over the ring of angels in the great Botticelli "Coronation of the Virgin"—those angels, studied lovingly and long by him ; or over the birds and foliage round Ghiberti's baptistery doors—all studied in cheap photographs.

> I got a few photos at the Louvre, including the two Botticelli frescoes. These are the finest paintings in

the Louvre, *je le déclare*, and the way they are placed is a vile scandal—in the very darkest and dingiest corner of the whole Louvre, and out of the traffic altogether.

The bridegroom being introduced to Mesdames les Sciences—aren't the latter too gracious, sweet, natural, old-fashioned, yet ever-presently real for words?

III

The fatherliness which was felt by his fellows of the Boulac compound was felt still more by his Arabic flock, indeed for some starved lives it was the only warm and rich affection that they knew. As their own children left them, he and Mrs. Gairdner gave to their Egyptian children some things that had been at the centre of their family life: the little crêche at Christmas, the Easter tomb-model with its entrancing little garden plants in shells or acorn-cups, were now transferred from the home to the church, and dark heads instead of fair ones clustered round them.

The children of Menouf in the Delta used to call Canon Gairdner "The *qasees* who loves us," and it is as shepherd of children that he will be oftenest remembered by his Egyptian friends: playing nonsense-games at a party; giving them rides on his bicycle in the desert; taking a little Syrian family group for a picnic on the fortieth day (the black day in the East) after their father's death; flashing in on the first Christmas of their orphanhood to play with bricks on the floor; these are the little things which memory guards.

And if a little child died, they knew that he wept with them.

> I can't forget his tears when she died. . . . He was ill, and I said, Don't trouble to come, but he replied, I *must* share this with you. Isn't he my son as well as yours? I've prayed and prayed for him. . . . He came at once and was as sad as if his own son had died. He took the mother's hand and led her away and comforted her.

"He came one day to our house," one more Egyptian friend said, "and the three children clustered round him. He carried one on his shoulder and the other two, one in each arm. He said to them, 'Tell me who I am?' (for he always loved to hear a little child say, 'You are my *qasees*'). One child answered him, 'You are the *qasees*.' He turned to the second and she said the same. He asked the third, and she, familiar with a certain Figure in a picture that carried a lamb on His shoulder, said, 'You are the Good Shepherd.'"

IV

But he was not a children's shepherd only. "The Canon has helped me more than almost anyone to understand and love and honour the Egyptians," says an American friend. And therein lies the secret of his power. His people felt that he *liked* being with them:

> We had a "Quiet Day" at Zeitoun in his last year of life [one of them says]. At the recreation time he found a group of us in the desert and singing a native tune. He began to sing with us, and soon had us all clapping and dancing as we sang. When they came to call him to food, he said, "No, no, *it is good to be here*."
>
> His letters to us always began, "My dear colleague, my dear comrade," as though he were one of us.
>
> I was angry and he wanted me to forgive someone. He put his hands on my shoulders and said, "Don't think of Gairdner the big, or the *qasees*. Think rather of your brother. Have we not both a big nail [a stake] to endure?"
>
> His judgment between two people was amazing. I say before God, he must have been filled with the Spirit. He could tell a lie from truth.
>
> Once my wife was angry with me and went away in anger and stayed away three months, and would not come back because of her vexation with me. I went to Boulac and told this trouble to Canon Gairdner.

> He was just starting for England. He said, "My son, I shall have three special points on my mind to pray for while I am in England. The first two concern my own life, the third is your relationship with your wife. These shall be the things that I pray for earnestly every day." As soon as he got back from England he came and hunted for me and said, as one who expected his prayers to be answered, "Is your wife with you now?" She was.
>
> Another time when we had not been getting on well together he came to the house and knelt down with us two and laid his hands on our two heads and made perfect peace between us. He always made peace.

Of Church instructions Gairdner poured out during his Egyptian life a whole series of small Arabic leaflets—lessons for baptism, for confirmation, preparation for Holy Communion, leaflets innumerable of special services, canticles, special instructions, the last, published during his illness, being on the keeping of the great fast.

> No one else taught us as he did [says his friend Yusef Effendi Tadros]. Other teachers taught us how to refute Islam; he taught us how to love Muslims. He made us feel we understood them and felt with them. When he told us about the beginnings of Islam, we felt as if we were sons of that time and knew the first Muslims.
>
> He would ask each of us in turn to give his thoughts [another pupil says]. I can never forget how he, who knew so much more than we, would sit with his head on his hand listening to us as if what we said was quite new and fresh to him, and he would seem the most touched of all by what we said and always took the lessons to himself, although he was our teacher.
>
> When we came to questions of modern criticism, we felt safe with him. He was a man of the old *and* of the new; we felt he would guide us through. He was gentle with us, but he made us see that there are many possibilities.

He would jump up and stamp and clench his fist in pure joy if he thought one of us had caught his thought.

When he was sitting among us teaching, I felt as if he was Christ and we were the disciples.

His friend Sheikh Bûlus er Rimâwi,[1] among many pastoral memories, cherishes this the most :

He asked me out to the Pyramids, and we supped together there. Then we walked together out to the west in the sunset till we were quite alone in the desert. He reminded me that I was now forty years old, and he said how he longed that I who was his son should die an evangelist. Then we sat down together on the sand. In a few minutes he said: "Let us pray together. Let us confess our sins. Before you is a big step [Sheikh Bûlus was to begin some evangelistic work in the city]; let us get cleansing for our past."

He knelt on the sand and we prayed together. In prayer he said : "Use this my son, O Lord, like a humble servant of Thine in his new work." Presently he said to me : "I want to pray in your name, and you after me." I shall never forget the words he said for me that night, while the stars came out. "Here am I," he said ; "send me. Make me ready afresh to bear Thy Cross in new ways. Make me forget and forsake the world afresh. Make my new work holy, done in Thee and for Thee. Make me do the work of an evangelist. Let me lay my life a sacrifice at Thy feet, O Jesus."

Then he said, very solemnly, "Remember that while we are here with God, Mr. Thornton's spirit is with us, and I ask you in his name and mine:

"Are you ready to put away all thought of the glory of this world ?"

And at last he said, with intense earnestness,

[1] See Chapter VIII, Section VII.

clenching his fist and shaking it as he spoke : " Are you ready to consecrate your life and to be an evangelist *unto death* ? "

Before I spoke, he said : " Don't answer me, my son. Kneel and make your answer to Christ."

I knelt then on the sand and we prayed with tears. He prostrated himself on the ground, but one arm strayed upwards that his hand might rest on me. It was one of the great moments of my life, and Christ was there with us.

That " let us confess our sins together " was very characteristic. " If he discovered that he himself had been in the wrong, he always ran back to confess it," says one of his flock.

Such a nice thing happened to-day [Gairdner said in a letter to a friend], a carelessly treated affair (on my part) had grievously offended, or led to the grievous offending of a member of my congregation, who wrote me an indignant letter that made me feel very bad, as I feared that he might be *offended* in the New Testament sense of the word. I was restless and ill at ease, as I had no way of getting at him till the morrow: and I could settle to nothing. I had prayer, and then remembered that I had *once* seen him sitting at a little café in Sharia Madabegh, so on the off-chance, and in order to do something, I got on my bicycle and rode slowly down the street, keeping my eyes wide open. No sign of him. . . . Suddenly I caught sight of his *back* just walking round the corner ! I say, I felt that I just knew there is a God in heaven. I went right up and had it out with him. He was melted, and largely because I had taken that way of finding him You can imagine how happy I am this evening.

And his Arabic Church Committees recall how he associated himself with them in every act of contrition They remember him, at a Quiet Day at Maadi, confessing to them with effort, almost with tears, the sins that weighed down his spirit. He would be made in all things like unto his brethren.

And they gave him some moments of exquisite joy when they showed their love and appreciation. After the presentation of a photograph of the Church Council and himself among them, he broke out characteristically:

> There was so much *love* knocking about that one felt there was something not only happy but also holy and heavenly about it all. The truly golden side of our friends' character came out, and I do truly love them for it.
>
> Well, there is no excuse now for not going forward with a good heart. Somehow I feel that if so many of God's little ones are pleased with me, He cannot be very displeased. So I take heart of grace.

V

There was a mellow happiness over his last years of work, yet, while outsiders still marvelled at his youthful vigour, to those who were working most closely with him it was obvious, before Gairdner's last furlough of 1926–7, that a deep-seated fatigue had hold of him. He himself felt that his furlough must be given to some recharging of mind and spirit. He dreamed of an Oxford term, of " finding out what they are doing in theology," of a return to Greek literature with his daughter, of a spiritual retreat with his friend Brother Douglas Downs at his Franciscan home in Dorset.

When, before he left Egypt, he rather forlornly confided to his friends that his Society had asked him to give special help with the great " World Call " then sounding in England, two of his comrades wrote to the Society and begged for a furlough of freedom.

> Give him six months' rest [said Dr. Lasbrey's letter]. He probably knows full well that he ought not to " deputate." This year he ought to be free from all calls of this sort.

He was not put to any long spell of speaking, but neither was he set quite free—a summer school at Malvern, lectures and college "squashes" at Cambridge, a lecture to a training-college in London, more college squashes at Oxford, a speech to a congress at Chester, to a clergy gathering at Exeter—each one costing him, with his high standards and his tired brain, hours of preparation; and the dates of them so spaced out, as he sadly said, as to make it impossible for him to follow any lectures through the Oxford term.

"My time at Oxford has been hopelessly cut up. It has not been a good time in respect of intellectual renewal," he told a friend; "I might almost as well have been at Pittsville as at Oxford." And coming back to his University, a foreign missionary and outside the normal rhythm of her life, he found it hard to renew contacts. "No Trinity don has once invited me inside the gates; it is sad," he told his son.

It was suggested to him that he should regain this sort of intercourse by offering himself for the Oxford degree of Doctor of Letters, and he went so far as to write to his friend Professor Clement Webb about it.

> I conceive that what would disqualify me straight away would be the question of quantity. It may be true that only two works are submitted. But doubtless the Faculty would immediately consider the submitter's output as a whole. . . . Now really I have only published three works of the sort that could be submitted to an academic Faculty: (The three works are a treatise on the esoteric side of El Ghazzali's philosophy, *The Phonetics of Arabic*, and *Egyptian Colloquial Arabic, a Conversation Grammar*.) I think these three have "class." But they are smallish works in bulk and as few in quantity as *three* is!

To his son he wrote: "I reckon that the cost of this little concession to 'family pride,' which Mr. Gilbert tells us 'should be denied and mortified,' would be over £70. . . . I am certainly going no further in the matter." This aspect of his furlough was only in line with the steady denial to him all his life of outward signs of success, God having reserved some better thing for him.

But as regards his children it was a time of delight. He watched with joy the expansion of a son's musical nature at the Festival at Worcester. He spent a holiday on the Whitby moors in "a year of unusual heather-glory," with bathing, French cricket, readings of *Pickwick* and Shakespeare, and "demonstrations" of music on an "indescribable, broken-winded, toneless hack of a so-called piano, lacking even its middle C," and all this was pure joy:

> Oh fortunate mortals to have such a succession of rich joys. And yet they are essentially simple ones after all—joys of the natural affections, of the mind and the soul.

And indeed the predominant memories of that last furlough are of joy. He enjoyed the Oxford home provided by his sister-in-law at 10 Bradmore Road. Visitors found him gloating over "the glorious photograph of the French restoration of the Parthenon frieze," or leaping over the back of a chair to reach the piano when the afflatus suddenly came upon him.

A friend in a convent at St. Albans recalls his visit to her:

> We went round our Home for Incurables, and he threw a ray of sunshine on everyone he talked to—they have never forgotten him. He noticed everything—the pictures on the walls, Arundels most of them. He pointed out beauties—a detail of drapery that had its meaning and value for the whole design. Then he went to see our new church which was nearing completion. We talked of Arabic architecture and its influence on later styles; the inward unity that underlies all man's attempts at expressing his idea of the greatness of God. An appointment with the Bishop

of St. Albans called him and with a few words of farewell he flashed away, leaving me full of joy and thanks.

The furlough ended with four days of great glory in Paris, mastering, as he loved to do, the historic outlines of the city, building up in his mind the Paris of the Middle Ages, glowing at the Sainte Chapelle, or living over at Versailles the ominous last days of royal glory.

VI

Yet at the beginning of February 1927, when he returned to his Egypt, he found himself "singularly unrefreshed," as he confided to his closest fellow-workers.

But he was happy that year in his home and work with a very contented happiness. His daughter Eleanor was with her parents, and on his Monday "half-holiday" he played tennis with her, or with her stepped out barefoot his projected restoration of the dances that went with the Greek choric odes! And in his work he had no longer the sense of frustration, for recruits had joined him. "Had ever a man such colleagues," he would say, "at once so able and so devoted!"

> To make an exclamation of approval was very characteristic of him [says one who came to know him in these latter years]. He constantly let drop little remarks of amused comment or words of encouragement or thanks that left one with a sense of invigoration.

Already, with the coming of new colleagues, he was envisaging a retirement for himself from the full leadership of the Arabic Anglican community "to my sadly neglected literature work," and he did turn now to his desk and pull out the manuscript, for many years untouched, of a commentary on Galatians, with an essay at a fresh Arabic translation of the Epistle, nearer the spirit and the idiom of the *κοινή* Greek. By this slender book he inaugurated a new Biblical literature in Arabic, for this was the first serious commentary written with the needs in view of a Church whose main witness must be to the surrounding Moslem world. This he was able to finish in the summer of 1927, but those who knew him best, and only they, could see over all his vigorous doings a shadow of fatigue, due, no doubt, to the insidious onset of the disease that was to reveal itself ere the year was out.

> One day [says his friend the Rev. Girgis Bishai] he looked at me and said, " We are both tired to-day." I said, " I am feeling that the time has come for rest," but he said to me, " We must witness till we draw our last breath." " But we are getting old," I said (I was eight years older than he). " Yes, we are getting old," he answered, " but with age will come power and grace to witness to the very end."

And especially did fatigue show itself with any call for a new departure of thought. When a request came in the summer of 1927 from Dr. Mott that he would write a paper for the great meeting of the International Missionary Council on the Mount of Olives, he felt a curious reluctance :

> So great was the distaste with which I turned from the prospect that I felt that this alone should determine my refusal, for how could such a task be properly performed if assumed and carried with a sense of utter unwillingness and distaste? I felt so keenly that I had been put to this job again and again until I have got stale to it ; and that the younger generation of workers must be given these tasks now.

But at the last moment, by a saving thought, he enlisted the help of his friend Dr. W. A. Eddy. " To get a new fresh young mind on that material, and that mind as fine a one as Eddy's, may just eliminate the staleness I feared, and add the freshness I was despairing of." His old pleasure in working with another keen mind returned, and he was able with this help to give to the Church his own summary of his life's teaching on *The Values of Christianity and Islam*.

VII

In October 1927 the whole family life was crowned by a silver wedding, made glorious by children and Cairo friends, with gifts and little ceremonies and lover-like letters and all that commerce of affection that was so dear to him. The first wonder was the discovery that his naval son would have shore-leave in Cairo for the very day.

> Do you know where I saw it? I had gone out to spend a day in the desert for reflection and meditation and happened to buy an *Egyptian Mail*. I was glancing it through, lying among some rocks near Maasara, and my eye fell on a very inconspicuous passage I might quite well have missed. You can imagine the depth and height of the subsequent chortling. It was *too* neat! Well, mine boy, thrice welcome: and you shall well and worthily represent your brothers and sisters, and we will have a beautiful time.

"A beautiful time" they had for a whole "festal week," "our week of wonders," and at the end he summed up the joy of it all in writing to thank one of his children for a silver-wedding letter:

> What is it that keeps a letter like this from being an exceedingly unhealthy experience for the two who read it—the two who are no more immune than the average mortal from temptations to egoism, vanity and conceit, and whose deeper temptations, struggles and evil characteristics are veiled to the eyes of lover children? Just the salt, the creative and preservative principle of love. I won't say that, even so, there resulted *no* "puffing up," both as a result of the things you said and the silver wedding in general, but it could never go far. For one thing, the delicious

hyperboles you went in for in your filial enthusiasm often created such a solvent of happy laughter that conceit-germs at once gave up the struggle for existence and expired ! And, much more important, as I said before, *love* continually stepped in with its wonderful power of keeping everything healthful. For love is life. . . . The love and admiration of children are healthful and pure, things that therefore simultaneously exalt to the stars and humble to the dust : like the Cross of Christ itself, to which I can assure you I have often taken your letter.

What is " the thing that remains " after a letter like yours, and after all the discountings, the momentary temptations to complacency, the smiles, and so forth ? Just that we are yours and you are ours—for the remaining years of this existence—and, because love is *the* thing that abides, for eternity. I told you that during a sleepless night, when I had a temperature, I composed in my head a letter to you in return for yours, down to the turns of phrases. One thing I do remember about that thought-epistle : it ended by saying something which I will say now, that letters such as the one you wrote do constitute a sort of blessed permanent *Nunc Dimittis*, though the " Dismissal " may be postponed for years or decades. They constitute the most beautiful and soul-satisfying of farewells. For in truth a farewell like this is the pledge that Absence is not going to be the salient fact.

CHAPTER XIX

IN EXITU ISRAEL DE EGYPTO

1927–1928

They are, she answered, our country birds: they sing these notes but seldom, except it be at the spring, when the flowers appear! and then you may hear them all day long.—*John Bunyan.*

I

WHEN, in November 1927, Gairdner said casually in writing to his son, "I had a temperature," the words pointed to the beginning of the illness (dental sepsis which after the necessary extractions left septic complications in the lung) with which he was to fight a losing battle for the next seven months.

It quickens a man's trust in Providence as poet, to see with what quaintly tender firmness during these last months the final rhymes were added to the poem of his earthly life. Already, as we have seen, that pamphlet for Dr. Mott, summarizing his life's thought on Islamics, had been printed; already a friend had been laid under promise to give his last message to the Arabic Church; already his *Nunc Dimittis* letter to his children had been written; and to the last these fitnesses continued, last meetings, last occasions, last messages were granted, he never knowing them to be the last; for to the very end there was hope that his unusual vigour and vitality might be allowed to master the poison. And the unconsciousness of finality is what gives those final cadences their value and their beauty.

In Douglas Thornton's life Gairdner had written:

There is only one reason that warrants a biographer in dwelling on the sacred details of the passing of a soul. This warrant is not to be granted to sentimental demand, or even to that of mere dramatic completeness. But when the last hours are entirely of a piece with the whole of the life that has gone before, pointing its message, completing its inspiration, and perfecting its glorifying of God, then it becomes so essentially part of the life that the writer of the life cannot choose but set it down.

So was it in his case.

He had no mind to be ill, and it was for him a new experience to find illness slowly gaining its hold. At first he was full of all his old ploys: the Christmas Eve festival of music and the great Communion of the Feast he carried through; he visited several sick that day and came home spent; but the next evening, looking like a ghost, was able for some hours to be the humorist of a Boulac Christmas party. Then, finding himself really ill, he turned his thoughts again to literature. Much he hoped to do, but what he actually did in those weeks of illness has its significance.

He was probably the only Westerner of whom the *Muktataf*[1] (the leading Arabic literary review of Cairo) ever wrote that he "must be accounted an Arabic poet of genius." This master of the classical Arabic metres now turned to work in the simplest spoken language for Egyptian street-waifs:

> You know those hardy annual requests which have figured in every Literature Committee report for decades back [he wrote]: "A major want is versified Gospel stories and simple hymns." Well, I have been experimenting. . . .
>
> When we found out that simplified classical rhymes were useless for street-children, I started in at purely colloquial verse, but constructed on the strict and con-

[1] July 1917, p. 89

> sistent principles of the colloquial language (some former attempts were very go-as-you-please and their metrical system was loose to a degree). Some of the little hymns and Gospel stories which I did for our ragged Sunday school have proved successful. I should add that all the metres adopted were those for which easy or popular *Arabic* tunes are available.

It was his last literary enterprise, this breaking through established classical forms for the sake of the souls of children. May he be the Cædmon to a line of children's poets!

One other task of literature was greatly in his thoughts. "I feel as if I wished we could turn to it just about next thing," he told his friend. It was a plan for the revision of the Arabic New Testament. He and many others had long felt the paramount need for a more perfect instrument than the existing translation, though that has greatly served. He would have brought to it, in addition to his Arabic and life experience as an exegete, the exact science of New Testament Greek. Meanings would have shone out afresh. That task must wait, but not, please God, for ever.

> Deep in one's heart [Gairdner wrote in these days to his friend Mr. A. T. Upson] one knows and is sure that the dislike for the project, and opposition to it, are based, as so often in these lands, on *fear*: fear of what the Christians will say, what the Mohammedans will say, what the Americans will say, what the two Bible Societies will do, and so forth. But fear is a miserable basis for permanent action or inaction—unbelieving, untruthful, sterile. I refuse to be bound by it in so far as any given subject relates to my own life-work. . . .
>
> I am inclined to think . . . that the thing to strike for would be a Supplementary Revised Version, which might be considered at first a mere study-companion-version, as indeed the English Revised Version has become, and would take its chance of becoming or

not becoming the "authorized" one of the future, *according to the will of God.*

With these words, unconsciously, he bade his farewell to Arabic literature.

II

His farewells to the Arabic Church were as fitting. When on Friday, March 2nd, an X-ray examination revealed that his wearing and obstinate fits of coughing were due to an abscess in the right lung, he asked for a week-end to settle his affairs before going to Heluan for rest and treatment. And in that week-end he met for the last time his ex-Moslem children in the faith, with a great physical effort saying words of peace to them whom he addressed that day as "My beloveds, my *most* beloveds"; and he was for the last time present in his own church at the Holy Communion with his people. He might not preach, but very simply begged their prayers and their continuance of the work he left.

He left them, but even before the serious nature of his illness was suspected he had written words of cheer to the leaders of the Church who thought him indispensable:

> I was once more and for the thousandth time touched by your love. But—just look at the growing strength and rootedness of the native Church. Much, I know, remains to be done here, but the process is going on and my removal would not stop or arrest it. And then the point is of fundamental importance that the removal of some apparently indispensable worker always releases unsuspected forces and resources. . . . All of which really means, "We believe in the Holy Ghost, the Lord and Giver of life," and not in any one man or in man at all.

III

He grew slowly into the life of an invalid, impatient at first of the interruption to his work—"Stupid illness seems such an irrational thing "—but never anything but patient in his acceptance of personal limitations, and with a half-humorous and curiously objective interest in his own illness. "He showed me the photograph of his lung in a detached sort of way and proceeded to talk about plans for literature work," says a friend. And Canon Oliver Quick, who was able to visit him at Heluan, says :

> What struck me most of all was his intellectual unselfishness—possibly the rarest form of that cardinal virtue. I am sure he was absolutely interested in God's world rather than in his own or in any particular set of views about it ; he was one who has the child's single-minded faith that the world above all things is worth *watching*. The power and interest of θεωρία seems to be almost departing from this modern world, and it is greatly refreshing to meet for an hour or two one who has succeeded in keeping it.

He read Conrad and Hardy with vigorous, enthusiastic comments, and he made his first acquaintance with W. H. Davies : "That Shepherd book is simply great : a tonic : a bracer : an enlarger."

But the hope of cure by rest and sunshine failed. On Tuesday, March 20th, a consultation with the Swiss specialist revealed that the trouble was on the increase, and from a sofa-life in an hotel it was necessary to move him into the Heluan Sanatorium for "artificial pneumo-thorax" treatment. It was a desert hospital, built on a barren rock in wonderful clear air. Here he was forty days—"a kind of Lent, and I would not have missed one of them."

It was a time of deep and deeper retirement as he grew less able to see visitors, and to his wife, who had ever generously shared him with Eastern and Western friends, were granted weeks of almost sole companionship. His hospital room became strangely a home and a centre. "I have never seen so patient a man," said one of the

Egyptian doctors. "He would always greet one of the nurses, who was Italian, with a cheery 'Viva,' and told his wife that her presence there made the days 'a sort of extension of our silver wedding.'" Moreover, he drained thankfully every draught of beauty :

> I say, that Pompei Flora is just wonderful : everybody, including my shrill-voiced Italienne sister, has admired it. It might be a quattrocento, a Botticelli !

The Cantorian panels of Luca della Robbia were hung on a bare cupboard opposite his bed, and he traced in them likenesses to Arabic babes of his congregation. He had, too, a little "altar" with a wooden cross and a Leonardo da Vinci reproduction ; his best flowers must always be set there.

But shadows drew in.

> It is a good thing that all those joblets and chorelets were tackled and finished off in those palmy days [of the beginning of the illness]. In the present phase one just has to lie passive and listless. For this discipline the Palm Sunday Collect is the ideal prayer. . . .
>
> I will tell you one thing which that vile cough suggested to my mind with a suggestion that stuck : namely, that not more horrible, stinking, diseased, alien to the healthy self was that foul sputum than is self-admiration, love of praise, or working for thanks, to the soul. Things to be spat out if they're there ; and to have the system utterly cleansed of if one desires to be whole.

Holy Week he spent in a passion of intercession for his people. On Palm Sunday he took to himself the Collect and made his friends pray it for him daily, but with this gloss to its meaning, that a share of the patience and humility of Christ might be his own, and that the corresponding share in resurrection power should be for the Arabic Church. He was greatly content when he heard of the depth and reverence of their services, and they on their part said, "We knew that he was there with us ;

we could feel his spirit. Our Canon is helping us now more than he ever did by any sermon." And the ti grew ever closer between him and the people from whom he was now completely withdrawn.

> I was in Heluan on Easter Day, conducting ser vices [says the Rev. R. S. Macdonald]. In the train coming back to Cairo afterwards I met three effendis members of the Church of the Saviour. They had been out to Heluan, not with any hope that they might be allowed to visit the Canon, they had not even asked for that, but because they felt they would like to be near him on the Feast.
>
> Love says foolish things [one of his people con fessed], and I asked my wife if she thought we might offer to God the life of one of our children for the recovery of the Canon.

Many who had loved his fatherly presence were slowly learning the love that enters into the unseen and the eternal, and works by way of prayer.

IV

On the Monday after Easter a rapid and dangerous suppuration in the pleural cavity set in, which must have proved fatal but for an emergency operation to drain the pleural cavity. Those were days of terrible anxiety and harder nights. On April 19th, the crisis day of operation, and for eight succeeding days, the temperature of the air was over 105° (one day at least reached 113°), while he sat propped with countless pillows and swathed round in bandages.

And in those days were seen two wonders, the wonder of the answer to his request for patience and the wonder of the fellowship of prayer.

He asked patience, and praise was given to him.

"This has been a day of praise, a day of praise," he murmured after the operation on April 19th, and of his early-morning devotions he said, "That's when the lauds and alleluias and praises begin to flow." "Thank God for the holy ice," was another of the words of those days ; and with a twinkle to the doctor, " I suppose I'm the coolest man in Heluan ; no one else gets so many iced drinks." When he thought he clutched too greedily at an offered drink, he pushed it aside a moment while he gave thanks, saying, " Grace, not paganism ! " Yet all this was not easily won.

> Last night a terrible thing nearly happened. You were sitting by me between the duties of the day and night sisters [he told his wife]. A horror came over me that this was to be yet another night of restlessness, and *I all but cried out*. Then a sudden inspiration came that I could turn on my side and get some relief.

Meanwhile, outside that room wonders and beauties were working out among his people, and amongst more than they. Their love was passionate. By day and night in his own church and in the hospital chapel at Old Cairo prayer was made without ceasing, and in many a Cairo home. "I always think there's something specially holy when the *families* get to work," Temple Gairdner said. And outside his own Church, Coptic priests, American missionaries, Armenians, Greeks, Egyptian Presbyterians, even Moslems were united in a great wave of love and prayer. " Surely," said an American missionary, " nothing has ever happened to draw us so closely together in prayer for so many long weeks. I believe it has done more for Christian unity in Egypt than all the conferences."

And almost daily, as the representative of this praying multitude, his friend Maurice Richmond entered his room and found it full of the sense of living, invisible comradeship. " As I visit him, the prayer, the silent prayer, and the hands laid on in blessing are offered in the power of all prayers prayed for him." And Temple Gairdner asked to send this message to his praying friends :

> One of the wonderful things which I attribute to

> your ministry of prayer is . . . that when the mind was restless, the restlessness would somehow find its expression in pleasant, friendly, humorous, sometimes even beautiful thoughts. And the Name and atmosphere of the great Risen Jesus has been very pervasive.

V

On Sunday, April 29th, it was decided that the only hope lay in an unusual and pioneer operation which would require the constant supervision of the leading surgeon in Egypt. For this reason it was necessary to move the patient from Heluan to the Anglo-American Hospital in the green island called Gezira at Cairo.

Temple Gairdner once wrote of the last hours of an Egyptian friend:

> Apart from his inward possessions he had little indeed on earth that gladdened existence. Was it not, then, beautiful of God to vindicate the truth and worth of his inner life during those dull days here, by simply overwhelming him with an experience of heavenly beauty and delightsomeness?

And now to himself, whose life had been so full of artistic renunciation, was granted an ecstasy of joy in colour and sight. It dominated the days of waiting for operation, and in the days of weariness that followed, it gave way to an inward quietness and shining peace.

As he was moved on a stretcher to the ambulance that was to carry him from one hospital to another he asked for a pink rose from beside his bed, and the little group, tense with anxiety at moving so sick a man, saw him go off waving his flower and calling out, "I'm a regular sybarite." At the end of the drive of nearly twenty miles he said, "I've had a regular joy-ride and that plucky little rose kept up nearly all the way."

He found himself brought back from the desert to the green earth:

It was *enough* that first sweet dawning [he told a friend] to catch sight of a section of one tree in the garden below, and to know I was back in the earth again: a bit of earthly Paradise after that blistering rock. And birdlings, too, twittering and cheeping, and *one* with a low little song. My sister Ailie's spirit and mine came together where that spring tree is.

Amid the curious mix-ups of the matter is that in the *lavish* way my illness is being done for me (I am merely passive) elements of sheer luxury have been and are here and there all the time, and the strange thing is that these one enjoys with the absolutely sybaritic refinement of the Hedonist that is in one. I don't speak of this place only: the strand was weaving itself all the time on that *gabal* [mountain or desert], also where I was forty days—tempted of the devil—yes, sometimes.

The whole thing is a song, Thanks be to God for His unspeakable Gift, and gifts.

Benedicite was his sick-bed canticle ("There's just one clause I can't yet say—O ye fire and heat," he confessed, thinking of those days of fiery trial at Heluan), and to one who had sent him a present of wine he wrote:

FRIEND AND FRIEND OF OUR HEARTS,

It is a joy to me that I am now able to trace a few lines to yin twa freens as occasion offers. I was so conscious of the fluttering of the wings, so to speak, of those who came to Heluan so regularly to do me service, and though I saw no faces I was no end helped. Bless you three—or was it four?

And now I want you to know that it has arrived at my ears and intelligence *what* a gift I owe to a certain donor. I just want to tell you a little more about what this gift has meant to me (your wondrous justification for giving it is too remarkable for spifflication. Well, what of it? Love's all).

. . . At this place, where my illness is more and more becoming a form of luxury, I can't tell you the rich benefit these wines are to me. My daily dressing is still a very exhausting ceremony, and when it is finished I am pretty well clemmed and dead beat. Then comes that wondrous champagne, and, well slashed with cold soda-water (a holy thing), it runs through my veins and brings such refreshment and strength again. And I bless God for the vine and its fruit, that fundamental, almost sacramental thing, for the hillside that trained it, and the sun that ripened it and the hands that harvested it. I bless Him for the kindly fruit of the earth given so wonderfully for use and not abuse.

As for the red wines, they are always making me eat meals at times when I turn from food. And once again the blessed fruit of the vine and the cold soda-water make the impossible possible.

All this looks at first sight very casual stuff. But how little is it so! Your gift has got well into my enormously enlarged Benedicite which I recite nearly every day.

I bless the Giver of All: the Gift: the Donor.

Flowers, too, brought an ecstasy of joy. When he had blue anchusa it must stand between him and the light, so that he might catch the clear shining through its petals; "Like the body of heaven in its clearness," he murmured. And on the morning of his great operation, a day for which he chose the words, "Yea, I have a goodly heritage," a friend managed to carry to his room a trail of his well-loved "Morning Glory," and he had "two hours of pure joy watching it."

VI

"I shall never forget," says Maurice Richmond, "the perfect courage—the poise—of his mind as he quietly spoke of the two alternatives of his last operation." He knew well enough, as he had known from the beginning, that he was grappling for his life. And in moments of weariness he had found it hard not to long for the blessedness of death. But he resolutely turned his face to life. "If I didn't I should be a quitter!" he told his wife.

> I want to ask [he said on the day before this operation] that if they succeed it may be to the glory of God and to my joy, and if there be after it more trouble and suffering for me, in either case it will be under the hand of God and the Cross of Christ.

The operation, in spite of its great difficulty and danger, had to be performed under a local anæsthetic. It was long and exhausting, but the patient, with his eager yet detached interest in the science and skill of it, declared that he "would not have missed it for anything." It was successful in attacking the original seat of the disease in the right lung, but it soon became apparent that the poison had passed beyond the reach of local remedy.

There *was* "more trouble and suffering" in the days that followed:

> The *cough*. It has been heavier since the operation. No one knows what it means to me. I have had it six months. I have *never* asked for it to be taken away.

Then a friend, watching the lesson of his illness as it worked in many souls, wrote of the mystery that his suffering was a part of the "filling up" of "that which was lacking" in the Passion of our Lord.

> That such as I should have such honour. . . . But only, only up to the limits of my poor powers: the darker and more terrible things I could not have stood: and lo! they have not been demanded of me!
>
> Thanks be to God for His unspeakable gift: His unspeakable wisdom.

Henceforth, "no man troubling him," he lived in the

calm of this wonder, to which his last letter on earth returned once more : " Behold what tiny crucifixion He has asked of me. It was exactly and all I could offer. Mighty wisdom ! Well, there will be that much Resurrection power also."

And his inward calm grew into a sort of quiet ecstasy. It had troubled him, he told a friend, that his later years, burdened with the care of many works and many souls, had yielded little of that mystical experience which had glorified his earlier life in Christ. Now, as in heavenly endorsement of his life-work, the glory was restored. " Some say," of him as of another Pilgrim, " that the Shining Ones that had sometimes appeared to him on his journey were become his Companions."

VII

And throughout these last days his friends became conscious ever and anon that the man whom they were, as it seemed, sustaining with their prayers was all the time succouring them with a ministry of intercession. His wife offered to read him a book about prayer, but he answered, " Dr. X preached to his people so much about prayer as to *deave* their ears. The only way really to learn to pray is through a strong inward necessity."

And his many little messages unconsciously revealed his life in this respect.

> Never during these difficult times have you or your work been long absent from my mind and my prayers by night or day.
>
> I must and will get wonderful J. M. on my heart and soul in prayer.
>
> I am lying back resting on the ocean of God's love, borne there by the prayers of friends. . . . I am upheld by the wings of their prayers. All this might make me an egoist, but I offer up all these prayers to God, asking that they may come back in blessing on all who pray.

And the boon was given. Those who prayed were seeing their request refused and yet knew God to be so close that they, like Temple Gairdner, found themselves atoned to all that He might do. Once again was verified the truth learned by Gairdner at the deathbed of Douglas Thornton, "The opposite of joy is not sorrow, but sin. Pure joy and pure sorrow can live together."

> I have gone into his room [says Maurice Richmond] when there has been evidence of the working of the poison in his body and when he has been physically exhausted and distressed. I cannot explain it to you, but I merely know as a fact that time and again after sitting quietly by his side in silent prayer and giving him one divine sentence or promise from the Gospel and the blessing of God in Christ, I found myself coming out of his room filled with a spontaneous and an unusual joy.
>
> The highest spiritual thought one could offer him would be quietly met with, "That thought has been continually with me." "Everything in the room says Glory" . . . "The spiritual world is very perspicuous in the evenings, and in the early morning—very perspicuous" . . . "All songs, all songs"—such sentences showed the inward triumph of spirit as the "outer tabernacle was worn away." Time and again one left that room with an impelling sense of joy.

"Before we upward pass to heaven, we taste our immortality." But in that experience was nothing inhuman. Rather, did we see the human itself "put on" immortality. He lay there, half in heaven, but supremely normal, commenting on his children's letters, greeting his eldest son from India with a quaint jesting tenderness; wholesome and humorous to the very last, when on the evening of May 22nd he fell asleep and on his wife's shoulder slept his life away. His son, as he looked on the sleeping face, could only say, "Your joy no man taketh from you."

VIII

And to Temple Gairdner who was ever a sharer of his joys was granted that even now his friends should know some measure of that sharing. " We seemed to be left standing in a pool of light," said one of them.

> I was at the church when they came from the hospital with their precious burden [wrote an American friend]. I watched them. . . . I saw the beautiful flowers—I saw through a veil of tears. Then a strange thing happened. The church seemed to be filled with the sweetest music, and I heard Canon Gairdner's voice leading the joyous strains of song.
>
> It was so surprising and strange to have weeping suddenly turned into song that I felt confused. I went out into the street and up over the railway-bridge with songs in my heart, and saying to myself, " Canon Gairdner has brought so much music to my soul that I find myself singing at his funeral."

And thus while letters from a distance said, and truly said, " The earth is poorer," the group in Cairo chiefly knew that death was poorer and that Christ's Church held her living treasure still. It was Ascensiontide. And they returned to the city, with sorrow at their hearts, but also " with great joy, praising and blessing God."

APPENDIX

LIST OF PUBLICATIONS BY W. H. T. GAIRDNER

Titles printed in italics are works in Arabic
Titles marked with an asterisk are out of print

1897. Studies in Prayer*. British College Christian Union.

1898 and 1899. Helps to the Study of St. John's Gospel* (Parts I and II). British College Christian Union.

1900. Helps to the Study of the Epistle to the Romans* British College Christian Union.

1906. *Life of Joseph.* C.M.S., Cairo.
Ahmad and Bulus * (Dialogue on Moslem objections to Christianity). C.M.S., Cairo.

1906–12. *Life of the Messiah* (Parts I–IV). C.M.S., Cairo.

1907 *Abraham, Isaac and Ishmael.* C.M.S., Cairo.
The Gospel of Barnabas (with Selim Abd el Ahad. A refutation of the validity of a pseudo-Gospel written by a mediæval pervert to Islam). C.M.S., Cairo.

1908. The Gospel of Barnabas. Christian Literature Society for India.
What happened before the Hegira? (A dialogue refuting the Moslem assertion that the Christian Scriptures now in use have been tampered with and are not the Scriptures written in the first age of the Faith. Published in Arabic and English). C.M.S., Cairo.
Egyptian Studies * (with Douglas Thornton. A series of studies made for Egyptian students' meetings, concerning education, etc., in Egypt in 1908). C.M.S. Cairo.
Life of St. Paul. C.M.S., Cairo.
D. M. Thornton: a Study in Missionary Ideals and Methods. Hodder and Stoughton.

1909. Inspiration, a Dialogue * (a comparison of Muslim and Christian ideas). Christian Literature Society for India.

Life of Samuel, Ruth and David. C.M.S., Cairo.

The Muslim Idea of God. Christian Literature Society for India.

1909. The Reproach of Islam (revised and reprinted in 1921 as The Rebuke of Islam). United Council for Missionary Education, London.

1910. The Verse of Stoning (Quranic controversy). Christian Literature Society for India.

The Eucharist as Historical Evidence (i.e. of the Death of Christ at His Passion, denied by Moslems). C.M.S., Cairo.

Science and Faith in Whom ?* (a paper for the Cairo Discussion Society, and the resulting correspondence). Privately printed.

1911. Egyptian Hymn-tunes and Notes.* Privately published.

El Azhar Collegiate Mosque.* Privately reprinted from an article in " The East and the West."

The Doctrine of the Unity in Trinity.* Privately reprinted from an article in " The Moslem World."

1912. The Anglican and Coptic Communions in Egypt * (a small leaflet on friendly relationships). Privately printed.

Life of Joshua. C.M.S., Cairo.

The " Way " of a Mohammedan Mystic * (transcription of the Sufistic experiences of a Turkish mullah). Otto Harrosowitz, Leipzig.

Syrian Hymn-tunes.* Privately printed.

1913. *Inspiration, Christian and Islamic* (the most important essay yet published on this subject). C.M.S., Cairo.

1914. Al-Ghazzali's Mishkat al-Anwar and the Ghazzali Problem.* Reprint from " Der Islam," Strassburg.

The Moslem Doctrine of Tanzih (Transcendence). C.M.S., Cairo.

Vital Forces of Christianity and Islam (an essay for the volume with the same title). Milford.

1916. *Aspects of the Redemptive Act of Christ.* C.M.S., Cairo.

Aspects of the Redemptive Act of Christ. Christian Literature Society for India.

Preparation for the Holy Communion. C.M.S., Cairo.

1916. *God as Triune, Incarnate, Atoner.* C.M.S., Cairo.

God as Triune, Incarnate, Atoner. Christian Literature Society for India.

1917. The Metres of Arabic Poetry.* Privately published for the Cairo Study Centre.

Egyptian Colloquial Arabic: a conversation Grammar and Reader (completely revised in 1926). Heffer, Cambridge.

1918. Ecce Homo Arabicus * (a reply to claims made for Mohammed and remarks derogatory of Christ in "The Islamic Review"). Privately printed.

Mohammedan Tradition and Gospel Record, The Hadith and the Injil.* Reprint from an article in "The Moslem World."

1919. *The Last Supper*. C.M.S., Cairo.

1921. Joseph and his Brothers (an Old Testament Passion-play, illustrated by Elsie Anna Wood). S.P.C.K., London.

Joseph and his Brothers (an Arabic version of the play). C.M.S., Cairo.

A Modern Metre of Egyptian-Arabic Verse.* Reprint from "American Journal of Semitic Languages and Literature."

A Class-book of Arabic Accidence (with Atallah Athanasius). School of Oriental Studies, Cairo.

Passover Night (A Bible mystery-play). S.P.C.K., London.

Passover Night. C.M.S., Cairo.

1922. The Last Passover Night. S.P.C.K., London.

Saul and Stephen. S.P.C.K., London.

The Last Passover Night. C.M.S., Cairo.

Saul and Stephen. C.M.S., Cairo.

Brotherhood, Islam's and Christ's * (being a speech made at Glasgow to the Scottish Missionary Congress). United Council for Missionary Education, London.

1923. The Good Samaritan (a New Testament morality-play). S.P.C.K., London.

1924. *The Secret of Life* (a "Tract for the Times"). S.P.C.K., Cairo.

1924. *The Divinity of Christ* (another tract for the student class). S.P.C.K., Cairo.

Instructions for Catechumens (Lessons on Christian Faith and Life in Preparation for Baptism). S.P.C.K., Cairo.

Al-Ghazzali's Mishkat al-Anwar (The Niche for Lights) (a translation, with Introduction). Royal Asiatic Society, London.

1925. King Hezekiah (a tragical drama). S.P.C.K., London.
A Harmony of the Passion Story from the Four Gospels (Illuminated). S.P.C.K., Cairo.
Instructions for Catechumens. S.P.C.K., Cairo.

1926. *Preparation for Confirmation.* S.P.C.K., Cairo.
Lessons on Membership in the Anglican Church. Privately printed.

1927. *Who is the Founder of Christianity?* (articles on the meaning of the Cross). S.P.C.K., Cairo.
The Phonetics of Arabic. Oxford University Press.
The Values of Christianity and Islam (with Dr. W. A. Eddy—a preparatory paper for the Jerusalem meeting of the International Missionary Council). International Missionary Council.
The Book of Comforts (readings for mourning gatherings). S.P.C.K., Cairo.

1928. *Commentary on Galatians with a new Arabic Translation of the Epistle.* S.P.C.K., Cairo.
The Message of the Fast. Privately printed.

Note.—Canon Gairdner left almost ready for the press a complete edition of his Egyptian and Syrian Hymn-tunes, for publication by S.P.C.K., London.

Commentaries on Hebrews and Philippians, the latter with a new translation of the Epistle, were also left almost ready for publication in Arabic, as were also some Bible rhymes for children.

It is hoped to collect and republish some of the more important of his papers on Oriental subjects in a volume of Essays.

Made and Printed in Great Britain
by Hazell, Watson & Viney Ltd.
London and Aylesbury